DESCARTES'S *MEDITATIONS*

In this new introduction to a classic philosophical text, Catherine Wilson examines the arguments of Descartes's famous *Meditations*, the book which launched modern philosophy. Drawing on the reinterpretations of Descartes's thought of the past twenty-five years, she shows how Descartes constructs a theory of the mind, the body, nature, and God from a premise of radical uncertainty. She discusses in detail the historical context of Descartes's writings, and their relationship to early modern science, and at the same time she introduces concepts and problems that define the philosophical enterprise as it is understood today. Following closely the text of the *Meditations* and meant to be read alongside them, this survey is accessible to readers with no previous background in philosophy. It is well suited to university-level courses on Descartes, but can also be read with profit by students in other disciplines.

CATHERINE WILSON is Professor of Philosophy at the University of British Columbia, Vancouver. She is the author of *Leibniz's Metaphysics: A Historical and Comparative Study* (1989) and *The Invisible World: Early Modern Philosophy and the Invention of the Microscope, 1620–1720* (1995).

CAMBRIDGE INTRODUCTIONS TO KEY PHILOSOPHICAL TEXTS

This new series offers introductory textbooks on what are considered to be the most important texts of Western philosophy. Each book guides the reader through the main themes and arguments of the work in question, while also paying attention to its historical context and its philosophical legacy. No philosophical background knowledge is assumed, and the books will be well suited to introductory university-level courses.

Titles published in the series:

DESCARTES'S *MEDITATIONS* by Catherine Wilson

DESCARTES'S
MEDITATIONS

An Introduction

CATHERINE WILSON

University of British Columbia

CAMBRIDGE UNIVERSITY PRESS

PUBLISHED BY THE PRESS SYNDICATE OF THE UNIVERSITY OF CAMBRIDGE
The Pitt Building, Trumpington Street, Cambridge, United Kingdom

CAMBRIDGE UNIVERSITY PRESS
The Edinburgh Building, Cambridge, CB2 2RU, UK
40 West 20th Street, New York, NY 10011–4211, USA
477 Williamstown Road, Port Melbourne, VIC 3207, Australia
Ruiz de Alarcón 13, 28014 Madrid, Spain
Dock House, The Waterfront, Cape Town 8001, South Africa

http://www.cambridge.org

First published 2003

Printed in the United Kingdom at the University Press, Cambridge

Typeface Adobe Garamond 11/12.5 pt.   *System* LATEX 2$_\varepsilon$ [TB]

A catalogue record for this book is available from the British Library

Library of Congress Cataloguing in Publication data
Wilson, Catherine, 1951–
Descartes's *Meditations*: an introduction / Catherine Wilson.
p.   cm. – (Cambridge introductions to key philosophical texts)
Includes bibliographical references and index.
ISBN 0 521 80981 9 (hardback) – ISBN 0 521 00766 6 (paperback)
1. Descartes, René, 1596–1650. Meditationes de prima philosophia.   2. First philosophy.
3. Metaphysics.   4. God – Proof, Ontological.   I. Title.   II. Series.
B1854.W55   2003   194 – dc21   2003051553

ISBN 0 521 80981 9 hardback
ISBN 0 521 00766 6 paperback

For my children, Eva and David

Contents

Figures

xi

Introduction: About the Meditations

Descartes's *Meditations on First Philosophy*, first published in 1641, are devoted to the following philosophical questions: What can we come to know about the human mind and its powers? Is there a reality behind appearances, and, if so, how can we have access to it? Do our experiences arise from our bodies and our brains, or could we think, feel, and perceive without them? How can we recognize truth and distinguish it from false and confused opinion? Is there is a God, and, if so, is this God benevolent, malevolent, or simply indifferent to us? If this God is benevolent, how should we understand illness, error, and morally wrong actions?

This book is intended as a first introduction to the *Meditations* and, at the same time, as an introduction to some basic problems and terminology of analytic philosophy, including the theory of knowledge, metaphysics, philosophy of science, philosophy of perception, and philosophy of language. No previous experience in philosophy is presupposed. Chapter 1 is an introduction to the problem of knowledge in Cartesian terms and Chapters 2–11 lead the reader through the arguments of the *Meditations*, explaining and commenting on the important points along the way. Chapter 12 offers an explanation of the relationship of the *Meditations* to Descartes's other writings, and discusses the conflicting perceptions of Descartes in his own time. It outlines the relationship between Cartesian problems and doctrines and the evolution of modern philosophy. While the *Meditations* are unusual amongst philosophical works, insofar as it is possible to reconstruct and follow Descartes's main arguments without knowing anything about the seventeenth-century background, a brief survey of Descartes's life, character, and aspirations will help to set the stage for a detailed treatment of his text.

René Descartes was born March 31, 1596, in Touraine, southeast of Paris, and educated at the Jesuit college of La Flèche, to which he was sent as a boarder at the age of ten. His future role as the founder of modern philosophy was not foreshadowed in his early accomplishments and interests. Somewhat sickly and fond of his sleep – not unusual qualities in an adolescent – the young Descartes showed no signs of iconoclasm or even of philosophical acumen. He studied logic, grammar, poetry, and history, and although he was an avid reader and much favored by the schoolmasters, the literary side of his education interested him less than the mathematical. After leaving school, he acquired a law degree but he never practiced. He wrote to a friend that he would have been happy as an artisan.

Returning home, Descartes learned such skills of the minor nobility as how to ride a horse and handle weapons. He was, however, not satisfied with life on a country estate and his family sent him to Paris, where he continued to study mathematics. In 1618, he signed on with Prince Maurice of Nassau who was fighting the Spanish, to experience, he said, the theatre of the world, to learn its manners and customs. He left the Netherlands in 1619 on a long tour through Eastern Europe. Wintering in southern Germany, he sought out learned persons for discussion before moving to Prague, where he encountered Tycho Brahe's new cosmological system, a compromise between the earth-centered system of the universe still in great favor and Copernicus's heliocentric cosmology, which represented our sun as only one of a multitude of stars and our planet as an even smaller speck on the cosmic scene. He studied geometry, optics, mechanics, music theory, and animal physiology. He began to wonder how the mind fitted or did not fit into the world of physical objects and processes.

A series of dreams in 1619 convinced Descartes that he had been specially favored by God and was destined to be a philosopher, which, in the terminology of the time, meant one devoted generally to the pursuit of knowledge of all things. The dreams stimulated nine years of work attempting to perfect a method of discovery, but in 1623 Descartes was still searching for a profession. He had published nothing in philosophy, or in any other field, though his ambitions were grand. He announced to his friends that mathematics, as it was taught and applied in a haphazard and unsystematic way, was virtually useless, and stated his plan to invent a method of formal reasoning governing proportion and quantity of which ordinary geometry and arithmetic would compose only a part. This *mathesis universalis* or "universal analytical method" would embrace physical questions and, by extension, moral questions, insofar as these depended on human nature and the nature of the world. Returning to Paris, Descartes enjoyed an "agreeable and innocent" life, working on his universal method, and studying the theory of lenses. His *Rules for the Direction of the Mind*, formulated and partially written down in the early 1620s, presented some methodological ideas, along with some ideas about visual perception, but he was not sufficiently satisfied with them to publish them during his lifetime.

A popular image of Descartes represents him as a quiet and meditative person who enjoyed sitting still in his room and thinking. In fact, he was an unusually restless man who moved around and changed his residence frequently. Within a few years, he had decided to leave Paris, to escape the heat of the city, he claimed, and the press of crowds.

In fact, he was beginning to find the Parisian intellectual climate too conservative. The liberal atmosphere of Amsterdam enticed him back to the Netherlands, and, in 1628, Descartes settled there, to pursue his thoughts on philosophy in the broad sense, considering especially its claim to independence from theology. He was not interested, he decided, in theological subtleties and the mysteries of eternal salvation but in happiness in this life. It seemed to him that the union of medicine and mathematics through the formulation of a rationally intelligible account of the human body was the key to happiness, since both physical and emotional suffering had their basis in the body. He began to study the structure of animals, buying cadavers in butchers' shops to take home and dissect. He also sketched out a two-part treatise on natural philosophy. The first part would be concerned with the constitution of matter and light, the laws of nature, and the origins and structure of the cosmos, and the second part would be concerned with animal and human bodies, considered as machines.

The treatise was never published, though the first part was amplified and reworked and eventually published as the *Principles of*

Philosophy. Then, in 1637, at the age of forty-one, Descartes brought out anonymously three scientific *Essays*, the *Optics*, the *Geometry*, and the *Meteorology*, the last dealing primarily with celestial phenomena. He appended to them a personal essay, the *Discourse on Method*, that detailed his frustrations with his own education, the uselessness of traditional philosophy, his beliefs about the similarities and differences between humans and animals, and his hope to be able to introduce into other areas of science the analytical techniques he had employed successfully in the *Essays*. He advanced the view that a proper understanding of the functioning of the human body would contribute to the improvement of medicine and morals and that a well-founded theory of the physical world would render us "masters and possessors of Nature."

The *Essays* were followed four years later by the *Meditations on First Philosophy*. To the surprise of some of his followers, Descartes had turned his attention away from anatomy and physiology and from his theories regarding terrestrial and celestial phenomena. Instead, the *Meditations* took up the traditional topics of metaphysics – God and the soul – and the traditional topics of epistemology – truth, error, and the role of the senses in the acquisition of knowledge. Readers curious as to why Descartes set off in this new direction and what its consequences were will find further information and explanation, some of it necessarily speculative, in Chapter 12.

Descartes moved to a pleasant chateau near Leyden in 1643, shortly before releasing his complete system of the natural world as the *Principles of Philosophy* in 1644. Recalled to Paris, he objected to being put on display "like an elephant or a panther" and instead accepted the invitation of Queen Christina of Sweden to move to Stockholm to serve as her instructor, though she made little use of his talents. His interests shifted once more, this time from the physical sciences and metaphysics to what we would today call psychology and ethics. He wanted to understand the function of the "passions" that we suffer through our encounters with persons, objects, and events in the world, especially love, hatred, wonder, desire, joy, and sadness, and to determine how to overcome such psychological evils as anger, depression, and the fear of death. His last work, the *Passions of the Soul*, published after his death in 1650, developed out of an exchange of letters with the lonely and intellectual Princess Elizabeth of Bohemia. The *Passions* describe the physical symptoms attached to the emotions and offer moral advice about their management.

Descartes's personal life can be reconstructed from the five volumes of letters he left behind. These convey the impression of a proud, sensitive, somewhat emotionally volatile man, anxious as to his reputation and not always perfectly straightforward in his accounts of himself, but whose commitment to clarity and truth is beyond doubt. His irascible and jealous nature did not preclude warmth and tenderness. He had an illegitimate daughter who died in early childhood and for whom he grieved for a long time. His letters touching on love and the passions have recently begun to intrigue commentators, some of whom note the first intimations of a theory of the unconscious.

THE *MEDITATIONS*

Many earlier philosophical books had purported to answer the questions of metaphysics and epistemology posed in the opening paragraph above. For all the precise and subtle reasoning employed by their authors, they were known to contradict one another. Worse, the plurality of opinions seemed to give rise to the following paradox: If we do not know what is *metaphysically* true about God, the mind, and the world, and what is false and confused, how can we establish that a particular philosopher's *epistemological* conception of how to distinguish truth from falsehood is not false and confused? At the same time, if we cannot have confidence in a particular philosopher's epistemology, how can we trust the metaphysical conclusions presented in the philosopher's writings?

The *Meditations* address this paradox. Descartes makes no direct reference in this text to past philosophers and their writings. He does not build on, or try to develop or refute the ideas of other philosophers, at least not explicitly. Like a mathematician, he tries to formulate a self-contained proof. (Mathematically inclined readers will be reminded of the method of "indirect proof," in which we assume that a proposition that we suspect is true is actually false.) Like an experimentalist, he changes ordinary conditions to see what happens. (His contemporary Francis Bacon tried carrying a clock down to the bottom of a mine and stuffing the carcass of a chicken with snow; Galileo Galilei rolled a ball down a carefully constructed inclined plane.) Whether one sees the Meditator as trying out a thought-experiment in which customary ways of thinking are controlled and constrained like experimental objects, or as trying out the equivalent of an indirect proof in mathematics, the starting point of the *Meditations* is largely free of positive assumptions. The Meditator settles on a policy of radical and systematic doubt, uncertain at first whether anything is thereby to be gained. As it turns out, the policy is successful. It leads to significant discoveries in both metaphysics and epistemology – and to the discovery of some fundamental principles of natural philosophy concerning the human body and the bodies surrounding it. The Meditator even becomes convinced that, if future inquirers adopt his method, they will be able to make further discoveries about themselves and about the material world.

The *Meditations* are written from the first-person perspective of a narrator, the Meditator. Is the "I" of the *Meditations* René Descartes himself, recounting what he experienced and thought, over a period of precisely six days in 1640? Many introductions to the *Meditations* treat the Meditator as Descartes and describe Descartes as entertaining certain propositions or as coming to accept certain conclusions. I have not followed this practice for several reasons. First, the assumption that the "I" of the *Meditations* should be identified with the historical Descartes seemed methodologically unsound, insofar as the Six Days of Meditation never occurred, at least as far as we know. A number of the insights that suddenly occur to the Meditator – including the insight immortalized in the phrase *cogito, ergo sum*: I think, therefore I am – had occurred to the historical Descartes years earlier. The historical Descartes had even long since worked out an entire system of the physical universe and the human body of which he was quite certain, which the Meditator gives no hint of having ever done. The Meditator is better regarded as a fictional character (who could have existed) in a story taking the form of a voyage of intellectual (rather than geographical) discovery. The historical Descartes tells the story of the Meditator to a certain purpose, as is explained in Chapter 12.

Descartes believed that anyone who started at the Meditator's starting point and who employed his reasoning powers appropriately would arrive at precisely the same conclusions as his Meditator does. He was not merely expressing the views *he* had arrived at by following a particular train of thought that could well have gone in a number of other directions. Everyone, according to Descartes, not only those with special aptitude and schooling, can be or become a philosopher. He wanted his audience to identify with his Meditator and to think along with his Meditator – and it is hard not to do so. While it might have seemed appropriate to refer to the Meditator as "It," especially since, for more than five of the six *Meditations*, the Meditator is unpersuaded of the existence of an external world and of the Meditator's own body, custom and clarity dictated the use of the anthropological pronouns, and I have accordingly alternated between "he" and "she," for the most part on a *Meditation*-by-*Meditation* basis.

Descartes believed that, while later investigators might add to the knowledge of nature indefinitely, the answers he had given in the *Meditations* to the metaphysical and epistemological questions posed above were authoritative and final. His arguments were sound and his conclusions could not be overturned. Nor was there anything significant to be added to them. Are Descartes's claims about the nature of truth, God, the mind, and the world really authoritative and final? Many of Descartes's contemporaries – the more famous amongst them as well as the more obscure – strenuously denied that they were. Others became convinced Cartesians. Every reader of the *Meditations* has to try to decide the question for him or herself, by following the arguments and by applying to them the rigorous standards of critical thinking on which Descartes himself insisted.

The question whether Descartes's claims were all true and adequately demonstrated is of course different from the question of his influence on the history of modern philosophy and modern science. This influence is profound, and Descartes can be said to have defined the main problems of modern philosophy for his immediate successors, Spinoza, Malebranche, Leibniz, and Berkeley. The best reason for reading Descartes, however, is not that what he said is beyond criticism, nor that his historical role as founder of modern philosophy makes him a worthy author. Rather, reading Descartes is a good experience, the philosophical equivalent of a journey to an interesting territory undertaken in the company of an agreeable stranger. No matter how many times one has read and annotated a copy of the

Meditations, a fresh reading is virtually guaranteed to bring new ideas and insights.

Besides the sharp distinction preserved in this text between the historical Descartes – the seventeenth-century intellectual combatant, friend and foe of numerous illustrious philosophers – and his solitary Meditator, two other departures from past convention are worth mentioning. First, the present commentary proceeds in strict chronological order, taking the arguments in exactly the sequence in which they come. Each section is geared to a set of quotations from the *Meditations* that are identified by a reference to the standard edition of Descartes's writings. Second, discussion of the *Objections* to the *Meditations* and Descartes's *Replies* to them has been relegated to the end of the main chapters.

THE *OBJECTIONS* AND *REPLIES*

The seven sets of *Objections* and *Replies* that Descartes appended to his *Meditations* are indispensable to an understanding of his main text. Recognizing their importance, past studies have moved back and forth between exposition and interpretation of Descartes's doctrine and analysis of the reactions to it by the more notable of his commentators. As well as forcing the reader to identify Descartes and the Meditator, this treatment interrupts the flow of the *Meditations*. Descartes could have written a dialectical treatise, considering and answering objections as he went along. He explains his reasons for not doing so and, as they are entirely credible, I resolved to respect them, even when some explanatory digressions were required to explain the main text. Young persons of my acquaintance pointed out that some readers would be tempted to skip the discussion of the *Objections* and *Replies* at the end of each chapter. Well, an author is not after all a policeman . . . I can only hope that readers will not succumb to this temptation, even if it is only for self-interested reasons. The criticisms raised and parried not only clarify the meaning of the earlier text and deepen the reader's appreciation of the issues, but are an excellent source of topics for examinations and term papers.

Though I have tried to represent Descartes's arguments and intentions as objectively as possible, every commentary is at the same time an interpretation and the present commentary is no exception. I have taken the doctrine of the good body of *Meditation Six* to be Descartes's intended contribution to natural philosophy and have laid more than usual emphasis on the preoccupation of his critics with the possibility that God is fictional and that corporeal substance can think. My intellectual debts to the books and articles cited in the section on Further Reading and to colleagues and students are at the same time substantial. Discussions with Husain Sarkar and Gábor Boros helped especially to shape my understanding of Descartes's procedures on one hand and of the theodicy hidden in his metaphysics on the other. I am also grateful to Tim Christie for assistance with the Index, and to Hilary Gaskin for proposing the project and for sound advice along the way. The edition cited is *The Philosophical Writings of Descartes*, 3 volumes, translated by John Cottingham, Robert Stoothoff, Dugald Murdoch and Anthony Kenny (Cambridge, Cambridge University Press, 1984–91). References in the text (AT) are to the standard edition, *Oeuvres de Descartes*, 11 volumes, edited by Charles Adam and Paul Tannery (Paris, Vrin/CNRS, 1964–76). Citations are by volume number and page, as these are given in the English translation.

CHAPTER I

The situation of the Meditator is described and his desire to demolish everything and begin again is explored, while the Reader is introduced to some basic philosophical concepts

I THE MEDITATOR – THE BUILDING METAPHOR–"KNOWLEDGE-CONDITIONS" – SCIENTIFIC AND UNSCIENTIFIC MENTALITIES (AT VII:17–18)

> Some years ago I was struck by the large number of falsehoods that I had accepted as true in my childhood, and by the highly doubtful nature of the whole edifice that I had subsequently based on them. I realized that it was necessary, once in the course of my life, to demolish everything completely and start again right from the foundations if I wanted to establish anything at all in the sciences that was stable and likely to last. (VII:17)

Our first introduction to the Meditator finds him in a mood of disillusion but, at the same time, full of confident resolve.

The Meditator's aim, it seems, is to establish something in the sciences that will be "stable and likely to last." He has apparently just realized that he is going to have to "demolish everything completely" and start again "right from the foundations" in order to accomplish this task.

This announcement raises a number of questions. Who is the Meditator and why is he so disenchanted? How did the Meditator discover "some years ago" that the beliefs he had acquired in childhood and built on subsequently were falsehoods? Why did he wait so long to do anything about this grievous state of affairs? What is the plan to demolish "everything" completely and why does the Meditator think demolishing everything is the essential first step to establishing "something" firm in the sciences?

We know very little about the Meditator. He must be an adult, since he refers to his childhood as past. He seems to be at least temporarily relieved of the pressures of having to make a living, though he refers to "worries" that he has for the moment set aside. He has some leisure in which to reflect. Otherwise, we know nothing about the Meditator, not his age, his educational and family background, or his customary occupation, only that he is dissatisfied with the number of falsehoods he has accepted and that he sees the need to remedy this situation.

The sudden emergence of a decision to change one's life completely after years of inaction is not beyond comprehension. One who has lived in the same city for twenty years might come to the realization that a large number of the friendships established in childhood and maintained since are weighing him down. One who has lived all her life in an apartment inherited from her deceased parents might come in time to appreciate the inadequacy of the roof, the faulty plumbing, and the defects in the appliances. Regardless of feelings of familiarity and attachment, one might become convinced that these fixtures have to go.

Of course, in order to build, it is not usually necessary to demolish "everything completely." Even if your circle of friends seems tiresome, there are usually one or two you would just as soon keep. Sometimes an old flat can be restored and refurbished. At other times, partial measures do not seem to work. The old structure can get in the way of the new structure. The old building may have to be dynamited and carted away before new construction goes up.

The two vignettes capture something of the Meditator's situation. Like familiar companions and familiar surroundings, his old beliefs served him well enough for a time, but increasingly he sees them as unsatisfactory, in the same way that the people and surroundings of one's childhood can come to seem limited. The Meditator even expresses his dissatisfactions through an analogy between what might be called his "knowledge-condition" and an old building he inhabits. An individual's knowledge-condition can be thought of on analogy with his or her "health-status" or "financial condition." My knowledge-condition is the good, bad, or indifferent condition I am in with respect to possessing knowledge, as opposed to possessing health or money.

There are many respects in which possessing knowledge is not much like owning or living in a house. There are, however, several similarities that make the analogy work, beyond the fact that both knowledge and houses can be expensive to acquire. A house is *constructed*: it is built up out of various materials – wood, metal, sand – collected in the environment or acquired from others. These are not thrown into a pile together, but are given a structure. Knowledge, too, is built up out of observations collected in the environment or acquired from others. The data of experience have to be assembled in a certain way or we will have nothing more than a chaos of sensations such as we suppose infants to have. A house is *functional*: it offers a place to eat, rest, and store things. A mind well-stocked with knowledge-items provides psychological nourishment and recreation. Moreover, being well informed is a precondition of making sensible decisions in practical matters. Finally, a house can be *expanded* and *improved*: I can clean out musty corners, upgrade the plumbing or wiring, add rooms, terraces, balconies, or entire stories. My knowledge can be upgraded, expanded, and improved as well. I can rid myself of misconceptions, refine my knowledge of particular topics, and master entirely new subject areas.

There are several further similarities. A house can be erected carelessly, without a proper foundation, leaving it in danger of collapse. A house, however elaborate and ornate, can also be only a dream-castle that has no substantiality and that will vanish as soon as I wake up or come out of my reverie. Analogously, my knowledge-condition can be without good and proper foundations and accordingly shaky, or even purely illusory.

When a sweet illusion vanishes – say, the illusion that one was going to capture some attractive prize with little trouble – one's feeling is often that the props that were holding up one's view of the world have been kicked out and that something has collapsed. Nevertheless, the Meditator has two distinct worries, one about the *foundations* of his knowledge, another about its possibly *illusory* character. A dream-edifice cannot collapse – though it can be dreamed to collapse. Dream castles do not come with dream-foundations, or dream-plumbing and wiring, for that matter. An edifice without a foundation cannot, in the ordinary course of things, vanish into nothing. Still, what is "groundless" or "unfounded" merges in our experience with what is delusory. Both are threats to the stability and permanence of the house the Meditator imagines himself to possess.

The Meditator has not explained where his feelings of insecurity and doubt with respect to his knowledge-condition stem from. Why does he think that a complete overhaul of his existing beliefs is called for? This question is perhaps best approached by scrutinizing his wish to establish something in the sciences that is "stable and likely to last," since this is the avowed purpose of the planned destructive activity.

Which sciences is the Meditator interested in, one might wonder? After all, there are many sciences – anatomy, chemistry, mathematics, physics, physiology, astronomy – representing the various specialties. No one can seriously wish to contribute significantly to all of them. The Meditator does not say to which science he wishes to contribute. He does not present the familiar profile of the enthusiast for black holes, sharks, prime numbers, or some other particular type of object or phenomenon that has produced total scientific dedication in this person. The Meditator may, for all we know, be fascinated by some particular type of object, or some phenomenon, but he has not given any clue so far. All we know is that he has general scientific ambitions. So it is appropriate to ask: What differentiates the general orientation of the scientist from the nonscientist's? What is it to want, in a general way, to establish something in the sciences without being an enthusiast for a particular subject?

Here is a provisional, doubtless somewhat controversial, characterization: Both the scientist and the nonscientist are interested in "things" – natural things, manufactured things, social things, experienced things. The nonscientist (more precisely, the person whose attitude towards things at the moment is not scientific) thinks about, looks at, interacts with, describes, imagines, dreams of, tries to obtain, hopes for, ignores, or fears things. The scientist (more precisely, the person adopting at the moment the scientific stance towards things) is in pursuit of nonobvious truths about things – truths that can only be discovered by long observation, or by observation under controlled circumstances, by experimentation, by precise measurement. One can have either a scientific or a nonscientific attitude towards any and all of the following: dreams, tropical birds, hairstyles, soil . . . depending on whether one is trying to find out some nonobvious truth about them, or just thinking about them, or liking, or not liking, some of them.

Often, scientists voice the opinion that knowing nonobvious truths about things is useful, claiming that possession of the truth enables human beings to change the world for the better. Advances in scientific knowledge, it is often said, can be applied to the relief of physical and psychological suffering and deprivation, prolonging life and health and making us less susceptible to misfortune. Scientists may even explain why they wanted to become or are gratified to be scientists by reference to their altruistic motives. Yet – think on what happened to Pandora with her Box, or the development of the atomic bomb – the pursuit of nonobvious truths about what things are really like, or what is inside them, can be dangerous. Scientists can be deluded about the benefits to humanity that will flow from the pursuit of some nonobvious truth, or about the appropriateness of some kinds of science for someone with genuinely altruistic motives. Just as often, however, scientists express their opinion that the successful pursuit of nonobvious truth provides them with a unique kind of personal satisfaction that cannot be obtained in any other way. To have a scientific orientation is not necessarily to be interested in power and control, or even in providing benefits to humanity. One can want to be a scientist because one finds knowledge of nonobvious truths worth having for its own sake.

The scientist – whether practically inclined and altruistically motivated or disinterested – (we can ignore the rare malevolent scientist who truly wishes to worsen the condition of the world) – has a further, important, goal in addition to that of getting to know many nonobvious truths. He or she does not want to believe anything that is false. It is just as important not to accept as true many nonobvious errors and superstitions as not to be ignorant of the truth. Skepticism is an important feature of the scientific attitude.

The provisional characterization of the scientific attitude just given does not permit us decisively to classify all orientations towards a thing as scientific or nonscientific. Is my study of the prices, heights, and colors of tulips for sale over the Internet "scientific?" Yes, but only weakly so; for the knowledge I am seeking, though not obvious to everybody, is relatively superficial. Are the detailed investigations of a jealous lover into the beloved's behavior "scientific?" They are certainly intended to get at some nonobvious truths that will change the condition of the world for the better – in the eyes of the investigator, anyway. However, the distanced, skeptical attitude may be conspicuously lacking. There is a continuum between scientific and nonscientific interests, with some kinds of investigation resembling more closely our stereotype of scientific activity as laboratory work carried out in a white coat with a microscope. The definition given should, however, be enough to start with. As an aspiring scientist, the Meditator is oriented to the discovery of some nonobvious truths about things, and likely believes both that practical benefits will flow from their discovery and that their discovery is intrinsically satisfying.

There are two ways to address the question of the Meditator's dissatisfaction with his knowledge-condition, keeping in mind the analogy between knowledge and houses. One can take a *historical* perspective and ask why someone of a certain background, living like the author of the *Meditations* in Amsterdam in the middle of the seventeenth-century, might have come to doubt whether his or her knowledge was in good condition. One can also take a *timeless* perspective and ask why anyone, in any historical era – for example, in the early twenty-first century – might come to doubt whether his or her knowledge was in good condition. Let us take up the historical question first.

Today, we are accustomed to the idea that scientific discovery builds on previous discovery, that scientific knowledge is cumulative. From Copernicus's astronomy, the modern theory of the universe was born. From the theory of elements discovered in the eighteenth century, modern chemistry was born. Furthermore, our latest methods and techniques seem to build on our experience with previous methods and techniques. "Scientific method," as we know it, comprises certain tests and procedures. For example, it is often said that scientific hypotheses must be verifiable or falsifiable by experiment, that experimental results must be reproducible, and that quantitative relationships should be sought corresponding to all qualitative differences. Science also comprises certain techniques – the employment of statistical inference based on the laws of probability, methods for determining causal relationships such as regression analysis, and the use of instruments for visualization and measurement.

If an aspiring scientist today declared that it was necessary to demolish all existing knowledge in the sciences and to reject all the canons of experimental practice and the interpretation of data in order to establish stable and lasting results, we could hardly regard him or her as a serious aspirant to the scientific life. Only a crank would make such a proposal. The Meditator, however, is a fictional character created by René Descartes in 1640 and the Meditator's situation reflects his creator's historical context. In 1640, the fundamentals of modern science have not been established. An omnipotent and benevolent God is widely believed in Christian countries to have created the cosmos from nothing in seven days, as reported in the Book of Genesis, and then to have created each type of animal, vegetable, and mineral in more or less the way it now appears on earth. Heaven and hell are considered to be real places, to which God will assign us after death. The Ptolemaic system, with the earth at the center of the universe, with or without certain modifications, is still taught in the universities. The laws of mechanics and the inverse-square law of gravitation have not yet been stated. The nature of light is unknown. It is still a mystery why living creatures need to breathe air and what warms their blood. The chemical elements, their attributes, and their principles of combination have not been identified. Doctors can do little except set broken bones, lance abscesses, and induce sleep. The microscope and the telescope, however, have just come into use. Galileo, following Copernicus, has insisted that the earth orbits a stationary sun, which, he somewhat implausibly claims, is another star.

Meanwhile, the moral and philosophical treatises of ancient authors, long lost or forgotten in Europe, have been recovered and translated, published, and reread. Many of these texts contradict Christian theology and Christian ethics. Among the recovered works are the systems of the ancient Stoics, with their "world soul," and their ethics based on personal virtue and the ideal of self-sufficiency. The ancient Epicureans are discovered to have denied the existence of a providential God who created and supervises the universe. They propound the doctrine that the world and all its creatures, including human beings, came into existence by chance from clusters of atoms moving aimlessly in a void and will dissolve into atoms again.

Who, amongst all these speculators, self-proclaimed authorities, ancient eminences, and powerful dispensers of official knowledge, is to be believed?

The printing press, invented almost 200 years earlier is, by 1640, pouring out essays, treatises, polemical works, astronomical tables, strange descriptions of distant lands, people, and wild beasts, and books of recipes and cures for every manner of illness. A few heretical treatises and dialogues cast doubt openly on the existence of the Christian God. It is not clear what anyone should believe, for the books contradict one another. Can salamanders live in fire? Do all diseases come from the stars? Are there witches? This is the Meditator's time-bound predicament: He doesn't know what to think about himself, the world around him, or God. He is like someone who has come into a room in which many noisy arguments are going on. People with raised and sometimes barely intelligible voices are making competing claims, credible and incredible. It is no wonder that he has a strong compulsion to put his hands over his ears and block out all the noise.

Nor is there much in 1640 by way of knowledge of scientific method. Although mathematics employs certain standard methods of analysis for the solution of problems and although Francis Bacon has proposed a novel method of classifying observations in order to arrive at a knowledge of nonobvious truths in his *New Organon* of 1620, there are no established canons of experimental practice, laboratory manuals, or statistics textbooks. The Meditator is a would-be scientist who is convinced that the question of method is as fundamental to inquiry in the natural sciences as it is to mathematics, but who has no proven techniques and instruments and who has no trustworthy body of scientific data to ground his inquiries. His impulse to demolish is not, taken in its proper context, the whim of a crank. We could put the point as follows. If in our time it would be counterproductive to demolish everything in order to become a scientist, this is chiefly because creatures like the Meditator succeeded in *becoming* scientists when there were none before.

The problem of knowledge can also be considered from a timeless perspective. Think of my knowledge-condition as a model, or *representation*, of the world existing in my mind that enables me to think certain thoughts, to write or speak certain sentences, and to pronounce certain opinions and beliefs true and others false. If, for example, I am asked to describe the room in which I am sitting, I can report that the walls are a biscuit color, that there are sofas and carpets, pictures and ornaments, a piano, a view to the west, and so on. I can explain how some of the mechanisms in the room work; for example, how to turn on the lights and heating, and how certain objects came to be as they are, such as the cushion whose edges were nibbled by mice. Going beyond my own room, I can describe my city, explain how some of its institutions work, and give some account of its history and evolution.

My knowledge-condition with respect to my room and even my city is, I might think, not too bad. A little reflection, however, will show that confidence in the adequacy of my representation with respect to descriptive, explanatory, and historical accuracy is unjustified. I do not know the name of the species of palm in the window, or how the heating system actually works, or in what year the picture of a small boat tied to its dock was painted. There are corresponding deficits in my knowledge of Vancouver, Canada. The more detail I try to provide about my surroundings, the more mis-statements will creep into my account and the more evident my ignorance of features of even my immediate environment will become. When it comes to my overall representation of the world outside my room and my city, my knowledge-condition is even poorer.

One might suppose that I at least have considerable knowledge of myself. However, reflection again suggests that my representation or model of myself is not as good as I am inclined at first to think. It is true that I remember many events of years past, but these constitute after all only a fraction of my past experiences. I imagine that I know things about myself that no one else knows, but introspection does not teach me as much about myself as I might at first suppose. What am I really like? Am I courageous? Generous? Do I like Brahms? In some circumstances, yes, in others, no.

Imagine being asked to write a descriptive essay that contains everything you know. For this experiment, you are given piles of paper and pencils, as much time as you need, and proper rest and nourishment. You are not, however, permitted to consult any books, newspapers, websites, or other media, or to ask questions of anyone else. Whatever you know about the fundamental particles of physics, geography and the world-economy, astronomy and cosmology, the behavior of animals, snow, sleet and hail, aerodynamics, human physiology and psychology, and what you are like as an individual, has to come out of your own head and will therefore represent your knowledge-condition, more or less as it is.

If I were required to write such an essay, it would be, even under the most favorable writing-conditions, rather short – at most, a few hundred pages. It would also be somewhat ridiculous, to the eye of the expert at least. This is not because I am an ignorant person. My "explanation" for why it snows might even employ such specialized concepts as water molecules, freezing points, crystallization, and the stability of the hexagonal form. To a meteorologist, however, it would probably appear hilariously garbled. My account of poverty and wealth, though I fancy I have some insight into these matters, would be considered hopelessly naïve by each of: an economist, a sociologist, a social worker, and an entrepreneur. My interpretation of my own personality and past behavior might seem self-serving to a psychologist or any more objective observer.

The situation is the same for all of us. Our individual representations of the world in which we are situated, no matter how insightful or well-read we consider ourselves to be, are like the Meditator's house, without solid foundations. We know that there are protons, molecules, labor-markets, weight, neurotransmitters, horses, genes, rituals, speed, feathers, asteroids, gravitational and electromagnetic forces. We have the vague idea that some of these terms are more basic than others – "molecules," for example, and "forces." None of us, however, can claim to be certain what the foundations of the world actually look like, what concepts are truly fundamental. We know as well that our so-called explanations for why things happen and our historical reconstructions of the past are largely fantastic. So we know on reflection that our personal knowledge-edifices are not built on very solid foundations and that we spend much of our time in dream-houses.

Nevertheless – one might think – there are people who know about protons, and the economy, and genes, and all these matters, including the physicist, the meteorologist, the paleontologist, the biologist, and so on. They are experts, and if you want your house to have better foundations and to have fewer imaginary features, you need only consult them. Think of the millions of volumes in the great public libraries of the world. No single mind could embrace the knowledge they contain. It is unreasonable for an individual to aspire to a knowledge-condition that represents everything fully and accurately. Collectively, though, "our" representation of the world has good foundations and is solid. On this view, the Meditator's timeless concerns about the foundations, solidity, and reality of his house are needless. There is no particular reason for any individual to be too worried about his or her own knowledge-condition. Each of us has as much knowledge as we need to get through the day and to earn a living, and it is only rarely that we feel we lack some key piece of information. Moreover, we all make up a part of humanity, which, taken as a whole, is very well informed indeed.

Well, that is an optimistic view. But it is problematic. Confidence in the collective knowledge of humanity is hard to sustain. Surely the contents of the great libraries of the world contain, if not more falsehoods altogether than truths, at least plenty of falsehoods? Why else do textbooks have to be revised year after year? Further, the experts disagree about many things, starting with such simple matters as what a person ought to eat to remain healthy, which you might think had been settled long ago, and going on to such matters as whether the universe will come to an end in a huge explosion or will endure forever. We can refer in a vague way to "the wisdom of the human race at the dawn of the twenty-first century." However, while it makes sense to speak of *my* representation of the world, *my* knowledge-condition, there is no representation of the world – thought or written – that we could designate as *our* representation of the world, the knowledge-condition of the collective mind, for there is no collective mind. There are only many books, many experts (and frauds), many opinions. It is perhaps fair to say that we humans know a good deal and seem to be in a reasonably good knowledge-condition, relative to gorillas or birds. Nevertheless, wherever we can point to a material artifact that contains vast quantities of knowledge, such as an encyclopedia, we can be certain that no mind contains it. Any actual collection of minds contains much that is mere illusion and that lacks good foundations. So there is little comfort to be had in the thought that there is a collective representation of the world that is adequate.

Suppose it is up to me and I want to improve my representation of the world. I shall try to identify and learn from those persons whose expertise I have reason to credit. Trying to improve my knowledge is an active process, not passive reception. *I* have to decide *where* to look and *when* I have looked long and hard enough and this implies that I have to make some decisions about where *not* to look. *I* have to decide *whom* to trust and how far – and this means deciding *not* to trust some self-proclaimed authorities: – maybe all PR spokespersons, some sales-people working on commission, and most members of ideologically constituted "think tanks." I have to ignore *some* claims for my attention and credence if I am to make any headway. I even have to rule out as unworthy of further consideration some explanations about how things happen without making a full investigation. The Meditator's decision to demolish everything and to begin laying his own new foundations for science still needs some explanation, however.

2 THE AIMS OF AN IDEAL SCIENTIST – SORTING-PROCEDURES – BELIEF-SETS – SKEPTICISM AND CREDULITY – CONFORMITY AND AUTHORITY (AT VII:18)

To see more clearly what is involved in upgrading one's knowledge-edifice and why a general demolition of one's existing opinions might be conducive to that end, the notion of a *sorting-procedure* will be helpful. A small investment of time at this stage with respect to some further basic concepts of epistemology will pay large dividends later with respect to understanding the complex philosophical architecture of the *Meditations*.

Suppose my ambition, like the Meditator's, is to become a scientist. Not only do I want to become a scientist, I want to approach as closely as I can to the condition of an ideal scientist. The opinions I accept – my beliefs – must reflect the nonobvious truth about things. I also want my representation of the world to be not just accurate, but ample. My knowledge-edifice should not only have good foundations, it should be large and elaborately detailed.

An "opinion," for the purposes of the present discussion, is any claim expressible as a declarative statement in a meaningful sentence of English. It is a proposition that *could be* believed by someone, whether or not anyone actually believes it or has ever believed it. It is customary in ordinary language to separate "facts" from "opinions," to refer to "mere opinions," or to what is "only an opinion." This common usage, however, should be ignored in all that follows. The statements below can all be considered to express opinions:

Cows eat grass
Cows climb trees
The normal lifespan of a cow is less than ten years
The number of stars is even
The number of stars is odd
$2 + 2 = 5$
Snow is white
Cows are large animals

Imagine a computer program that generates English sentences like these and then presents me with a list of them. In principle, I can sort any such sentence I am confronted with into one of three classes: BELIEVE, DISBELIEVE, and UNDECIDED. I can do the same with most sentences encountered in a book, or a newspaper article, or vocalized by an acquaintance, or thought up by me:

BELIEVE: Opinions *I* agree with and accept.

DISBELIEVE: Opinions *I* disagree with and reject.

UNDECIDED: Opinions *I* am not convinced of either way.

For example, if I am presented with the sentences *Cows eat grass* and *Snow is white*, I will put them into the BELIEVE category. I agree that cows eat grass and that snow is white. The opinion that *Cows climb trees* will go into the DISBELIEVE category, along with $2 + 2 = 5$. Finally the sentence *The normal lifespan of a cow is less than ten years* will go into the UNDECIDED category; for I do not know enough about the normal lifespan of cows to agree or disagree. *The number of stars is even* and that *The number of stars is odd* will go into UNDECIDED as well. I suppose one or the other must be true, but I do not know which.

I can perform this sorting procedure for as long as I like, provided I have the leisure in which to do so and a source of new sentences. It has never until now occurred to me deliberately to wonder whether I am actually mortal; and no one has formally presented the claim *CW is mortal* to me for my assessment. Yet if I now present the opinion to myself, I have no hesitation in placing it into the BELIEVE category.

The procedure just described sounds simple enough, but there is a complication. A single English sentence can correspond to more than one opinion. Many sentences are *ambiguous* and susceptible of multiple interpretations, e.g., *This drill is boring*. Other sentences are *vague*. In ordinary life, the context in which a sentence is uttered or written helps to pin down the meaning we should attach to it. The proposition asserted by a speaker or writer, using a particular English *sentence*, is the opinion he or she is actually expressing. And until I have decided what a sentence means, what opinion I should take the sentence as expressing, I cannot assign it to the category of BELIEVE, DISBELIEVE, or UNDECIDED.

Take *Shooting stars can be entertaining*. It is susceptible of at least three interpretations, corresponding to three different thoughts or opinions that might be expressed by the sentence and that can be paraphrased as follows:

a) Shooting firearms at the stars can be a fine sport.
b) A show of meteors at night can be pleasurable to watch.
c) Taking photos of celebrities is good fun.

If I am presented with the sentence *Shooting stars can be entertaining*, I have not been presented with an *opinion*, for I do not know which opinion – (a) or (b) or (c) – is being expressed. I might believe the opinion expressed in (b) but not that expressed in (a) and (c).

Or, take the vague sentence *Cows eat grass*. I know that cows eat other food besides grass – maize, for example, and hay, as well as processed feed. Probably there are some cows that have never eaten grass in their lives, only synthetic cattlefeed. Does the sentence *Cows eat grass* express the opinion that Cows eat *only* grass and that *All* cows eat grass? If so, I should place the sentence in the DISBELIEVE category. If, however the meaning of the sentence is, *With some exceptions, cows eat grass given the opportunity; grass is the usual and preferred food of a cow*, I should place it in BELIEVE.

Cows are large animals is another vague sentence. When presented with it, I can not tell whether to disagree or agree, for cows are larger than some animals but smaller than many others. Reflecting on these matters, I might put each of *Cows eat grass*, *Cows are large animals*, and *Cows climb trees* into the UNDECIDED category. (I have never seen a cow climb a tree, but perhaps they can get a little way up into the branches of low-spreading trees; it depends on exactly how the word "climb" is to be understood.)

When I am asked to classify *sentences* generated by a computer that have not been uttered or written by a speaker or writer in a meaning-fixing context, then I am likely to experience some difficulties. Even when I am classifying sentences produced on some occasion by another human being, I may experience difficulties on account of vagueness and ambiguity. On a little reflection, it is apparent that deciding what I should place into the category BELIEVE – what I should believe – is no simple matter. Nevertheless, each of us can be said unproblematically to hold many opinions (our own) for true and to hold many other opinions (those of irritating newspaper columnists) for false.

Call the set of opinions that are believed by Person X, X's "belief-set." We can ask about anyone's belief-set: How good is it? Is every opinion Person X holds for true *really true*? Is every opinion Person X holds for false *really false*? Are *all* true opinions contained within Person X's belief-set? Are *no* false opinions contained within X's belief set? In other words, is Person X omniscient? I can ask the corresponding questions about myself, too. Is every opinion I hold for true *really true*? Is every opinion I hold for false *really false*? Are *all* true opinions contained within my belief-set? Are *no* false opinions contained within my belief-set? In other words, am I omniscient?

The hypothesis that any other living or dead person is or was omniscient seems clearly untenable. It is therefore exceedingly unlikely that *I* am omniscient. I can figure this out by reasoning as follows. It is quite apparent that other people harbor numerous false beliefs about geography, medical matters, etc., and fail to believe certain true things. It would be strange, however, if I were one of the few human beings in the world who had *no* false beliefs along the same lines. Moreover, I often discover that I *was* wrong about something that I firmly believed. I have frequently believed that the road I was driving along would take me to my destination, when this was untrue, as I discovered on pulling over and consulting a map. I have also often failed to believe certain true things, such as the fact that I had a dentist's appointment on some particular day. Relativists sometimes insist that whatever a person believes is "true for that person." If so, many things that are "true for" some person or other are, at the same time, false and can be discovered to be false by that same person.

It seems that we are an error-prone species. I have good evidence that I am not exempt from the tendency to err and that no one else is either. My belief-set is constantly undergoing revision as I discover that I was wrong about certain things and as I expunge false beliefs from my belief-set, and learn new facts.

To make my belief-set correspond to reality, I must find a way to accomplish the following three subtasks. Perhaps I cannot accomplish each of them perfectly. But the better I am at accomplishing each of them, the more closely I will approach to the knowledge-condition of an ideal scientist:

Subtask (1) Decide which opinions currently believed or disbelieved are actually TRUE.

Subtask (2) Decide which opinions currently believed or disbelieved are actually FALSE.

Subtask (3) For all opinions that are currently undecided, decide whether they are TRUE or FALSE.

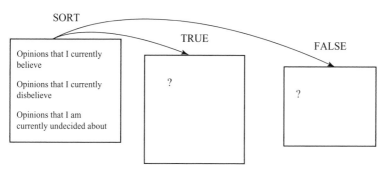

Figure 1   The overall task of becoming an ideal scientist

But how should I go about the overall task?

Suppose I have the opportunity to choose one fundamental *sorting-procedure* in the hope that it will enable me to complete the overall task appropriately. I should first consider the array of sorting-procedures that I could use and pick the best, the one that looks as though it is most likely to produce the best results in terms of getting my beliefs into the right boxes, TRUE & FALSE. How, though, can I choose any procedure? For, if I do not yet *know* what is true and what is false, how can I *know* that one procedure gives better results than another?

All I can do, it seems, is pick a method that looks promising and, once I have tried it out for a while, make a decision as to whether it is working. I can tell if it is working if I am satisfied with the results. One might compare this process to that of friend-selection. Suppose I want to sort persons of my acquaintance into two boxes: Good Mates and Bad Mates. Unfortunately, I do not know in advance what the characteristics of Good and Bad Mates are. If I already knew what the characteristics of Good Mates and Bad Mates were, I could assess each candidate against the criteria. I need, however, to develop these criteria on the basis of my experience with the candidates. The experience of socializing with a humorless person might, for example, encourage me to introduce the criterion of "having a sense of humor" into my set of criteria for a Good Mate. When I reach the point where all the candidates I encounter either fulfill the criteria I have built up or fail to fulfill them *and* no experience with new candidates induces me to change my criteria, I can be confident that my criteria are good, and that my sorting procedure for Good and Bad Mates is reliable.

In looking for a fundamental rule for inquiry, I have to follow the same procedure. I have to consider various criteria for classifying opinions as true or false, on the basis of my experience with the opinions themselves. Just as experience with different sorts of people can disclose to me that humor is important in a friend, but a knowledge of fine wines is irrelevant, experience with different sorts of opinions can disclose to me that some characteristics are important for truth, others are not.

Consider several sorting-procedures for opinions that can be quickly rejected as inappropriate to the overall task. First, there is a method that might be designated the Method of Total Credulity:

> Method of Total Credulity: Whenever an opinion is presented to me, I shall deem it TRUE. I shall further review all my previous opinions and deem them all TRUE, no matter how I regarded them before.

Figure 2   The Method of Total Credulity

A person who is able successfully to employ the Method of Total Credulity will hold all opinions for true. She will believe that *The number of stars is even* and that *The number of stars is odd* and that *Cows climb trees* and that *Snow is black*. She will even hold for true the opinion, *All my opinions are false*, while holding all opinions simultaneously for true.

Is it possible seriously to imagine someone employing the Method of Total Credulity? It is hard to understand what could be involved in holding all the above propositions for true and being happy to believe contradictions. And even if we can imagine someone successfully deciding to believe everything, mechanically accepting all opinions does not fit with our intuitive idea of what a scientific method should look like: the Method of Total Credulity can hardly help anyone to improve his belief-set. By employing it, the inquirer will come to accept as true many new falsehoods. Equally unfortunately, he will not expunge from his belief-set any existing falsehoods that, in his current state of partial ignorance, he accepts.

Another method, Total Skepticism, will purify my belief-set very well – down to nothing:

> Method of Total Skepticism: Whenever an opinion is presented to me, I shall deem it FALSE. I shall further review all my previous opinions and deem them all FALSE.

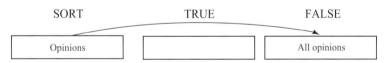

Figure 3 The Method of Total Skepticism

By employing Total Skepticism, an inquirer can purify her existing belief-set of all errors. She will also have a method for dealing with all currently undecided propositions – reject them all. However, in light of the fact that *some opinions are true*, she will end up with an empty belief-set that fails to reflect reality.

Perhaps, then, an inquirer should trust his instincts and follow a Subjective Policy?

Subjective Policy: Whenever I BELIEVE a proposition, I shall deem it TRUE. Whenever I DISBELIEVE a proposition, I shall deem it FALSE. If I am UNDECIDED, I shall simply ignore the proposition.

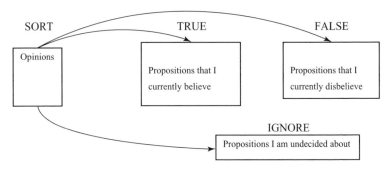

Figure 4   The Subjective Policy

It is hard to see how the Subjective Policy can help me make any progress towards the goal of becoming an ideal scientist. For the reason I decided to try to sort my existing beliefs was that I had reason to suspect that many of them were false. As well, deciding to ignore all opinions I am currently undecided about can hardly extend my knowledge of nonobvious truths.

The three Methods considered – Credulity, Skepticism, and the Subjective Policy – all supply *criteria* for truth. A criterion can be thought of as a filter that selectively lets something through, as a coffee filter lets coffee through but holds back grounds, or as a criterion for friendship excludes some people from the role of friend. What collects beyond the filter is clear coffee or acceptable friends, and what is left in the filter can be discarded or ignored for purposes of drinking or friendship. The Methods of Total Credulity and Total Skepticism are not effective filters, for one lets everything through and the other lets nothing through. They are nonselective. The Subjective Policy is selective, but it is evident that it is not selective in quite the right way.

If I can choose the right filter for opinions, what collects beyond the filter will be what is TRUE. A good selective filter can be used on propositions I already believe or disbelieve, and it can also be used on undecided propositions. Consider some other selective filters that might be useful for deciding what is true: the Authority Principle and the Conformity Policy.

> Authority Principle: Everything a particular designated Authority (for example: elders, technical journals, religious authorities) says is true I shall deem to be TRUE. Everything that the Authority says is false or that it does not explicitly state to be true, I shall deem to be FALSE.

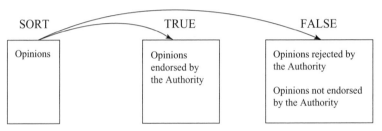

Figure 5   The Authority Principle

Conformity Policy: Everything most other people believe I shall deem to be TRUE. Everything most other people reject or fail to believe I shall deem to be FALSE.

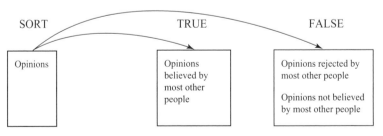

Figure 6   The Conformity Policy

Both the Authority Principle and the Conformity Policy can change my belief-set. In case I have been using the Subjective Policy up to now, introducing the Authority Principle or the Conformity Policy will make a difference to what I hold for true. If I learn that 75 percent of the population believes that UFOs have visited Earth, I will hold this for true if I am employing the Conformity Policy, regardless of my previous disagreement with the opinion. We now need to ask, however, whether either of these filters is any good if my aim is to acquire new beliefs about what is nonobviously true. A criterion tests beliefs, but we also have to test criteria, or filters, to see if they do what they are supposed to do.

I can check whether my paper filter really "performs as advertised" to filter cryptosporidium cysts by examining the filtered water with a microscope for the presence of cryptosporidium cysts. If I am very worried about the condition of my water, I had better have this assurance. At least, I should be assured that the fine print on the filter box that says that the filter has been tested by some expert is not a forgery. How, though, can I check whether the Authority Principle or the Conformity Policy "performs as advertised" to separate true from false propositions? Well, since there is no fine print to look at, it seems that all I can do is scrutinize propositions that made it through the filter and see whether they really are true. The reason I need a filter, though, is that I do not know what is TRUE!

Suppose I look at the opinions that made it through one or the other of these two filters and compare them with the opinions that were held back. Suppose that, when I see what the outcome is, I am tempted to believe that *Some things the Authority has certified are just not TRUE* or that *Some things that most people think are true are just not TRUE.* How can I decide whether I should (a) change my conception of what is true, or (b) simply reject the Authority Principle or the Conformity Policy?

Truth is a philosophically perturbing subject. It seems that if I try out a proposed filter for a while and see what propositions come out as TRUE and FALSE, I will think the filter is good if and only if all the propositions I now believe come through and all the propositions I now disbelieve are trapped. This implies, however, that with a good filter, I will not refine my belief-set. A good filter is supposed to help me refine my belief-set! What is the way out of this dilemma? The next chapter shows how the Meditator manages to extricate himself by ignoring (temporarily) the question what a truth-filter looks like and how it is to be certified. Instead, the Meditator begins to experiment with his existing belief-set.

CHAPTER 2

Meditation One
The possibility of a malevolent Demon is raised and the Meditator resolves to doubt everything he can possibly doubt

I THE WITHHOLDING POLICY – CAN THE SENSES BE TRUSTED? – THE DREAM ARGUMENT – THE MALEVOLENT DEMON ARGUMENT (AT VII:18–23)

> I am here quite alone, and at last I will devote myself sincerely and without reservation to the general demolition of my opinions.
>
> . . . Once the foundations of a building are undermined, anything built on them collapses of its own accord; so I will go straight for the basic principles on which all my former beliefs rested.
>
> (VII:18)

The Meditator's overall ambition is to establish something in the sciences that is "stable and likely to last." The previous chapter suggested that we should understand his aim to be the discovery of nonobvious truths about the world and that he needs especially to add significant true opinions to and eject significant false opinions from his belief-set, while shrinking his set of undecided opinions. We can take him as having realized that all the sorting-procedures described in Ch. 1 Sec. 2, including the Methods of Total Credulity and Total Skepticism, the Subjective and Conformity Policies, and the Authority Principle, are inadequate for this purpose. To be sure, the Meditator has not explicitly reviewed each of the five methods and found each wanting. Yet the Authority Principle and the Conformity Policy, the only two that showed any real promise, are alluded to in the text. Most beliefs acquired in childhood are either inculcated in us by certain authorities, or they are the consensus beliefs of the people around us.

The Meditator reiterates his intention to demolish the entire edifice representing his knowledge-condition. He will bring it down by knocking out the foundations of his existing beliefs:

> Reason now leads me to think that I should hold back my assent from opinions which are not completely certain and indubitable just as carefully as I do from those which are patently false . . . And to do this I will not need to run through them all individually, which would be an endless task.
> (VII:18)

Note that the Meditator has *not* decided to adopt the method of Total Skepticism, holding all propositions for false. In fact, he is not even trying to sort his opinions into the categories TRUE and FALSE. Instead, he has decided simply to sort his opinions into two categories, BELIEVE and DOUBT, ignoring the problem of truth. We can assume that his aim is ultimately to come to know what is true and what is false. He has no way, however, to get out of the trap that the problem of stating and justifying a criterion for truth has just been shown to lead us into. Perhaps he senses that he can only make headway by backing away for the moment from the large, mysterious, problematic concepts TRUE and FALSE.

The Meditator has decided that he should "hold back . . . assent" from any opinion held by himself, or anyone else, that is not "completely certain and indubitable." He will employ the following policy:

Withholding Policy: If an opinion appears to be at all uncertain, or if it is possible to doubt it, I will withhold assent from it, i.e. I will not BELIEVE it.

The Withholding Policy is a departure in two respects from the ordinary way of filling in and sometimes kicking beliefs out of our belief-sets.

First, I normally distinguish between propositions I *actively disbelieve* and hold for absurd and propositions that I merely doubt or have not decided about. I *actively disbelieve* the proposition that our Earth has two different suns that appear on odd and even numbered days of the month, whereas I have merely *not decided about* the proposition that there is intelligent life elsewhere in the universe. I *actively disbelieve* that I shall live to be 200 years old, whereas I merely *doubt* that I shall live to be 100 years old. The Withholding Policy instructs me to ignore this distinction. It tells me to withhold assent from any proposition that is either absurd in my view, or plainly wrong, or probably not right, or unproved, or dubious, or questionable, or maybe false, or simply possible to doubt. All such propositions are to be treated in the same way and relegated to a single category, the category of propositions I do not believe.

But what about the propositions the Meditator currently believes? What will happen to them as a result of the Withholding Policy?

This brings us to a second interesting feature of the Withholding Policy. There are many propositions that I believe to be true without being *completely certain* that they are true. For example, I believe that *I locked my office door when I left it*, and I believe that *There are fewer than eleven planets*. I believe that *I shall live to be at least seventy years old*. But I am not *completely certain* of any of these propositions. I would perhaps bet $100 on not being shown to be wrong where the planets are concerned. I would not, however, bet $100,000 that I locked my office door when I left it, or on the planetary proposition either. I do not consider those propositions impossible to doubt, and, by dwelling on my hereditary and acquired weaknesses, it is possible for me to feel uncertain that I will live past the age of sixty-nine, though I do not actually believe that I will not. The Withholding Policy instructs me to refuse to believe any opinion of which I am not completely certain, any opinion that it is possible to doubt.

But will the Withholding Policy really help with the completion of subtasks (1)–(3)? It is unclear at this stage whether it will help very much. If the Meditator is currently undecided about an opinion, he should withhold assent, according to the Policy. He should withhold assent from all opinions that he currently disbelieves as well. Evidently, if the Meditator is undecided whether buying a new horse would be a good idea, or undecided whether the Copernican system or the Ptolemaic system is true, the Meditator should not believe that buying a horse would be a good idea, or that one or the other system is true. It isn't clear, however, how this is going to lead to a beneficial revision of the Meditator's belief-set, not in the direction of the total make-over the Meditator is seeking. Establishing something stable and lasting in the sciences is a goal whose relation to the Withholding Policy is, at this stage, far from clear.

The Meditator does not know where the Policy will lead. It might turn out to be a dead end. Nevertheless, the Meditator has to start somewhere and he knows that certain other policies and procedures do not work or involve untestable filters. The Meditator can appreciate that those methods are useless for approaching the condition of an ideal scientist. Since he is also convinced that many of his existing beliefs are false – even if he does not know which they are – and that he has in the past accepted them despite their dubiousness, the Withholding Policy seems sensible.

The Withholding Policy is the basis of a sorting-procedure, and it is a selective filter. It is not, however, as observed earlier, a filter that is intended to hold back false beliefs and let though only true beliefs. It filters propositions that the Meditator thinks he ought to assent to from propositions from which he thinks he should withhold assent. The filter will change the composition of the Meditator's belief-set. The Meditator may hope he will, in time, discover a much more useful filter, one that will actually separate true from false propositions. For the moment, however, the Meditator has resolved simply to undertake a sorting-procedure that will separate opinions as follows:

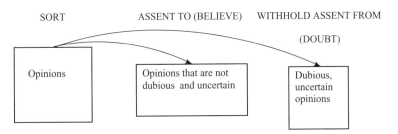

Figure 7   The Withholding Policy

Resolved to try out the new Withholding Policy, the Meditator realizes that he cannot consider each of his opinions individually to see which ones are dubious, unproved, less than fully certain, and otherwise of poor quality, since this would be an "endless task." It would be truly exhausting to have to consider all his own opinions, as well as all of other people's opinions, one-by-one and to try to decide whether he is dead certain of each of them. All the propositions about cows . . . about the sun and stars . . . skeletons . . . numbers . . . snow . . . children and animals . . . chemicals . . .! Rather than making an enormously long list of sentences and trying to consider them as individual propositions with definite meanings, the Meditator has to resort to some "chunking" procedures, considering entire categories of opinion. What *kinds* of opinion has he believed in the past? Which kinds are the least bit doubtful?

At this stage, the Meditator's condition can be represented as follows:

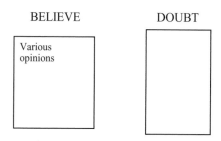

Figure 8   The Meditator's belief-set at the beginning of *Meditation One*

What opinions should be placed into DOUBT? It would be appropriate for the Meditator to place all superstitions, lies, and popular falsehoods of which he is aware into DOUBT. What about Sensory Propositions, based on experiences and memories of experiences, such as the following?

The sky is blue
The desktop is hard
Roses smell sweet
There are many stars in the sky
I am surrounded by people and objects

Are these propositions certain and indubitable? They do not seem to be superstitions, lies, or popular falsehoods. Is it permissible to believe them? The Meditator observes that most of his current opinions, which he acquired in childhood, are derived from his sensory experience – what he has seen, tasted, and handled. Are they really impossible to doubt?

The Meditator recalls that he has sometimes been deceived by sensory experience and he ventures the thought that it is prudent never to trust a source that has ever been less than perfectly reliable.

> Whatever I have up till now accepted as most true I have acquired either from the senses or through the senses. But from time to time I have found that the senses deceive, and it is prudent never to trust completely those who have deceived us even once.
>
> (VII:18)

For example, the sun often looks no larger to our eyes than a dinner plate and flies do not look as though they have hairy legs. Regardless of how it looks, I know the sun to be larger than a dinner plate, and, on examination with a microscope, flies can be seen to have hairy legs. Our naked eyesight is not entirely trustworthy. Perhaps our other senses are just as defective and all Sensory Propositions should be placed in DOUBT.

The Meditator is here toying with a policy, the policy of Radical Mistrust, wondering whether to accept it or not. According to the policy, if a certain source has *ever* been found untrustworthy or deceitful, then propositions issuing from that source are dubious and assent should be withheld from them all. If Radical Mistrust is justified, *all* opinions about how things are that are based upon vision, touch, and the other sense modalities should not be assented to. We should doubt that *Snow is white*, that *Grass is green*, and that *Rocks are hard and solid*.

The Meditator is not able to endorse the use of the policy of Radical Mistrust, however, recognizing that it is overly severe. Consider an everyday application of the policy: If you are *even once* given an answer by Person X that you later come to regard as deceitful, *everything* Person X *ever* tells you from that point onwards should be doubted. Radical Mistrust seems an extreme policy. Suppose you have good reason to think that X has given you a deceitful answer to the question "Where were you last night?" Why not simply decide that X is an unreliable informant on this kind of issue and avoid placing too much confidence in him or her where such issues are concerned? X might, after all, be a perfectly good informant concerning the time of day or how to ski. Maybe there is even reason to think that X will give more honest answers to the question "Where were you last night?" in the future. We humans have, it might be said, trusting dispositions, as well as a thirst for knowledge. It is hard to cut off potentially good sources of information just because, on some particular occasion, they have deceived us about something or other.

The Meditator comes to the corresponding conclusion where his senses are concerned. There is no particular reason to doubt most claims about what I see, touch, taste, smell, and hear. Some immediate sensory experience seems to be indubitable. The Meditator cannot doubt, he confesses, "that I am here, sitting by the fire, wearing a winter dressing-gown, holding a piece of paper in my hands . . . that these hands or this whole body are mine." To doubt such evident things would be to resemble, he says, those madmen, "whose brains are so damaged by the persistent vapours of melancholia that they firmly maintain that they are kings when they are paupers, or say they are dressed in purple when they are naked, or that their heads are made of earthenware, or that they are pumpkins or made of glass." If the ultimate aim is to become a scientist, to purge one's false beliefs from one's knowledge-edifice and to add only new truths, the method of mistrusting one's own senses does not seem to lead in the right direction.

Unexpectedly, however, it occurs to the Meditator that he does sometimes resemble a madman. Some of the experiences he has while asleep and dreaming are like those madmen have while awake and are just as bizarre. Other dream-experiences are not at all bizarre but they are just as delusory. In fact, the Meditator realizes, the experiences he has while asleep are often the same as the experiences he has while awake. The Meditator might in fact be asleep and only dreaming that he is meditating and only dreaming that he is writing about dreaming . . .

> How often, asleep at night, am I convinced of just such familiar events – that I am here in my dressing-gown, sitting by the fire – when in fact I am lying undressed in bed! Yet at the moment my eyes are certainly wide awake when I look at this piece of paper; I shake my head and it is not asleep; as I stretch out and feel my hand I do so deliberately, and I know what I am doing. All this would not happen with such distinctness to someone asleep. Indeed! As if I did not remember other occasions when I have been tricked by exactly similar thoughts while asleep!
> (VII:19)

The Meditator decides that, while he may be dreaming that he is meditating and writing – perhaps he is even a creature without hands and a human body dreaming that he has hands and a human body – not everything that is seemingly revealed by his immediate experience should be doubted.

Perhaps eyes and heads do not exist and are merely imaginary, but, the Meditator decides, "it must at least be admitted that certain other simpler and more universal things are real. These are as it were the real colours from which we form all the images of things, whether true or false, that appear in our thought." When painters depict imaginary sirens and satyrs, "they . . . simply jumble up the limbs of different animals" without inventing "natures which are new in all respects." I should not doubt that, even if I am dreaming, there are certain simple and universal forms that are not imaginary but real. In other words, dream-objects and situations, however bizarre, are made up of combinations of well-known forms, and these well-known forms are themselves made up of simpler forms that really exist.

If this combinatorial theory is correct, the Meditator reasons, perhaps the opinions of arithmeticians and geometers which are based on simple and at the same time abstract concepts ought to be believed, but not the propositions of natural science:

[A] reasonable conclusion ... might be that physics, astronomy, medicine, and all other disciplines which depend on the study of composite things, are doubtful; while arithmetic, geometry and other subjects of this kind, which deal only with the simplest and most general things, regardless of whether they exist in nature or not, contain something certain and indubitable.

(VII:20)

"For whether I am awake or asleep, two and three added together are five, and a square has no more than four sides." By contrast if I am only dreaming that I have seen the moon, or read that bodies accelerate as they fall and that there are nine planets, or that I have found out somehow that I have internal organs, such a heart and a liver, these things are doubtful and possibly false, though I have believed them up to now.

The Meditator realizes, however, that it would be just as unwise to trust mathematical propositions that seem true as to trust physical, astronomical, and medical propositions. For, when adding up long columns of figures, I often make careless mistakes. If this happens with long columns of figures, why can't it happen to me with a shorter column? When I work through a long geometrical or algebraic proof, I can become convinced of the proposition on the last line even when certain errors have slipped in unnoticed that vitiate the conclusion. If this happens with a long proof, why not with a short proof? Perhaps, the Meditator reflects, he goes wrong every time he tries to add 2 + 3, or to count the sides of a square. Perhaps even simple and universal forms do not exist and are purely imaginary and the results of arithmetic and geometry as well ought to be doubted. The weakness of the human intellect and memory, and the carelessness to which he knows he is prone, seem to threaten even the simplest results of the so-called "exact" sciences.

A new thought brings the Meditator up short. Hasn't he been created by an omnipotent and benevolent God who surely has the ability and motivation to fashion a less pathetic creature than one who can not add 2 + 3 and get 5? Presumably there is a God – at least the Meditator has always thought so – and this God is omnipotent and benevolent – at least the Meditator has always thought so. This belief, however, was acquired in childhood and inculcated by certain authorities. It now occurs to the Meditator that the assumption that God is benevolent as well as all-powerful is at least somewhat doubtful.

Suppose there is a Deity and this Deity is omnipotent, but not benevolent. Then the Deity could bring it about that everything the Meditator thinks is real and existing is not. The Deity could make it the case that "there is no earth, no sky, no extended thing, no shape, no size, no place." A Deity could make it seem that simple arithmetical sums such as $2 + 2 = 4$ are false and that octagons have nine sides. I can hallucinate a ship, or a chair, or a person that is not there. Why couldn't a Deity cause me to hallucinate an entire world of people and things that were not there? Not only *could* a Deity deceive me in this fundamental way, but a certain kind of malevolent Deity *would* take pleasure in deceiving me. The existence of just such a malevolent Deity might seem improbable, but it seems to the Meditator that it is not impossible. Is anyone willing, he asks to *deny* that there is an omnipotent Deity? Is anyone willing to *assert* that an omnipotent Deity could not bring it about that there only seemed to me to be a world of colorful, moving objects and people when there was not? The Meditator now realizes that this is how things stand:

If there exists a malevolent Demon who enjoys deceiving me, then . . .

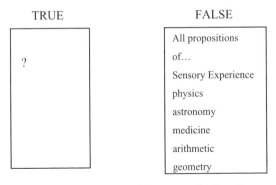

Figure 9   How things stand if there is a malevolent Demon

Having realized how things stand, what should the Meditator believe and doubt? The Meditator does not know that there exists a malevolent Demon, and he does not positively believe that there exists a malevolent Demon. Nevertheless, the possibility of a malevolent Demon can not be excluded. Therefore, the existence of a good God is doubtful. Consequently, the Meditator is forced – for the time being – to doubt all his existing opinions pertaining to sensory experience as well as all opinions pertaining to mathematics and physics. We can represent the Meditator's current belief-set as follows:

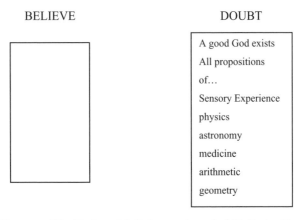

BELIEVE   DOUBT

> A good God exists
> All propositions
> of…
> Sensory Experience
> physics
> astronomy
> medicine
> arithmetic
> geometry

Figure 10   The Meditator's belief -set at the end of *Meditation One*

Compare Figure 9 with Figure 10. Notice that although the left-hand (TRUE/BELIEVE) and right-hand (FALSE/DOUBT) boxes have nearly identical contents, Figure 10 appears without the heading "*If there exists a malevolent Demon who enjoys deceiving me then . . .*" and the DOUBT box in Figure 10 contains the proposition *A good God exists*. The Meditator has reasoned as follows:

1) God, if He exists, is omnipotent and He is either good or malevolent, I do not know which. I acquired a belief in childhood that God exists, and is omnipotent and good, but I do not know if this belief is TRUE.

2) If God is omnipotent and malevolent, all propositions of Sensory Experience and all the opinions of the physicists, the mathematicians, the doctors, etc., are FALSE.

Now:

3) In accord with the Withholding Policy, I should DOUBT the proposition acquired in childhood but now seen to be dubious, that a God exists who is both omnipotent and good.

Further:

4) Insofar as I am not certain that there does not exist an omnipotent and malevolent Demon, I should DOUBT all Propositions of Sensory Experience and all the opinions of the physicists, the mathematicians, the doctors, etc. (Figure 10 expresses the content of (3) and (4).)

> I will suppose therefore that not God, who is supremely good and the source of truth, but rather some malicious demon of the utmost power and cunning has employed all his energies in order to deceive me. I shall think that the sky, the air, the earth, colours, shapes, sounds and all external things are merely the delusions of dreams which he has devised to ensnare my judgment. I shall consider myself as not having hands or eyes, or flesh, or blood or senses, but as falsely believing that I have all these things.
>
> (VII:22–3)

At the conclusion of *Meditation One*, the Meditator has resolved to doubt all the opinions of alleged experts – including learned authors, physicists, mathematicians, and doctors, and also the truth of all his own former opinions, including the opinion that he has hands, a body, and all the propositions he came to believe on the basis of his senses. He currently believes nothing about himself or his world, or the existence of any natural or supernatural entities.

One might wonder why the Meditator does not decide to doubt the existence of a malevolent Demon on the basis of the Withholding Policy, since the existence of a malevolent Demon is, after all, very uncertain. The Meditator does not believe that the Deity is a malevolent Demon. He is just as doubtful and uncertain whether a malevolent Demon exists as he is whether a good God exists. So, in accord with the Withholding Policy, the Meditator is not entitled to believe that a Demon exists anymore than he is entitled to believe that a good God exists.

There is perhaps a good and simple reason why the Meditator does not resolve to doubt the existence of a malevolent Demon in accord with the Withholding Policy. The Withholding Policy is specifically meant to apply to existing opinions, especially those acquired in childhood (that is to say, inculcated by authorities or adopted in order to conform to popular opinion). The hypothesis of a malevolent Demon is not one of these "received beliefs." The Meditator can *suppose* that or *posit* that a malevolent Demon exists without violating the Withholding Policy. To suppose that P is not to believe that P ("Suppose you have just won the lottery . . .") and to suppose that P exists is not to believe that P exists ("Suppose there is a highly contagious mutant virus that kills its victims within six hours . . ."). We still, however, need some explanation for why the Meditator decides to suppose or posit that a malevolent Demon is deceiving him.

Recall the Meditator's general dissatisfaction with his knowledge-condition, his feeling that he needs to "demolish everything," and his observation that it would be too time-consuming to sort through his existing opinions one by one in order to improve his belief-set. This impatience led him to chunk his existing received beliefs into categories of belief, including Propositions of Sensory Experience and the propositions of arithmetic, astronomy, medicine, etc. If a malevolent Demon existed, he realized, all these beliefs would be false. The Withholding Policy, together with uncertainty as to the existence of a good God, provides a reason to doubt propositions in every major category of received opinion. At the same time, only the supposition that there exists a malevolent Demon makes it psychologically possible to apply the Withholding Policy in an effective way. For it would be difficult simply to *decide* to doubt that one had hands, that humans need water to survive, and that stars are real flaming objects in space unless one could envision a scenario under which these propositions only seem to be obviously true but are not.

The application of the Withholding Policy, backed up by the supposition of the malevolent Demon, is a thought-experiment aimed at disclosing information that is hard to get by ordinary means. Just as I can come to realize something new about myself by seeing what occurs to me when I imagine myself the beneficiary of some unexpected good fortune, and just as a society can learn something about itself by considering what would likely happen if a fast-acting lethal virus came into existence, so the Meditator can hope to learn something by seeing what occurs to him when he posits the existence of a malevolent Demon.

The Meditator is now in an awkward position. Can he really, should he really adopt the supposition in question? The Withholding Policy, the Meditator observes, is difficult to apply and accordingly daunting: "A kind of laziness brings me back to normal life . . . I happily slide back into my old opinions and dread being shaken out of them, . . . for fear . . . that I shall have to toil . . . amid the inextricable darkness of the problems I have now raised." To suspend belief in what for most people were and still are everyday commonplaces – that we are animated living bodies that move about in three-dimensional space, surrounded by variously colored physical objects, some of which, like the stars, exist at a great distance from us, in a world created and watched over by a benevolent Deity – is not easy and it is emotionally perturbing. The opinions of normal life predicate us as *belonging* to an essentially friendly world. The Meditator has abandoned this comfortable belief. He no longer has a place, a social role, and various duties and responsibilities, though he seems to do so. He has posited only one real, external thing, and with this thing he exists in a hostile or at least alienated relationship, as the victim of that being's deceptive powers.

2 OBJECTIONS TO *MEDITATION ONE*

The Objectors to *Meditation One* are critical of the reasoning processes of the Meditator. Above and beyond their commitment to good reasoning, they are concerned with the intentions and beliefs of the Meditator's creator, Descartes. A fundamental objection to Descartes's presentation of the Meditator is raised by the theologian Antoine Arnauld:

> I am afraid that the author's somewhat free style of philosophizing, which calls everything into doubt, may cause offence to some people. He himself admits . . . that this approach is dangerous for those of only moderate intelligence . . .

> I rather think that the First Meditation should be furnished with a brief preface which explains that there is no serious doubt cast on these matters but that the purpose is to isolate temporarily those matters which leave room for even the "slightest" and most "exaggerated" doubt; it should be explained that this is to facilitate the discovery of something so firm and stable that not even the most perverse skeptic will have even the slightest scope for doubt. Following on from this point, where we find the clause "since I did not know the author of my being," I would suggest a substitution of the clause "since I was pretending that I did not know . . ."
> (VII:215)

Arnauld expresses a worry about discipline and control. Philosophy, according to a common conception of its role at the time, ought to serve theology by giving rigorous demonstrations of the truths of religion in order to combat atheism. Atheism takes root in skepticism and doubt. It is dangerous to society because, when a person comes to doubt that there exists a transcendent God or to doubt that there is a rational reason to believe in a single God, or in the God revealed by the Christian texts, his beliefs may lead to further skepticism about morality, or even about the obligation to obey the laws of the state and its rulers. Even if Descartes does not mean to stir up trouble, Arnauld fears that his text might have subversive effects.

Though Descartes does not assert in *Meditation One* that the existence of God or God's benevolence are doubtful, Arnauld is particularly concerned about the way in which the Meditator turns over in his mind the supposition that an omnipotent God might possibly be a malevolent Demon rather than a benevolent divinity. He thinks Descartes ought to make clear that the Meditator does in fact know all along that a good God exists although he is "pretending" not to know.

In response, Descartes compares the *Meditations* to "fire and knives" that cannot be handled by careless people or children but that are useful for human life precisely because of their destructive powers. In his earlier, autobiographical, *Discourse on Method*, he had disclaimed any intention to cause harm or even to have others imitate him.

> My present aim . . . is not to teach the method which everyone must follow in order to direct his reason correctly, but only to reveal how I have tried to direct my own . . . I hope it will be useful for some without being harmful to any, and that everyone will be grateful to me for my frankness.
>
> (VI:4)

He explains in response to Arnauld that he did not raise the issue of pervasive doubt in the *Discourse*, which was written in French, for a broader class of readers. He has reserved it for the (originally Latin) *Meditations*, which he knows to be accessible only to "very intelligent and well-educated readers." These people, he implies, should know how to handle the intellectual equivalent of fire and knives. The interested Reader will find more information on the intentions behind Descartes's writing of the *Meditations* and on its theological implications in Ch. 12.

Another pertinent set of objections is offered by Pierre Gassendi. Gassendi writes that he approves the Meditator's project of freeing his mind from all preconceived opinions. He thinks Descartes's construction of a situation of radical doubt for the Meditator, does not really work, however. "Why . . . did you consider everything as false, which seems more like adopting a new prejudice than relinquishing an old one?" (VII:257–8):

> This strategy made it necessary for you to convince yourself by imagining a deceiving God or some evil demon who tricks us, whereas it would surely have been sufficient to cite the darkness of the human mind or the weakness of our nature . . . Whatever you say, no one will believe that you have really convinced yourself that not one thing you formerly knew is true . . . Would it not have been more in accord with philosophical honesty and the love of truth simply to state the facts candidly and straightforwardly rather than, as some critics might put it, to resort to artifice, sleight of hand and circumlocution?
>
> (VII:258)

Descartes ventures in reply that it is not so easy to free ourselves from preconceived opinions. In order to straighten out a curved stick, we bend it around in the opposite direction (VII:349). Moreover, just as in geometry, we may draw imaginary lines in a diagram in order to prove truths, so we may assume imaginary falsehoods in philosophy in order to prove truths. It is rhetorical showing off on Gassendi's part, he says, to suggest that this is philosophically dishonest (VII:350).

Finally, there are some lengthy and confused objections by Father Bourdin, a Jesuit priest. Bourdin asks how I can ever be absolutely positive that my senses are deceiving me or that I am dreaming. "What if the demon has convinced you that you sometimes dream?" he asks.

Descartes's Meditator, however, never claimed to be certain that he was dreaming or that his senses deceived him, so all this seems to be beside the point. Descartes shrugs off this barrage as irrelevant and repeats what he said to Arnauld: The *Meditations* should be read "only by those of a fairly robust intellect," implying that Bourdin is disqualified. Those who are inclined to precipitate judgments, who have no patience for orderly thinking, should keep clear of them. Those who have little capacity to distinguish truth and falsity should follow the opinions of others (VII:475).

Modern commentators have raised several additional difficulties. Can the Meditator really decide what to assent to and what to doubt, they wonder? To assent to a proposition is to believe it, and isn't belief involuntary? Whether it is a question of supposedly "deciding" to believe what an authority tells me, or what the consensus is, or to believe nothing or everything, belief seems to be outside my control. (Only the Subjective Policy seems to take this into account.) I can not just decide to believe that snow is blue. Nor can I just decide to doubt that I have arms and legs on the basis that it is logically possible that I do not have arms and legs, or even on the basis that it is logically possible that there exists a being who deceives me into thinking I have arms and legs.

To this objection, it might be responded that, although beliefs do form in us spontaneously and can be hard to shake, we have some control over what we believe. Suppose you decide that you have been too gullible in the past. You might decide to cultivate an attitude of suspicion. You will no longer believe certain things without evidence. You will no longer take certain people's word on trust. Alternatively, you might decide that you have been too skeptical in the past. From now on you will be more trusting, and not interrogate others so exhaustively. The Meditator did not just decide to doubt that he had feet. Rather, he looked for and discovered a psychological inducement to apply the Withholding Policy. He realized that the self-frightening fiction of the malevolent Demon was a coherent and even somewhat plausible one.

Doesn't this mean, however, that the Meditator only *pretends* to believe that there is no world, no shapes or colors, etc.? Can a creature who is thinking through what it would be like if there were a malevolent Demon ever really doubt that there is an external world? These questions belong to the philosophy of mind and epistemology and are still to some extent unresolved. A related set of modern worries concerns the Meditator's report that he is often deceived in his dreams. Granted, when I am asleep, I fail to realize that I am in bed, unconscious, etc., and it follows that I do not "know" that I am in bed and unconscious. Do I, nevertheless, simultaneously believe something false – namely that I am doing whatever I am dreaming I am doing?

Suppose I dream that I am surfing. Does *someone* have the false belief, *I am surfing*? It seems that if anyone is to have a false belief, it would have to be either my dream-self or my waking self. My dream-self, however, does not appear to have any false beliefs. My dream-self has her mind on her surfing – and she is surfing. My dream-self cannot think about my waking self, or believe that my waking self is not sleeping and is instead surfing. Meanwhile, my waking self is not thinking at all, for I am asleep and unconscious. So it seems that there is no self to have the false belief and to be deceived. A related problem about thought and reference is discussed below at the end of Ch. 3.

CHAPTER 3

Meditation Two
The Meditator discovers an indubitable proposition and continues with an investigation into her ideas of herself and her ideas of corporeal things

I HYPERBOLIC DOUBT – AN ADDITION TO THE
MEDITATOR'S BELIEF-SET – "COGITO, SUM" (AT VII:23–5)

So serious are the doubts into which I have been thrown as a result of yesterday's meditation that I can neither put them out of my mind nor see any way of resolving them. It feels as if I have fallen unexpectedly into a deep whirlpool which tumbles me around so that I can neither stand on the bottom nor swim up to the top. Nevertheless . . . I will proceed . . . until I recognize something certain, or, if nothing else, until I at least recognize for certain that there is no certainty. Archimedes used to demand just one firm and immovable point in order to shift the entire earth; so I too can hope for great things if I manage to find just one thing, however slight, that is certain and unshakeable.

(VII:24)

The Meditator is in the grip of her supposition, experienced with the force of a vivid daydream, that she is deceived by a malevolent Demon. Whirled around in dizzy confusion, she is unable to set her feet on firm ground. As she cannot accept any proposition that she does not recognize as certain and impossible to doubt, she believes nothing: "I will suppose then, that everything I see is spurious . . . that my memory tells me lies, and that none of the things that it reports ever happened. I have no senses. Body, shape, extension, movement and place are chimeras."

Figure 10 from the last chapter represents the Meditator's state, the state of Hyperbolic Doubt. Hyperbolic Doubt is doubt-taken-to-the-limit, doubt in excess of everyday uncertainty and anxiety about what to believe.

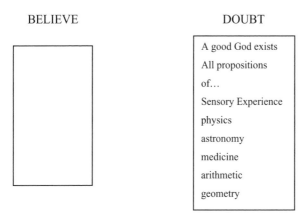

BELIEVE   DOUBT

A good God exists

All propositions

of…

Sensory Experience

physics

astronomy

medicine

arithmetic

geometry

Figure 11   The Meditator's belief-set at the beginning of *Meditation Two*

For anyone hoping to become an ideal scientist, the state of Hyperbolic Doubt is an uncomfortable one. If filters are tested by experience, according to whether what gets through the filter – good-tasting coffee, agreeable companions – is what we can appreciate that we wanted, the Withholding Policy does not seem too promising as a filter for beliefs. For it appears that the beliefs the Meditator currently possesses, i.e., none, are the same beliefs she would have possessed, had she resolved to adopt the method of Total Skepticism. Total Skepticism, we can agree, is not a method productive of knowledge.

There are, however, several respects in which the Meditator's Withholding Policy, which filters opinions into the categories of BELIEVE and DOUBT, differs importantly from the Method of Total Skepticism, which sorts *all* opinions into the category of FALSE.

First, it is difficult – perhaps impossible – to think of a scenario – a state of the world, taking the "world" to be whatever there is – under which the Method of Total Skepticism would be justified. What would the "world" have to be like for all statements, all propositions, to be FALSE?

Perhaps if the world were such that nothing existed, all propositions would be false? In that case, the proposition *Nothing exists* would be true. By contrast, it is possible to think of a scenario under which the employment of the Withholding Policy by the Meditator is justified. It is just the scenario in which the world has exactly two objects in it: an omnipotent malevolent Demon and a Meditator who have been assigned the roles respectively of deceiver and deceived and are playing them out.

Second, the Method of Total Skepticism would require the Meditator to disbelieve every future opinion presented to her, preventing her from ever acquiring a single belief. By contrast, the Withholding Policy need not prevent the Meditator from acquiring new beliefs. If any propositions are absolutely indubitable, if the malevolent Demon could never deceive the Meditator with respect to them, they may be believed.

Doubting everything that it is possible to doubt does not come to the same thing as doubting every possible proposition. There is reason to hope that the Meditator can begin to fill her empty belief-set under the Withholding Policy and that there are some truths about her condition and her world that she can eventually discover.

At this juncture, several candidates for propositions that might be believable occur to the Meditator. She considers whether she should believe that a Deity – benevolent or malevolent – exists and causes the Meditator to have the thoughts she is currently experiencing. After all, *something* must be responsible for the thoughts about being caught up in a whirlpool, Archimedes and his lever, radical deceit by a malevolent Demon, and her overall predicament, that the Meditator is experiencing.

Before beginning her meditative exercise, the Meditator might have supposed that such thoughts were caused by her own brain or her past experiences. Since she now doubts that there are any objects with shape and color – and brains are certainly objects with shape and color – she cannot believe that the brain is the cause of her current thoughts. Since she doubts that her memory reports the past to her accurately, she has to doubt that she had any particular past experiences, that any events actually occurred in the past that she now seems to remember. Should she also doubt that there is any nonmaterial cause of her thoughts? "Is there not a God, or whatever I may call him," she asks, "who puts into me the thoughts I am now having?"

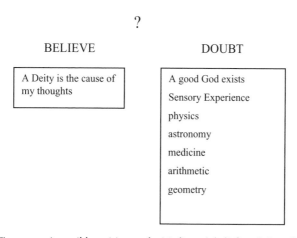

Figure 12   A possible revision to the Meditator's belief-set (rejected)

Can the proposition *A Deity is the cause of my thoughts* be doubted? Because she doubts that a benevolent God exists, the Meditator cannot believe that a benevolent God has caused her to have certain thoughts. However, even if a malevolent Demon is the cause of her thoughts, the proposition *A Deity is the cause of my thoughts* will be true. So perhaps that proposition should be assented to and the revision in Figure 12 is appropriate. In that event, the Meditator will have added a first item to her belief-set.

Unfortunately, the Meditator realizes, the proposition in question is after all doubtful. The thing that is responsible for the Meditator's thoughts might just be . . . the Meditator herself, unaided by a Deity, benevolent or malevolent. "I myself may be the author of these thoughts." This suggests the following revision:

?

BELIEVE   DOUBT

Either a Deity is or I myself am the cause of my thoughts

A good God exists
Sensory Experience
physics
astronomy
medicine
arithmetic
geometry

Figure 13   Another possible revision to the Meditator's belief-set (rejected)

It is not easy to decide whether the Meditator should add this new proposition *Either a Deity is or I myself am the cause of my thoughts* to her otherwise empty belief-set. Again, a short digression is in order.

The questionable new proposition is *disjunctive*: It consists of two alternatives, linked by the word "or." One might wonder how I can believe a proposition of the form *A or B*. On reflection, however, this is not so puzzling. Suppose I believe that my husband is either in the kitchen or in the laundry-room. This is tantamount to believing that he is in the house, but not in the dining room, the living room, etc. *A or B* can represent a genuine belief with plenty of content so long as the disjunction rules out one or more *relevant alternatives*.

There is some reason to suppose that some disjunctive propositions of the form *A or B*, namely, tautologies, can not be believed. A *tautology* like *Either it is raining or it is not raining* fails to rule out any state of affairs. It is true no matter what the state of the world is. A philosopher might insist that tautologies cannot be believed, because we cannot represent to ourselves the specific condition of the world a tautology expresses. There could be no difference, she might argue, between "believing" that *Either it is raining or it is not raining* and "believing" *Either snow is white or it is not white*.

The claim that we cannot believe tautologies is not perfectly convincing. One of the two tautologies above is *about* rain and the other is *about* snow. They seem to express thoughts with different "contents," even if both are true in the same states of the world – namely all possible states of the world. Nevertheless, it is easier to understand what is involved in believing *It is raining* than in believing that *Either it is raining or it is not raining.*

In any case, the proposition *Either a Deity is or I myself am the cause of my thoughts* is not a tautology. It is rather a doubtful and uncertain proposition, precisely because there is at least one relevant alternative that it excludes. Perhaps the Meditator's thoughts are not caused by anything. Perhaps they just happen. It might seem impossible that the Meditator's thoughts come from nowhere, but the Meditator has no reason to believe that there are no uncaused things or events that simply come out of nowhere. Certainly, the Meditator has no overwhelming reason to believe the proposition *Every thought has a cause.* The proposition *Every thought has a cause* is at least somewhat doubtful.

So the Meditator should not add *Either a Deity is or I myself am the cause of my thoughts* to her belief-set. Should she add the following proposition?

> *Either a Deity is, or I myself am, or nothing at all is the cause of my thoughts*

The Meditator does not debate with herself whether to add this lengthy disjunctive proposition to her belief-set. Indeed, after raising the question whether it would be appropriate to believe in some cause or other for her thoughts, she abandons temporarily the whole subject of the origins of her thoughts. Intuitively, it is easy to see why. This procedure of making up longer and longer disjunctive propositions that seem to have less and less content the closer they come to being truly indubitable because they do not exclude any possible alternatives does not seem to be going anywhere. If I feel that I am trapped in a whirlpool and can not put my feet down anywhere, if I am looking for an Archimedean point to shift me over from total ignorance to a science with firm foundations, coming to believe a lengthy, complex disjunctive proposition verging on a tautology does not seem like much help.

At this point, the Meditator comes to a startling realization. No matter how the Meditator's thoughts have come to be, whether there exists a malevolent Demon or not, there is a subject that *has* the thoughts the Meditator is having. No matter what, it cannot be doubted that the Meditator has certain thoughts. The Meditator *thinks*, and, accordingly, the Meditator *exists*. The malevolent Demon can deceive the Meditator with respect to the existence of colors, sounds, material objects, other people, and the truth of any equation or mathematical proposition. The Demon, however, cannot cause the Meditator to have any experience when the Meditator does not exist, including the experience of thinking that she exists. The proposition *I exist*, when considered by the Meditator, cannot possibly be doubted by her. Whether there is a God, a Demon, or no Deity at all, the Meditator realizes, *she* is something, not a phantasm or a nonentity.

> Is there not a God . . . who puts into me the thoughts I am now having? . . . [But] . . . I myself may perhaps be the author of these thoughts. In that case am not I, at least, something?
>
> (VII:24)

Notice that the Meditator did not assert "I think, *therefore* I exist" (*Cogito, ergo sum*), though this famous formula appears elsewhere. Rather, the Meditator asserted that *whenever* she had the thought *I am* or *I exist*, she realized that the thought was "necessarily true." The thought-experiment of withholding belief from every proposition that can be doubted, performed with the artificial apparatus of the malevolent Demon, has produced an observation that, in the Meditator's experience, is new and unprecedented, an indubitable intuition of existence.

> I have convinced myself that there is absolutely nothing in the world, no sky, no earth, no minds, no bodies . . . [T]here is a deceiver of supreme power and cunning who is deliberately and constantly deceiving me. In that case I too undoubtedly exist, if he is deceiving me; and let him deceive me as much as he can, he will never bring it about that I am nothing so long as I think that I am something. So after considering everything very thoroughly, I must finally conclude that this proposition, *I am, I exist*, is necessarily true whenever it is put forward by me or conceived in my mind.
>
> (VII:24–5)

The situation is as represented in Figure 14:

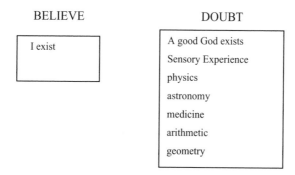

Figure 14   The Meditator's belief set at the end of p. 25, *Meditation Two*

This is progress. The experimental Withholding Policy has produced an unexpectedly decent result.

The Withholding Policy has turned out to be very different from Total Skepticism. It would be premature to suggest that the Meditator has discovered a *truth* (despite her claim that when she thinks about the proposition *I exist* she concludes that the proposition is "necessarily true"). However, the policy has at least produced a proposition that is a positive addition to the Meditator's belief-set. Archimedes boasted that, with a stable point and a long enough lever, he could move the earth. We do not know at this stage whether *I exist* can provide any leverage, but it is not a bad start. Will this proposition immune from doubt enable the Meditator to do the equivalent of shifting the position of the earth? If not, will *I exist* prove to be the only legitimate addition to the Meditator's belief-set that it is possible for her to make, leaving her still trapped for the most part in Hyperbolic Doubt? This remains to be seen.

What exactly, though, is the Meditator's "I," the now-believed-to-be-existing thing? Most sentences, as noted earlier, are vague or ambiguous. *Which* belief has the Meditator actually added to her formerly empty set of beliefs?

2 WHAT AM "I?" – FORMER OPINIONS DOUBTED – "I" MUST BE A MIND – *SEEING₁* AND *SEEING₂* (AT VII:25–30)

The Meditator recalls her former opinions about herself. She used to believe that she was a human being. But what is a human being?

Traditionally, philosophers had defined a human being as a "rational animal," or, with some frivolity, as a "featherless biped." The Meditator confesses that she never found the traditional definitions helpful. What is involved in being "rational?" What is an "animal?" These terms are vague and their meaning is hard to pin down. If one wanted to define "rational" and "animal" in such a precise way that no one could contest the definition, this could take (and waste) a lot of time. Without bothering about definitional precision, the Meditator muses that she had previously thought about herself – naturally and spontaneously – as a feeling, moving, living, food-consuming body. She also supposed that she had a soul that was something like a warm, vaporous infusion that maintained her life, sense, thought, and motion.

> [T]he first thought to come to mind was that I had a face, hands, arms and the whole mechanical structure of limbs which can be seen in a corpse, and which I called the body. The next thought was that I was nourished, that I moved about, and that I engaged in sense-perception and thinking; and these actions I attributed to the soul. But as to the nature of this soul, either I did not think about this or else I imagined it to be something tenuous, like a wind or fire or ether, which permeated my more solid parts.
>
> (VII:26)

Her own body, in the Meditator's former opinion, was a specific "mechanical" configuration of body in general. Body-in-general, she used to think of as "whatever has a determinable shape and a definable location and can occupy a space in such as way as to exclude any other body" and as whatever "can be perceived by touch, sight, hearing, taste or smell and can be moved in various ways, not by itself but by whatever else comes into contact with it." The Meditator's former opinion was that, without souls to animate them, all bodies were either corpses or somewhat corpse-like. They had no power of self-movement, or sensation, or thought. Dead people, rocks, books, and other such objects, had no souls. Hence, they were inert and could not feel, cause themselves to move, or think.

What should the Meditator believe about herself now? Can she know for certain that she is a construction of limbs whose faculties of nutrition, perception, and motion are attributable to her soul? The Meditator decides that these opinions do not merit representation in BELIEVE. For, on the hypothesis that body, shape, extension, movement, and place are all chimeras that the malevolent Demon has conjured up to deceive her, the Meditator is not nourished, does not move, and does not perceive the world. Even on the hypothesis of the malevolent Demon, however, the Meditator thinks:

> [T]hought; this alone is inseparable from me. I am, I exist – that is certain. But for how long? For as long as I am thinking. For it could be that were I totally to cease from thinking, I should totally cease to exist. At present I am not admitting anything except what is necessarily true. I am, then, in the strict sense only a thing that thinks; that is, I am a mind, or intelligence, or intellect, or reason. . .
> (VII:27)

"I am not," the Meditator continues, "that structure of limbs which is called a human body. I am not even some thin vapour which permeates the limbs – a wind, fire, air, breath, or whatever I depict in my imagination; for these are things I have supposed to be nothing."

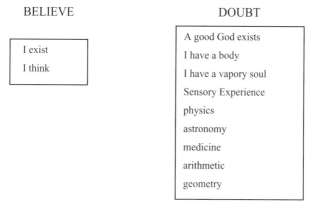

Figure 15   The Meditator's belief-set at the end of p. 27, *Meditation Two*

What are the faculties of a thing that exists and that thinks – an existing thinker? According to the Meditator, a thing that thinks is a thing that "doubts, understands, affirms, denies, is willing, is unwilling, and also imagines and has sensory perceptions." Each of these "mental actions" can be imagined as occurring in a bodiless being. A bodiless being can doubt that it has a body, understand the word "understand," affirm that it is a mind, deny that cows climb trees, and imagine that cows do climb trees.

How can I be willing or unwilling, one might wonder, if I do not have a body? For, if I do not have a body, it is hard to see how I can perform any voluntary action, such as raising my arm or refusing to get out of my chair, and hard to see how I can will to do so. However, on reflection, since I *seem* to have an arm, the "arm" the malevolent Demon has deceived me into thinking I have, I am able to will to move my arm, and since I *seem* to be sitting in a chair, I can will to remain in this (hallucinatory) chair. Further, I can be willing or unwilling to think about cows, even if there are no cows and the malevolent Demon has only made me think that cows exist and that I know what they look like.

Nevertheless, a contradiction is threatened here. The Meditator has just, in effect, stated that:

1) A thing that [only] thinks . . . [can have] sensory perceptions.

Having "sensory perceptions," however, seems to require having a body. For, only a page earlier, the Meditator said:

2) Sense-perception? This surely does not occur without a body.

How are (1) and (2) to be reconciled?

To help answer this question, it is necessary to take a temporary break from the flow of the Meditator's thoughts. Consider the following locutions:

I see a flowering tree in the garden
I saw the Prime Minister on television last night
I saw a flowering tree in my dream
After I had ingested the hallucinogen, I saw a flowering tree
Sinking to the bottom of the pool, I saw my life flash before my eyes

Apparently, there are numerous ways to "see" an object or an event. Concentrate on the difference between the kind of seeing that happens when I see a flowering tree "in my dream" and the kind of seeing that happens when I see a flowering tree "in my garden." We might call them *seeing₁* and *seeing₂*.

In *seeing₁*, there is a state of "awareness of" that does not imply the existence of an object or event that is perceived or misperceived. When I *see₁* a flowering tree in a dream, or in my imagination, I am undoubtedly having a perceptual experience. The question "Which tree did you see / are you seeing?" may even have an answer. I could report that in my dream I saw the dogwood tree at the foot of our old garden. I can also dream of, or imagine, an object that does not exist. Whether or not the old dogwood tree still exists, I can see it in my dreams. It is this kind of seeing – *seeing₁* – that the Meditator is evidently referring to in the following passage:

> For example, I am now seeing light, hearing a noise, feeling heat. But I am [perhaps] asleep, so all this is false. Yet I certainly *seem* to see, to hear, and to be warmed. This cannot be false; what is called "having a sensory perception" is strictly just this, and in this restricted sense of the term it is simply thinking.
> (VII:29)

Seeing₂ is more than a state of awareness, more than a way of "simply thinking"; it is a way of getting to know about the world outside myself. Something has to be added to an episode of *seeing₁* for *seeing₂* to occur. According to some philosophers,

$$(seeing_1 + x) = seeing_2$$

Philosophers of perception who accept this equation argue about exactly what feature x is that has to be added to *seeing₁* to get *seeing₂*.

One might suppose that feature x is the presence of the object, or its nearness to me. For me to *see₂* a tree, on this view, I must *see₁* a tree *and* there must actually be a tree in front of me and not too far away. However, the second condition does not seem to be entirely necessary. An object *seen₂* does not have to exist or be nearby. I can *see₂* a distant star that does not exist now, since it takes many years for light to travel from the star to my eye and the star might have exploded eons ago. I might *see₂* a tree that is behind me with a mirror or a distant tree with a powerful telescope. (Do I, however, *see₂* with a television set in the same way that I *see₂* with a telescope? This is debatable.) Nevertheless, it is necessary for *seeing₂* to occur that there be some entities "outside" myself.

The Meditator claims in effect that, even if she does not have a body, she can *see₁*. At the same time, because she doubts that she has a body and that there exists anything except herself, she doubts whether she can *see₂* anything at all.

How, though, does the Meditator know that she can really *see₁*? The answer is that a malevolent Demon, no matter how ill-willed and powerful, could not deceive the Meditator into believing that she was *seeing₁* a hand, a paper, a pen, when she was not. Nor could a Demon ever deceive the Meditator into believing that she was not *seeing₁* a hand, a paper, a pen, when she was. The upshot is that *seeing₁* is legitimately considered a kind of "thinking" along with the other mental activities enumerated – willing, feeling, and denying.

3 WHAT ARE "CORPOREAL THINGS?" – KNOWLEDGE OF [IDEAS OF] CORPOREAL THINGS – THE "PIECE OF WAX" – EXTENSION – INTELLECT PRIORITY – MIND PRIORITY (AT VII:30–4)

The Meditator realizes that, although she can imagine numerous things, she cannot imagine herself. She cannot form an image of herself with a certain shape and color. Indeed, if she could imagine herself, the Meditator would have to doubt that she existed, since she currently doubts that any object with a color and a shape really exists. Since the Meditator has been shown to exist, it follows that the self cannot be depicted in the imagination – or, for that matter, seen. The self is invisible.

This conclusion is worrisome to the Meditator. If a thing can neither be seen nor imagined, how can it be thought about and talked about? How can we have any knowledge of, how can we even think about, "objects" whose images we cannot even bring before our minds? Isn't it the case that the only proper objects of our thought and discourse are those things that we can either point to in the world or frame in our imaginations? We can think and talk about God or an angel, but to do so, it seems, we have to conjure up an image. In thinking of an angel, we avail ourselves of the image of a sweet-faced creature with wings and curly hair. In thinking about the Industrial Revolution, we conjure up a fleeting image of a stocking-machine or a laborer. In thinking about the taste of salt or the scent of violets we summon up gustatory and olfactory images. Even in thinking about something as abstract as the number seven, we raise up a figure 7 or an image of seven spots in our minds.

Those observations suggest that the things that we can come to know about must possess one or more sensory characteristics, such as color, shape, size, or taste. This raises the question how we can know anything about things that cannot be seen, or, more generally, things that cannot be sensed, including the self. The Meditator is already concerned with the disturbing tension between her ordinary view of knowledge as pertaining to corporeal things and the appearance of a new item in her category of BELIEVE: the invisible self – "[I]t still appears . . . that the corporeal things [i.e., material objects] of which images are formed in my thought, and which the senses investigate, are known with much more distinctness than this puzzling 'I' which cannot be pictured in the imagination."

The Meditator now embarks on a train of reflections that reveal that (even though they at first seem to present themselves to her in a complex, vivid, and individual way, through the senses of sight, touch, smell, taste, and hearing) corporeal things – or the simulacra that the malevolent Demon has supplied her with that she has always taken to be "real" – are in fact not understood very distinctly. Pondering the candle seemingly burning on her table, the Meditator considers a piece of wax that has congealed:

> Let us take, for example, this piece of wax. It has just been taken from the honeycomb; it has not yet quite lost the taste of honey; it retains some scent of the flowers from which it was gathered; its colour, shape and size are plain to see; it is hard, cold and can be handled without difficulty; if

you rap it with your knuckle it makes a sound. In short, it has everything which appears necessary to enable a body to be known as distinctly as possible. But even as I speak, I put the wax by the fire, and look: the residual taste is eliminated, the smell goes away, the colour changes, the shape is lost, the size increases; it becomes liquid and hot; you can hardly touch it, and if you strike it, it no longer makes a sound. But does the same wax remain? It must be admitted that it does; no one denies it, no one thinks otherwise. So what was it in the wax that I understood with such distinctness?

(VII:30)

Wax can be hard or soft, scented or scentless, sweet or tasteless, molded into any shape at all (think of Mme. Tussaud's museum), of various colors, resonant or silent, depending on what is done to it. Indeed, most material objects, although we think of them as having a typical picture-book look, are capable of undergoing changes in their color, shape, smell, or texture. Think of what happens to a piece of cheese left in the back of a refrigerator, or a bright cloth that is left in the sun day after day, or an egg left under a hen. They are still cheese, bright cloth, an egg (for a while). Their sensory properties, however, their qualities, are constantly changing.

What is there to know distinctly about a piece of wax? What makes it different from any other substance, such as chalk or cheese? Any particular material substance, it seems, can not only change its qualities without ceasing to be that substance, it can lose some of the properties that help us to identify it as "wax" or "chalk" or "cheese" without ceasing to be itself. Chalk, for example, can be dissolved in water. Wax can be vaporized. "Let us concentrate," the Meditator urges; "[T]ake away everything which does not belong [irrevocably] to the wax, and see what is left: merely something extended [occupying space], flexible, and changeable."

Isn't the wax, one might wonder, still known through the senses and the imagination? Isn't it my imagination, or my senses, that grasp what it is like to be extended, flexible, and changeable?

The Meditator decides that this is incorrect. The imagination and the senses cannot grasp the uncountable number of shapes that a flexible object can assume, all the changes that a changeable object can undergo, or all the ways in which it can be "extended": "I must therefore admit that the nature of this piece of wax is in no way revealed by my imagination, but is perceived by the mind alone . . . [T]he perception I have of it is a case not of vision or touch or of imagination . . . but of purely mental scrutiny. . ."

This is a surprising conclusion. The wax that I can see dripping from the candle, press between my fingers, and sniff, seems a consummate example of something that I come to know about by sensory experience, not by thinking, or by the use of my intellect. Getting to know the properties of the wax by applying all my senses to it seems to be a very different experience from thinking through an intellectual problem, even if vague images float through my mind in the course of trying to solve an intellectual problem. So the Meditator's conviction that the wax is apprehended by "purely mental scrutiny" seems implausible.

The key term is, however, the phrase "the nature of this piece of wax." There is, it seems, something *nonobvious* about the wax – its real nature – and this real nature is not available to the senses, which only apprehend its various shapes and textures, its changing color and scent. The intellect grasps that there is something that is the basis or foundation of all the perceptible changes the wax can undergo. There is a certain way that it *is*, such that it can *appear* in different ways, and only the ensemble of ways in which it can appear, and not the way that it is, can be apprehended by the senses.

According to the ordinary way of talking, the Meditator reflects, we can grasp the natures of things with our senses. For example, when the Meditator looks out of her window, she is frequently in a position to say that she "sees" human beings walking in the streets. What she is seeing is, therefore, evidently apprehended by her visual sense. Yet all that her senses really disclose to the Meditator, she realizes, are moving hats and coats that her mind *judges* to be human beings. The hat- and coat-covered objects could be automata moving hither and thither and not human beings at all; her sensory experience of them would be no different. The senses rest, as it were, on the surface of things, and do not inform us as to the nature of what we are seeing. As humans are literally "underneath" their hats and coats, so the true nature of the wax is metaphorically "underneath" the shifting sensory properties in which it is clothed. An animal perceives only the outward form of an object; the human mind can "take the clothes off, as it were, and consider [the wax] naked."

"I see humans walking in the street" is acceptable in ordinary language, the Meditator decides, even when what she really sees are moving hats and coats. However, "one who wants to achieve knowledge above the ordinary level should feel ashamed at having taken ordinary ways of talking as a basis for doubt." That is, ordinary language, which suggests that we can become aware of the nature and identity of things by using our senses, does not undermine the newly arrived-at view that the intellectual faculty of judgment, not the senses, arrives at a distinct knowledge of corporeal things.

So the Meditator's idea, acquired in childhood, that corporeal things are understood more distinctly than the thinking self is, and her former idea that the senses and the imagination are the basis of human knowledge, turn out to be, in her new and considered view, completely wrong.

The careful Reader will note that the Meditator represents herself as "not admitting that there is anything else in me except a mind." The same Reader might wonder whether the Meditator has forgotten that she is also supposed to have placed in doubt her old opinion that there were corporeal things outside her, such as wax candles and figures wearing hats and coats. If the Meditator is pretending that *Wax does not exist: there are only the ideas of wax in my mind planted there by a malevolent Demon*, it is hard to see how the conclusion that the Meditator's mind has come to know the nature of wax is justified. The proposition *Whether or not there is any wax, the nature of wax is known by my mind, not my senses* does not seem to be a good candidate for inclusion in BELIEVE. Nor does the Meditator propose to add this proposition to her belief-set. However, we can understand the Meditator's reasonings to apply to corporeal things, or bodies, if there turn out in the end to be any. The existence of material objects is currently in DOUBT, but they may exist.

Realizing nevertheless that in discussing corporeal things she seems to have gone slightly off her track, the Meditator decides that "it scarcely seems worth going through the contributions made by considering bodily things." By the end of *Meditation Two* the Meditator's belief-set has acquired four items:

BELIEVE DOUBT

I exist
I think, i.e., I doubt, will, imagine, perceive, etc.
Intellect Priority
Mind Priority

A good God exists
There are corporeal things external to me
I have a body
I have a vapory soul
Sensory Experience
physics
astronomy
medicine
arithmetic
geometry

Figure 16   The Meditator's belief-set at the end of *Meditation Two*

Note that, of the acquisitions the Meditator made for her belief-set in the course of *Meditation Two*, two concern the Meditator herself – that she thinks and that she exists – and two concern her method of acquiring knowledge. The Meditator has learned that:

1) The true nature of bodies (if they exist) is perceived by the intellect, not the senses.

2) Knowledge of the mind is more easily acquired than knowledge of bodies (if they exist).

(1) and (2) are designated in the BELIEVE box in Figure 16 as (1) the "(Principle of) Intellect Priority" and (2) the "(Principle of) Mind Priority".

The "Principle of Intellect Priority" implies that knowledge of corporeal things acquired by reasoning about them is more adequate, more profound, and certainly more nonobvious, than knowledge acquired by direct sensory experience. And where knowledge of noncorporeal things is concerned, direct sensory experience will not avail in any case. The "Principle of Mind Priority" is entirely different. It implies that knowledge of the corporeal world is harder to attain than knowledge of the mind. Knowledge of the self and the mind, arrived at through reasoning, is therefore the deepest and most adequate sort of knowledge that we can possess and also the easiest to acquire. Knowledge of corporeal things (if they exist) achieved through sensory experiences of their surfaces and emanations is the least adequate sort of knowledge we possess; perhaps it should not even be termed "knowledge," in view of the shifting set of superficial qualities that the senses reveal to us. Further, we are justified in inferring, on the basis of Intellect Priority and Mind Priority, that knowledge of corporeal things and their hidden properties achieved through the intellect is deep and adequate and well worth having, but also much harder to come by than knowledge of one's own mind. These three propositions contradict the Meditator's childhood beliefs. As a child she believed, like most of us, that she came to understand material objects very thoroughly by touching and handling them, gazing at them, and even by nibbling at them and sniffing them. She did not consider how she could acquire intellectual knowledge of corporeal things, and she did not understand how easy and at the same time how important it could be to acquire knowledge of one's own mind.

Note that the Principle of Mind Priority does not imply that it is easy to acquire knowledge of my own mental characteristics – for example, whether I am courageous or cowardly, even-tempered or irascible. Knowledge of myself as a distinct individual, with different characteristics from other people, is as difficult, if not more difficult, to acquire than knowledge of material objects. The mind or the Self that the Meditator insists that it is easy to know is mind-in-general, not what goes by the name of personality or character.

4 OBJECTIONS TO *MEDITATION TWO*

The Objections to *Meditation Two* are lengthy.

Pierre Gassendi in the *Fifth Set of Objections* proposes that the inference *I am thinking, therefore I exist* must be a condensed syllogism that would have to be unpacked as follows:

Premise 1 Whatever thinks, exists
Premise 2 I think
Conclusion: I exist

Gassendi says that Premise 1 is a preconceived opinion. We do not know it to be true, it should have been doubted, and therefore the conclusion *I exist* is not justified.

Descartes does not try to defend the truth of Premise 1, *Whatever thinks, exists*. Rather, he challenges Gassendi's assumption that the Meditator was relying on a syllogistic argument when she determined the certainty of *I exist*: "The most important mistake our critic makes here is the supposition that knowledge of particular propositions must always be deduced from universal ones" (IX A:205). Descartes explains that the crucial proposition *I am thinking, therefore I exist* is such that "When we examine it, it appears so evident to the understanding that we cannot but believe it, even though this may be the first time in our life that we have thought of it."

Descartes's point might be bolstered as follows. There are many "first-person" propositions, including *I walk* or *I am brave*, whose certainty is not immediately evident to anyone who thinks the proposition. There are also many "existence" propositions such as *God exists* or *Yellow cats exist* whose certainty is not immediately evident to one who thinks them. By contrast, the propositions *I am* and *I exist* are first-person statements (and the latter is also an existence statement) that have the following peculiar property: whoever thinks them cannot doubt them.

Arnauld claims that Descartes is committed to the view that there is nothing in the mind of which we are not aware and that this is obviously wrong; an infant in the womb has no thoughts of which it is aware (VII:232.) Descartes finds nothing strange in either the view or the implication that the fetus thinks. He ventures the following Awareness Thesis: "We cannot have any thought of which we are not aware at the very moment when it is in us." "I do not doubt," he says, "that the mind begins to think as soon as it is implanted in the body of an infant, and that it is immediately aware of its thoughts, though it may not remember them" (VII:246).

Does it follow from Descartes's Awareness Thesis that if I think I understand a sentence – say a sentence of a foreign language – or I think I am imagining St. Paul's Cathedral, or I think I am seeing the color "chartreuse," I must really understand the sentence, or be imagining that cathedral, or be *seeing₁* chartreuse? For if I cannot have a thought without being aware that that is the thought I am having, my knowledge of my own mental states must be incorrigible.

The claim that I have incorrigible knowledge of my own mental states seems implausible. I can certainly think I have understood a sentence of a foreign language when I have not, and my misunder-standing can be made embarrassingly clear to me. I can easily make a mistake about which building I am picturing in my mind's eye, or about the name of the color that is appearing to me. Perhaps the Awareness Thesis should only be understood to imply that, if I can introspect myself being in a certain state, I must be in that state. Perhaps I cannot be wrong about what I am *trying* to do –understand the sentence, imagine the cathedral, identify the color but I cannot introspect my success.

Objector 3, Thomas Hobbes, accepts the Meditator's conclusion *I exist*. From the fact that I am thinking it follows that I exist, he concedes, but not that I am a mind, an intelligence, or an intellect. If one is going to infer from *I am using my intellect* to *I am an intellect*, one might as well infer from *I am walking* that *I am a walk*. We should distinguish, Hobbes suggests, between a subject on one hand and its faculties and acts on the other. Thinking and walking are a faculty and an act, respectively, of a subject. The thing that thinks may be the same as the thing that walks, a subject that is surely not a mind: "Hence it may be that the thing that thinks is the subject to which mind, reason or intellect belong; and this subject may thus be some-thing corporeal. The contrary is assumed, not proved" (VII:172–3).

According to Hobbes, the subject that thinks not only could, but *must*, be corporeal. "For it seems that the subject of any act can be un-derstood only in terms of something corporeal or in terms of matter" (VII:173). When we assign various attributes to wax, we have to assign them to something corporeal, and when we assign mental activities, we have to assign them to something corporeal as well. Further, when we think, or reason, what we are doing is "joining . . . names or labels" referring to things in imagination. Insofar as imagination depends "merely on the motions of our bodily organs . . . the mind will be nothing more than motion occurring in various parts of an organic body" (VII:178).

Descartes states for the record that he will deal explicitly with the possibility that something corporeal in us, some element of our "organic body," thinks in *Meditation Six*. For now, he wants only to make clear that acts of understanding, willing, imagining, and perceiving fall under a conception of common consciousness. We refer them to mind, not to corporeal substance. Acts of thought have nothing in common with corporeal acts such as walking. One might as well conclude, he says, that the earth is the sky as that mind is a motion (VII:179). Moreover, reasoning is not the joining of names in the imagination. If it were, the French and the Germans could not reason about the same things since they use different names. Reasoning is rather the linking of things signified by the names, and so does not require or depend on the imagination (VII:178).

Mersenne, the author of the *Second Set of Objections*, had raised similar concerns about the possibility that thought is performed by the body:

> [Y]ou recognize that you are a thinking thing, but you do not know what this thinking thing is. What if this turned out to be a body which, by its various motions and encounters, produces what we call thought . . . How do you demonstrate that a body is incapable of thinking, or that corporeal motions are not in fact thought? The whole system of your body, which you think you have excluded, or else some of its parts – for example those which make up the brain – may combine to produce the motions which we call thoughts.
>
> (VII:122–3)

Since the time of the ancient physician Hippocrates, it had been observed that damage to the brain caused mental impairment. Recall that the Meditator too attributes madness to damage to the brain caused by the vapors of melancholia (*Meditation One*, VII:18–19). Because thought and experience seem to involve a kind of movement or flow, it is tempting to propose that there is some kind of motion in the brain that causes ideas to succeed one another. Mersenne does not pose his objection as a materialist; he is simply concerned that Descartes does not have a sufficiently forceful argument against materialism.

Descartes replies that he has not even raised the question whether the body is capable of thinking. The Meditator has not ruled out in *Meditation Two* the possibility that she has a body that is permeated by an airy or vapory soul, just as she used to suppose. In stating that she is *not* a body or a vapor, she means only that she currently doubts that she is, since she is assuming that the Demon has deceived her with regard to the existence of bodies and vapors. The propositions *I do not have a body* and *I do not have a vaporous soul* have not found a place in her BELIEVE box. Descartes, meanwhile, is willing to admit that one thing can appear under various forms and be taken for two things. (I might not realize that the person sitting next to me on the bus is the same as the clerk I deal with in the dry-cleaners because I do not see her face distinctly or have not memorized it.) This only shows, however, that the senses are not a reliable guide to the number of distinct entities existing in a given region (VII:132). It does not provide any reason for thinking that corporeal motions and thoughts are actually one and the same thing.

Further, Descartes insists, getting into the spirit of the argument after all, there is no positive reason to think that the brain forms thoughts. We can appreciate that damage to the brain seems to impair our thinking. However, we can infer from this observation only that the mind can be obstructed by the body; a defective body can impair the mind's expression of its thinking. Offering an analogy between the mind and the brain and legs and shackles, he points out that "if someone had had his legs permanently shackled from infancy: he would think the shackles were part of his body and that he needed them for walking" (VII:133). Descartes would perhaps have had a harder time explaining the action of drugs such as caffeine that enhance mental performance, by contrast with alcohol, which causes it to deteriorate, but he could have insisted that intelligence-enhancing drugs work by reducing the obstructive action of the body on the mind.

The hypothesis that that which thinks really is something like a wind or a vapor is advanced in all seriousness by Gassendi:

[W]hy is it not possible that you are a wind, or rather a very thin vapour, . . . which is diffused through the parts of the body and gives them life? May it not be this vapour which sees with the eyes and hears with the ears and thinks with the brain and performs all the other functions which are commonly ascribed to you?
(VII:260–1)

[I]t remains for you to prove that the power of thought is something so far beyond the nature of a body that neither a vapour nor any other

> mobile, pure and rarefied body can be organized in such a way as would make it capable of thought . . . You will also have to prove that this solid body of yours contributes nothing whatever to your thought. . .
> (VII:262)
>
> [W]hy should you . . . not be regarded as being, so to speak, the flower [of matter], or the most refined and pure and active part of it?
> (VII:265)

Gassendi maintained that all living creatures had a soul composed of very fine material particles, like those that compose flame. He called them the "flower of matter." Man, he agrees with Descartes, is the first and foremost of the animals. Nevertheless, both men and animals may have corporeal souls, for there is not much difference between them: "Men speak from impulse as dogs bark." Animals may have their own kind of thought, just as they have their own kind of language (VII:270). The brutes have nerves, animal spirits, and a brain, so why not a principle of cognition that they share with us? To prove that there is a difference in kind between men and animals that would warrant the attribution to men of an immaterial soul not to be found in animals, Gassendi thinks, Descartes should give an example of a capacity humans possess that animals lack (VII:270).

All Descartes has produced, Gassendi charges, are "negative results": "You should carefully scrutinize yourself and conduct a kind of chemical investigation of yourself, if you are to succeed in uncovering and explaining to us your internal substance. If you provide such an explanation, we shall ourselves doubtless be able to investigate whether or not you are better known than the body, whose nature we know so much about through anatomy, chemistry, so many other sciences, so many senses and so many experiments" (VII:277).

Gassendi's suggestion that, because the physical sciences have taught us so much about the body, we should employ a method analogous to chemical analysis or anatomical dissection to try to understand the mind is, of course, outrageous in the context of Descartes's program of doubt. So Descartes restates his argument for Gassendi's benefit: I can doubt that vapors – mists, wind, and flamelike substances – exist and still be certain that I exist. He accuses Gassendi of "repetitive verbosity" and stupid misunderstanding. He denies that the incompetence of infancy or drunkenness shows the dependence of the mind on the body. "[A]ll that follows from this is that the mind, so long as it is joined to the body, uses it like an instrument to perform the operations which take up most of its time" (VII: 354). "[T]he brain," Descartes says, "cannot in any way be employed in pure understanding, but only in imagining or perceiving by the senses" (VII:358). He insists that "I observe no mind at all in the dog . . . [I] believe there is nothing to be found in a dog that resembles the things I recognize in a mind" (VII:359).

Father Bourdin, Objector 7, raises the same questions about animal thought. He recounts the story of an inexperienced peasant who sees a wolf for the first time in his life and who concludes that it is not an animal because he knows that the animals are: the ox, the horse, the goat, and the donkey. Perhaps the Meditator simply failed to recognize thought as another function of the body. Bourdin proposes his own scheme (actually the traditional scheme of medieval Scholastic philosophy) (VII:506). On his view, the world divides into "Thinking substances" (animals, humans, angels, and God) and "Nonthinking substances" (minerals, liquids, plants, artifacts, etc.). Thinking substances subdivide into incorporeal thinking substances (God, angels) and corporeal thinking substances (humans, animals). Corporeal thinking substances divide into those with an unextended soul (humans) and those with an extended soul (animals). So, while humans differ from animals, they belong to the same category of corporeal substances as animals and are entirely unlike God and the angels.

Descartes's response is to mock Bourdin. In doing so, he shows profound disrespect for Scholastic natural philosophy, saying that it is "as if [Bourdin] had got his information from some oracle." He even claims superior theological rectitude by insisting that Father Bourdin's scheme is irreligious. To suppose that the soul can under any circumstances be extended or divisible is "exceedingly dangerous and entirely at variance with the Christian religion" (VII:520). The supposition that some souls are divisible raises the possibility, even if the classification scheme formally excludes it by fiat, that the human person can be destroyed by division, like any other material object.

A group of unnamed philosophers in the *Sixth Set of Objections* proposes that "when you say you are thinking and that you exist, someone might maintain that you are mistaken and are not thinking but merely in motion, and that you are nothing else but corporeal motion" (VII:413).

> [W]e cannot go so far as to assert that what we call thought cannot in any way belong to a body subject to some sort of motion . . .
>
> [A]nd since you confess that without a divine revelation no one can know everything which God has imparted or could impart to any object, how can you possibly have known that God has not implanted in certain bodies a power or property enabling them to doubt, think etc.?
> (VII:420–1)

This variation on the objection we have already heard from Hobbes, Mersenne, and Gassendi is noteworthy, for it raises the possibility that it is God himself who has conferred on matter the power to think. Descartes takes advantage of this innovation in his response. He points out that the critics have proposed an *alternative hypothesis* – that God has conferred on matter the power to think and that thinking is accomplished by means of motions in the brain. They have not addressed *his* arguments or found difficulties with *his* inferences (VII:446–7). If his arguments are good, their speculations must be incorrect, so there is no need for him to refute their claims as well as demonstrating his own.

Another fundamental criticism of Gassendi's concerns the Meditator's conviction that she understands the nature of wax through her intellect according to the Principle of Intellect Priority. The substance of the wax is not, Gassendi protests, distinctly conceived by the intellect:

> Besides the colour, the shape, the fact that it can melt, etc. we conceive that there is something which is the subject of the accidents and changes we observe; but what this subject is, or what its nature is, we do not know. This always eludes us; and it is only a kind of conjecture that leads us to think that there must be something underneath the accidents. So I am amazed at how you can say that once the forms have been stripped off like clothes, you perceive more perfectly and evidently what the wax is.
> (VII:271–2)

Though Descartes said nothing about "substances" in *Meditation Two*, Gassendi ventures his own view that a substance is an unknown substratum. We suppose or posit it as a "something" that supports qualities and activities. Its real nature, however, eludes us, since we can only observe its qualities and activities. Substance lies outside the realm of experience and is therefore, contrary to what he takes Descartes to be implying, unknowable.

The incorrigibility problem, as it is termed, is still alive. Do I have privileged access to the contents of my own mind? Are there things I know about myself that no one else can know? Is my current knowledge of myself incapable of correction by someone else or by my later self? Under psychoanalysis, people claim to discover that they loved or hated Person X for years without being aware of it. Perhaps they are just wrong about this. Descartes seemed to think that *if* we experience an emotion, we cannot fail to be aware that we experience *that* very emotion (AT XI 348–9). He is not so clear on whether, if we *have* an emotion at a particular time, we must experience ourselves as having it. Suppose it is possible to discover that one had thoughts, ideas, and emotions that one did not know one had at the time. Is the Awareness Thesis necessarily false? It need not be. Perhaps the discovery involves my suddenly remembering something that I thought or felt and was aware of earlier but have forgotten that I thought or felt. Perhaps love and hate are not forms of "thinking" but rather certain dispositions to act that should not be regarded as thoughts. Still, it is possible that love and hate are emotions that involve certain thoughts. If psychoanalysis can unexpectedly reveal certain emotions that we now have, not merely emotions we remember having had, then the thesis that we are aware of all our thoughts whenever we have them must be false.

Another puzzle related to self-knowledge can be constructed as follows: Suppose there are two Minds, A and B, existing in two independent Worlds. A exists in World A, B exists in World B. World A contains stars, people, animals, etc., along with Mind A. World B contains (and always has contained) only Mind B and a malevolent Demon. Suppose Mind A is at this moment aware that she is seeing an array of stars, including the constellation Orion. Suppose Mind B is in the same state as Mind A. Is Mind B aware of herself as seeing an array of stars, including the constellation Orion? Can she know about herself that she believes that she is seeing an array of stars and that she believes that she is seeing Orion? According to some philosophers, however paradoxical this might seem, Mind B cannot know these things about herself, leaving it open in what respect Mind B can be imagined to be in the same state as Mind A.

CHAPTER 4

Meditation Three (1)
The Meditator discovers how to distinguish true from false propositions by reference to the clarity and distinctness of his ideas and considers whether God is merely a subjective idea

I CLEAR AND DISTINCT PERCEPTION – TRUTH (AT VII:34–6)

I will now shut my eyes, stop my ears, and withdraw all my senses. I will eliminate from my thoughts all images of bodily things, or rather, since this is hardly possible, I will regard all such images as vacuous, false and worthless. I will converse with myself and scrutinize myself a little more deeply; and in this way I will attempt to achieve, little by little, a more intimate knowledge of myself.

(VII:34)

The Meditator continues with his experiment in Hyperbolic Doubt, maintaining the fiction of the malevolent Demon. When we left him at the end of *Meditation Two*, his belief-set was as it is represented in Figure 17. The Meditator reasons that he can add a new, significant item to his belief-set. He now "knows what is required for being certain of anything." He is in a position, he finds, to lay down a general rule that will serve as the sought-for filter that can separate TRUE from FALSE. The filter is the test or criterion of the clarity and distinctness of his perceptions. Justifying, or certifying, this filter as "performing as advertised" takes up, as one might expect, the entirety of *Meditation Three*.

BELIEVE   DOUBT

I exist
I think, i.e., I doubt, will, imagine, perceive, etc.
Intellect Priority
Mind Priority

A good God exists
There are corporeal things external to me
I have a body
I have a vapory soul
Sensory Experience
physics
astronomy
medicine
arithmetic
geometry

Figure 17   The Meditator's belief-set at the beginning of *Meditation Three*

> I am certain that I am a thinking thing . . . In this first item of knowledge there is simply a clear and distinct perception of what I am asserting; this would not be enough to make me certain of the truth of the matter if it could ever turn out that something which I perceived with such clarity and distinctness was false. So now I seem to be able to lay it down as a general rule that whatever I perceive very clearly and distinctly is true. (VII:35)

Up to now, the Meditator has been directly concerned with the question what he may believe, not what he knows to be true. The Withholding Policy permits him to sort opinions into BELIEVE and DOUBT on the basis of the question: *Could a malevolent Demon deceive me about this matter?* On this basis, the Meditator has begun to revise his former opinions. They are no longer identical with the set he acquired in childhood. Still, the question raised in connection with *Meditation One* has not been answered. What reason is there to suppose that the Withholding Policy, the supposition of the existence of a malevolent Demon, and Hyperbolic Doubt have been useful in helping the Meditator to come to believe truths and to eliminate falsehoods from his belief-set? For the Meditator's original aim, it will be recalled, was not simply to *change* the contents of his belief-set and to acquire different beliefs. Various methods, as we saw, will accomplish that. Rather, he aimed to revise his belief-set in such a way that it would reflect reality better than it would have had the Meditator employed the Authority Principle or the Conformity Policy, not to mention the Methods of Total Skepticism and Total Credulity. The Meditator's overall task was to sort his own existing opinions as well as sundry undecided propositions and opinions of others into the categories of TRUE and FALSE.

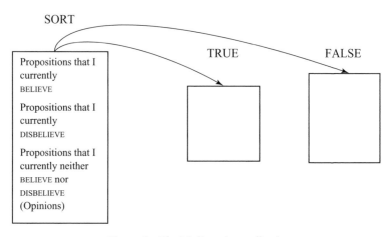

Figure 18   The Meditator's overall task

At the start of *Meditation Three*, the Meditator considers the list of propositions that he now believes. He is convinced that what he believes can be moved into the rectangle marked TRUE. (He is not, however, convinced that what he still doubts can be moved into FALSE.)

The Meditator is convinced that he *knows to be true* the principal items he has so far ranked under BELIEVE. He now asks himself what those items have in common, and what the items remaining under DOUBT have in common. The best answer he can supply is this: The

propositions under BELIEVE, in particular the "first item of knowledge" – *I exist* – are each and every one such that the Meditator clearly
and distinctly perceives them, while the items under DOUBT were
never perceived clearly and distinctly and still are not. The Meditator
can therefore "promote" his current beliefs to the status of known
truths. Moreover, if he encounters further propositions that are
clearly and distinctly perceived, they can be immediately classified as
TRUE. Clarity and distinctness are criteria that can appropriately filter
opinions.

> Clarity and Distinctness Filter: Whatever I clearly and distinctly
> perceive is TRUE.

The introduction of the Clarity and Distinctness Filter and the
promotion of BELIEVE to TRUE are somewhat problematic. The
Reader may feel that the Meditator is not really justified at this stage
of the argument in claiming that *it is true* that he exists and that the
other propositions he perceives clearly and distinctly are all TRUE.
He is unable to doubt that he exists, but what has this to do with the
hard problem of truth? Three questions arise:

1) What is it for "what I am asserting," as opposed to some physical object, to be perceived clearly and distinctly? Doesn't this
   mean that I perceive some proposition clearly and distinctly *to
   be true*? But if I still do not know what truth is, how can I know
   whether I have clearly and distinctly perceived a proposition to be
   true?

2) On what basis has the Meditator determined that his belief-set
   contains known truths, not just opinions he is psychologically
   unable to doubt? Hasn't he just turned to the useless Subjective
   Policy discussed earlier (Ch. 1 Sec. 2)?

3) On what basis has the Meditator determined that, if a certain
   characteristic, namely clarity and distinctness, pertains to all and
   only his current true beliefs, then all the truths he will come to know
   in the future will have the characteristic of clarity and distinctness
   as well?

Something of an answer, perhaps less than an ideally satisfactory
answer, can already be given to each question. Fuller answers to
(2) and (3) are given later in *Meditation Three* (see Ch. 5 Sec. 3 below).

Where the first problem is concerned, if the Meditator were interested in *defining* truth, it would not be informative for him to suggest that truth is what is clearly and distinctly perceived to be true. However, the Meditator is concerned not with the definition of truth but with the provision of a criterion of truth. If I wanted to define "beauty," it would not be informative to say *Beauty is whatever museum directors and fashion writers deem beautiful.* If, however, I wanted to provide a *criterion* for something's being beautiful, I might well say *Beauty is whatever museum directors and fashion writers deem beautiful.* I would in that case have offered a (controversial) theory of the beautiful. For it would be open to anyone to insist to the contrary that the criterion of beauty is enduring appreciation down through the ages, or the possession of "significant form," or to advance some other criterion that could be used to filter objects. If someone were then to wonder how to apply the criterion, asking "What is it to perceive a proposition clearly and distinctly," the response on behalf of the Meditator would have to be "It is to perceive it in the same way that you perceive the proposition *I exist* when you consider that proposition yourself."

The second problem arises because the Meditator does not give a defense of the claim that *I exist* and *I think* are true propositions. In *Meditation Two*, the Meditator only said that he found himself forced to conclude that they were true. He reported a subjective, psychological fact about himself, namely, that he could not doubt them. According to the old Subjective Policy, whatsoever I happen to believe is true, and one might think that it is just as subjective to insist that whatever I cannot doubt and feel compelled to believe is really true. However, as we have seen, the Subjective Policy does not alter my belief-set. The Clarity and Distinctness Filter does, so the criterion of truth it provides cannot be same as that provided by the Subjective Policy.

A short excursion, developing the point made in connection with first-person existence statements in Ch. 3 Sec. 4 above, is now in order.

Consider the items that survived the supposition of the malevolent Demon and that were sorted into the Meditator's category BELIEVE: *I think*, *I exist*, etc. Are these propositions contingent or necessary? Are they indexical or nonindexical?

When a proposition is *contingent*, it is possibly true and possibly false. That is to say, we can imagine possible worlds in which it is true and possible worlds in which it is false. Suppose there is a red chair in my room. In some possible worlds, this very chair in my room is blue. The proposition *The chair in my room is red* (ignoring problems of vagueness and ambiguity) is accordingly contingent and possibly false. The proposition *The moon has risen* is true in worlds in which the moon being referred to has come to be above the horizon and false in worlds in which it is still below the horizon. It too is contingent; in some possible worlds the moon is up and in others it is not.

The propositions about the chair and the moon just cited are *indexical* as well as contingent. They have a more-or-less definite meaning, and can be assessed as true or false only when they are considered as asserted by a particular speaker, *S*, in a given place, *p*, at a given time, *t*, pointing at or otherwise indicating a given object, *O*. *I am hungry* and *I am sorry* are similarly indexical. *I am hungry* said by Person X means something different from *I am hungry* said by Person Y. One proposition may be true and the other false.

The indexical proposition *I am hungry* is true or false on the various occasions on which it is thought or uttered. Whenever it is true, it is at the same time possibly false. Suppose I am hungry now and the proposition is true when indexed to me. Nevertheless, in some possible worlds, I am not hungry now. In those worlds, if I uttered the sentence "I am hungry," what I said would be false; I would be mistaken or lying. I can assert *I am hungry* with the intention of deceiving someone. So the proposition is both indexical and contingent.

I exist and *I think* are also indexical propositions. They mean something different when asserted by different speakers. When Person X says "I exist," X means that X exists, and similarly for Person Y. Both propositions – *I think* and *I exist* – are contingent: I can imagine a world in which I do not exist and a world in which I do not think. I cannot, however, imagine a world in which I could utter or write down the sentence "I exist" and be either mistaken or lying. Nor can I imagine a world in which I could utter or write down the sentence "I think" and be either mistaken or lying. (You might think I could be unconscious and produce those words by reflex or as a result of electrical stimulation of my vocal chords whilst being aerated with a bellows, but I still would not have said or written something false.) So these two propositions seem to belong to a special, interesting category. They are unlike most other indexical propositions including *It is raining*, *I am hungry*, and *My brother weighs 70kg*. These can be used to say something false. Neither *I think* nor *I exist* is, in terms of modern logic, necessarily true, any more than *Bears exist* and *Lions are lazy*. At the same time, I cannot possibly be mistaken about whether I exist and think, or deceive others into thinking I exist and think when I do not. No matter who speaks or writes the sentences "I think" and "I exist," whenever they have a determinate meaning, they are true. If a cleverly fabricated automaton were to write the sentence "I think" with a mechanical pen, the automaton would not have asserted a false proposition, namely, that the automaton was thinking. Nor, of course, would it have asserted a true proposition. A mechanical doll cannot assert a proposition because it cannot mean anything by the sounds or letters it produces.

Why, though, should the Meditator suppose that the characteristic he has identified these two unusual belief-items as having – being clearly and being distinctly perceived – should characterize any and all true beliefs? This question raises the problem of *induction*. Suppose I notice that all cars ever owned by me in my lifetime up to now have a certain characteristic in common. They have each cost less than $10,000. Can I infer that I will never own a car costing more than $10,000 (in today's dollars)? To make that inference, I should have to believe that there is an underlying reason why a car owned by me will never cost more than $10,000. The underlying reason might be that I am of modest means, or that I have no appreciation for fine automobiles, or that, although wealthy, I have an ethical principle against spending much money on cars. If I can know that I possess (and will continue to possess) one or more of these properties, I may be in a position to predict that I will never own a car costing more than $10,000 and my prediction should come out true. To make the corresponding inference regarding true beliefs, I should be able to cite an underlying reason why clearly and distinctly perceived propositions are true. I also need to have an underlying reason why that reason will continue to be an underlying reason.

Skeptics about induction doubt that I can predict the future accurately, no matter how much I know about the past and the present.

For, to infer from already observed regularities to future instances of the same thing, I have to assume that the future will resemble the past. To infer, on the grounds that I have never yet owned a car costing more than $10,000, that I never will, I have to assume that my properties (and perhaps those of the "world") insofar as they are relevant to car purchases will remain the same. What good reason can I find in turn for that hypothesis? People can change: Why shouldn't I come into a fortune, or develop an interest in fine automobiles, or reject my current ethical principle? So the Meditator needs to have a good reason why the Clarity and Distinctness Filter will work to filter our other true beliefs in addition to the ones he has already accepted as true, and a good reason as well to suppose that that reason will remain in force.

The Meditator believed, before he began to scrutinize his beliefs, that he clearly perceived the earth, sky, and stars, and other things outside himself and that these things were the source of his experiences. He now realizes that he only clearly perceived that he was experiencing "ideas" or "thoughts" of those objects and not their sources or causes. But what about mathematics? Did he formerly perceive certain arithmetical propositions, for example that $2 + 3 = 5$, clearly and distinctly? If so, the proposed criterion of truth must be useless. If the malevolent Demon can deceive us about simple arithmetical propositions and if these are clearly and distinctly perceived, the Clarity and Distinctness Filter is badly flawed; it lets some false propositions through.

The Meditator is perturbed by this realization. On one hand, he feels quite confident that he perceives the truth of $2 + 3 = 5$ clearly and distinctly. He also feels confident that he perceives the truth of the proposition that it cannot be the case that, although he exists now, sometime in the future the Meditator will never have existed. On the other hand, the Meditator has to admit that the malevolent Demon could have given him a nature such that he was always wrong about mathematics. How can the Meditator obtain complete confidence in the Clarity and Distinctness Filter? Evidently, to obtain this confidence, he must refute the hypothesis of the malevolent Demon. This means that the Meditator must establish that there exists a nondeceiving God rather than a malevolent Demon, before being fully confident that his belief-set is a genuine knowledge-set, consisting only of what is true: "For if I do not know this [that a nondeceiving God exists], it seems that I can never be quite certain about anything else."

2 IS THE DEITY (MALEVOLENT OR BENEVOLENT) MERELY AN IDEA? – IDEAS AND THEIR SOURCES – SUBSTANCE, MODES, ACCIDENTS – DEGREES OF REALITY AND DEGREES OF PERFECTION – MATERIALLY FALSE IDEAS (AT VII:36–46)

The Meditator tackles the question of the nature of the Deity – true to his Principle of Mind Priority – with a consideration of his thoughts and ideas, his mental contents. Some ideas, he recognizes, are just images: for example, our usual imagistic thoughts of a man, the sky, or an angel (wings, halo, sweet face), or of God (white-robed, beard), or of a malevolent Demon (grimacing, pointed ears). Some thoughts seem to be composed of an idea of a thing or a state of affairs and an attitude or emotion directed towards the thing or state of affairs. For example, when I hope that it will snow tomorrow, my thought represents a state of affairs – the event of its snowing – and I seem to direct the emotion of hope towards that imagined state of affairs. If I were to fear that it will snow tomorrow, the same state of affairs – the event of its snowing – would be represented in my thoughts, but the emotion directed towards it would be fear, not hope. Whether I love X or despise X, the object of my thought is the same person, and whether I want an apple or am hoping not to have to eat one, the object of my thought is the same kind of fruit.

Ideas, the Meditator reflects, considered simply as images, cannot be true or false. An image-idea of a chimera is on the same footing as an image-idea of a goat. I can imagine one in as much detail as the other, although goats exist and chimeras do not. Emotions and attitudes – both "ideas" in the Meditator's terminology – are no more true or false than images are. If I love or hate something, I have an emotion towards that object and whether the emotion is appropriate to the object or justified makes no difference to the intensity of the emotion. I can have emotions towards and thoughts of nonexistent objects with as much facility as I can towards and of existing objects.

Perhaps my old enemy has just died, but nothing in my thought has changed and I still burn with grudges and grievances against him. So image-ideas, along with emotions and attitudes, just "are" without being true or false.

It is possible that one or both of the idea of God and the idea of the Demon are inventions of the Meditator's mind, mere figments of his imagination. In fact, there is reason to think that both are probably figments. After all, there are many cultures that appear to have made up their gods. The Greeks and Romans were known to have had a whole pantheon which Christians regarded as imaginary. Hermes with his winged sandals who flew hither and thither bearing messages and Athena with her owl who gave wise advice to the Athenians were, most of us suppose, invented ideas of the Greeks. They did not correspond to anything real. Why, though, should we think otherwise of the Christian God, sometimes represented as an elderly man with a white beard, who seems even more ubiquitous than Hermes and who is as prone to advice-giving as Athena? The conundrum of God's existence will be hard for the Meditator to solve. For reasons tending to show that the malevolent Demon does not exist will also tend to cast doubt on the existence of a benevolent God, and reasons tending to show that a benevolent God exists must render somewhat more plausible the existence of a malevolent Demon. This double-bind accounts for the great difficulty and obscurity of the arguments of the first part of *Meditation Three*.

Getting started on his investigation into the existence and nature of Deities, the Meditator comes to the conclusion that he has ideas of three distinct types which he designates as follows:

Innate ideas: Ideas found within myself

Adventitious ideas: Ideas that present themselves as coming from an outside source

Invented ideas: Ideas made up by me

The Meditator decides to concentrate on "ideas which I take to be derived from things existing outside me," that is, on ideas that seem to be adventitious. For if the idea of a Deity can be shown to be adventitious rather than invented, there is reason to think that the Deity really exists. Given that he has certain ideas, which ones, the Meditator wonders, ought he to believe are ideas of existing things outside himself? Which existence-claims should be added to his belief-set? It is difficult to decide this question when the Meditator continues to doubt the existence of an external world and to suppose that he is deceived by a malevolent Demon. Nevertheless, his efforts to discover, merely from a consideration of the nature of certain of his ideas, whether those ideas correspond to anything external are impressive.

The Meditator notes that he tends to judge spontaneously that certain ideas do come from outside himself and that these ideas resemble the things from which they are derived. The ideas about which he so judges are those that do not depend on his will. For example, the idea of warmth (the sensation of warmth) that I have when sitting close to a fire is not dependent on my will. If I could produce the idea of warmth merely by willing it, I would not need the fire to keep warm. Moreover, I tend to judge that the fire throws off something – warmth – that gives me a warm sensation. I may also suppose that the idea of the fire (the visual image of its flames) is thrown off by the fire itself. But spontaneous beliefs are not trustworthy. Perhaps the sources of my ideas do not resemble them. Perhaps the sources of my ideas are not even external to me. After all, I seem to produce my own ideas when dreaming, so why should I not do so when awake?

On reflection, the Meditator realizes, many of his ideas do not resemble the things they are ideas of, or from which they are supposed to come. For example, the Meditator finds within himself two very different ideas of the sun. One idea represents the sun as a globe "several times larger," as the Meditator puts it, than the Earth. The other represents it as a disk about the size of a dinner plate. At least one of these ideas, and maybe both, does not resemble the sun. Yet, according to the Meditator's existing astronomical beliefs (which admittedly may all have been implanted by the malevolent Demon), the idea of the larger sun resembles better the item from which it originates. In fact, the little-sun-idea can be asserted to have no resemblance at all to the object of which it is the idea.

Still keeping in mind his aim to discover whether there is a Deity, and, if so, whether this god is benevolent or malevolent, the Meditator now reflects on the meanings of the traditional terms "substance," "accident" and "mode":

Substance: A thing capable of existing independently, such as a stone or myself.

Accident: A feature of a substance, such as greenness, blueness, sweetness, heaviness, or warmth.

Mode: Another attribute of a substance, such as extension, movement, perception, or imagination.

A "finite substance" is understood to be a creature, such as an individual human, an animal, or a material object, by contrast with infinite substance, which is God.

The Meditator now advances a scheme that we might term the Hierarchy of Ideas. He decides that ideas of substances have more "objective reality" than ideas of modes and accidents. Further, the idea of God – an infinite, eternal, immutable, omniscient, all-creating substance, has more "objective reality" than the idea of any finite substance. There is a hierarchy that looks like this:

Idea of God
Ideas of finite substances
Ideas of accidents and modes

When we consider ideas in themselves, they are all on equal footing, the Meditator says. However, when they are considered as representing something other than themselves, ideas higher up the scale have more objective reality.

The notion of "objective reality" is puzzling. The French version of the *Meditations* equates having more objective reality with "participating by representation in a higher degree of being or perfection." Still, it is not entirely clear what is meant.

To understand the Meditator's rather innovative thought, it helps to recall traditional conceptions of the Hierarchy of Being (not the Hierarchy of Ideas) that looked something like this:

God
Angels
Humans
Animals
Plants
Minerals
Earth

Items towards the top end of the scale were considered more perfect than items towards the bottom. The characteristics of the things on each level explained their assignment to lower or higher ranks; i.e., humans are more perfect than animals because they have reason, but less perfect than angels, because they are sinful.

Because the Meditator continues to doubt the existence of all the items in the Hierarchy of Being, he is hardly in a position to make such a ranking. He decides to do something analogous: to make a ranking of his ideas, given the characteristics of those ideas. As an idea of an infinite substance, the idea of God is more perfect and more real than the idea of a finite substance, and the latter is more perfect still than an idea of an accident or a mode. Ideas of accidents and modes, the Meditator will discover shortly, in a series of reflections that continue the train of thoughts on the elusive nature of the piece of wax, have a certain *flimsiness* to them that contrasts with the *stability* of the idea of God and the relative stability of the idea of a finite substance.

To the Hierarchy of Ideas, the Meditator adds a further assumption – the Causal Noninferiority Principle: "There must be at least as much reality [or perfection] in the efficient and total cause [of an effect] as in the effect of that cause." This assumption is somewhat easier to understand than the Hierarchy of Ideas. Evidently, a thing of some given degree of reality or perfection cannot cause something more real or perfect than itself to exist:

> A stone, for example, which previously did not exist, cannot begin to exist unless it is produced by something which contains, either formally or eminently everything to be found in the stone; similarly, heat cannot be produced in an object which was not previously hot, except by something of at least the same . . . degree . . . of perfection as heat, and so on. But it is also true that the *idea* of heat, or of a stone, cannot exist in me unless it is put there by some cause which contains at least as much reality as I conceive to be in the heat or in the stone.
>
> (vii:41)

The intuition here is clear. Sherlock Holmes cannot cause Arthur Conan Doyle to exist, since fictional characters are "less real" than historical persons; but Arthur Conan Doyle can cause Sherlock Holmes to exist, since Arthur Conan Doyle is more real than his character. I can create the idea of an imaginary chimera, but an imaginary chimera cannot create the idea of me, or even the idea of a chimera in me. Accordingly, if I find in myself the idea of something of a higher degree of reality or perfection than myself, I can be certain that it is not the effect of a cause less real and perfect than I am or no more real and perfect than I am.

Here are the conclusions the Meditator is heading for:

1) Ideas of things less perfect than myself can be wholly invented by me.

2) Ideas of things more perfect than myself cannot be wholly invented by me.

"It is clear to me by the natural light," the Meditator says, "that the ideas in me are like pictures or images which can easily fall short of the perfection of the things from which they are taken, but which cannot contain anything greater or more perfect."

Introspecting, the Meditator finds that he has ideas of other human beings, animals, corporeal and inanimate things, and also of God and angels. He finds that there is a kind of *flimsiness* about ideas of corporeal things that makes it somewhat plausible to suppose that the Meditator himself is the source of his ideas of corporeal things. (The possibility that the Meditator was himself the author of all his thoughts was one he had toyed with briefly at the beginning of *Meditation Two*.) The Meditator decides that he could produce himself, or put together from simpler components, ideas of human beings, animals, corporeal and inanimate things, and even angels, provided he had an idea of God: "I can see nothing in them which is so great or excellent as to make it seem impossible that it originated in myself." Only the idea of God, the Meditator decides, could not originate in himself.

What is so inferior about the ideas of corporeal things? As he contemplated the piece of wax in *Meditation Two*, the Meditator perceived that corporeal things are extended in three dimensions, and therefore have shapes, that they can change their position, endure for a certain time, and exist in quantity. "But as for all the rest, including light and colours, sounds, smells, tastes, heat and cold, and the other tactile qualities," he confesses, "I think of these only in a very confused and obscure way, to the extent that I do not even know whether they are true or false, that is, whether the ideas I have of them are ideas of real things or of non-things." So unclear and confused are his ideas of sensory qualities that he does not even know if his idea of "cold" is an idea of anything real. Is "cold" as real or less real than "heat?"

There is some reason to think that cold is just the absence of heat, and dark the absence of light, but it is not easy to decide whether cold and dark exist. If cold and dark are necessarily non-things, the ideas of them are "materially false." (If the malevolent Demon is deceiving the Meditator, nothing in the world is really cold or hot, but if "cold" is a materially false idea nothing *could* really be cold, regardless of the existence or nonexistence of a Demon.)

The notion of "material falsity" is exceedingly puzzling. Truth and falsity, as noted earlier, pertain to some judgments, but not to any images, emotions, and attitudes. One can recognize a judgment by its sentential form: e.g.,

Goats are omnivorous
X is lovable
Hope springs eternal
Chimeras do not exist
I desire an apple

"Cold" is not a judgment. "Dark" is not a judgment either. So what is there to be false?

The answer to this riddle is that there is a kind of derivative truth and falsity that can be considered to attach to ideas, insofar as I can be considered to judge that they are or are not ideas of something positive that *could be* real. Materially false ideas represent as something positive something that is only an absence and therefore could not be real. The ideas of a chimera, a unicorn, or Sherlock Holmes for that matter, are ideas of nonexistent things, but they are not materially false. Candidates for material falsity include the following:

Cold
Dark
Hell
Void
Rest
Evil

For there is some reason to think that these terms signify only the absence or privation of heat, light, divine grace, body, motion, and goodness respectively. Light, for example, consists of light waves, but dark does not consist of dark waves. Heat is the motion of particles, but cold is not the motion of "cold particles." Cold is only the relatively slow motion of particles without any temperature. For many theologians, Evil was a real force and Hell was a definite place. But many philosophers were not so sure.

As a perception or feeling, however, dark is just as real to me as light, and cold as heat. The ideas of heat and cold, dark and light, seem to be all on the same footing. Perhaps, the Meditator reasons, all sensory ideas are materially false. (One might conclude the same of heaven and hell, good and evil – since ideas of heaven and hell, good and evil, seem to be equally vivid.) If so, the Meditator concludes, it would be the case that they all "arise from nothing – that is, they are in me only because of a deficiency and lack of perfection in my nature." If, on the other hand, sensory ideas are materially true and correspond to things, "then since the reality they represent is so extremely slight that I cannot even distinguish it from a non-thing, I do not see why they cannot originate from myself."

Accordingly, when corporeal things are considered as collections of sensory properties such as shape, color, taste, and smell, the Meditator is convinced that he could be the source of the ideas of them. His own mind might have generated ideas of colorful, scented, and variously shaped objects, presenting them as independent of him. At the same time, corporeal things can also be considered abstractly, under the headings of substance, duration, and number. These ideas too, though they are ideas of intellectual and not sensory properties, the Meditator thinks he could have got from himself, for he is aware that he is a thing "capable of existing independently" (substance), that he has existed in the past (duration), and that he has various thoughts that he can count (number). He is aware of himself *as an enduring substance with a multiplicity of thoughts.* Although a thinking thing does not seem able to generate the ideas of extension, shape, position, and movement that the intellect ascribes to corporeal objects, merely by thinking about itself, the Meditator decides that this is not a serious problem. These "modes" of a substance might be contained in the Meditator "eminently" and available to him on reflection.

The upshot is that the Meditator might be the source of all his ideas of corporeal objects, sensory and intellectual. No external source need then be posited. He may have invented and produced on his own the world of corporeal objects that he *sees$_t$* and thinks about.

Now an interesting set of questions arises. Could the Meditator be the cause of the idea of a good God that he finds within himself? Could he have invented or constructed the idea when no such thing exists outside his mind? Could the idea of a good God be, like cold and dark, materially false – perhaps only the negation of the ideas of finitude and deprivation that the Meditator can find within himself by reflecting on his limitations? To these questions, the Meditator gives a negative answer, and he elaborates upon this answer in the remainder of *Meditation Three.*

> By the word "God" I understand a substance that is infinite, eternal, immutable, independent, supremely intelligent, supremely powerful, and which created both myself and everything else (if anything else there be) that exists. All these attributes are such that, the more carefully I concentrate on them, the less possible it seems that they could have originated from me alone. So from what has been said it must be concluded that God necessarily exists.
>
> (VII:45)

3 OBJECTIONS TO *MEDITATION THREE* (I)

Caterus, the First Objector, expresses doubt that an idea needs a cause. "[B]eing thought of," he says, "or having objective being in the intellect, is simply a thought of the mind which stops and terminates in the mind. And this can occur . . . without the thing in question existing at all. So why should I look for a cause of something which is not actual, and which is simply an empty label, a nonentity?" (VII:92)

Descartes replies that an idea is not a nonentity, and that the occurrence of any idea demands an explanation for how that idea could and has come to be. His argument helps to clarify the somewhat obscure argument for the existence of God based on the Hierarchy of Ideas:

> [I]f someone possesses in his intellect the idea of a machine of a highly intricate design, it is perfectly fair to ask what is the cause of this idea. And it will not be an adequate reply to say that the idea is not anything outside

the intellect and hence that it cannot be caused . . . For in order for the idea of the machine to contain such and such objective intricacy, it must derive it from some cause; and what applies to the objective intricacy belonging to this idea also applies to the objective reality belonging to the idea of God.

(VII:103–4)

Not just any human being, Descartes implies, can have the idea of an intricate machine. Someone with neither mechanical training nor the visual or tactile experience of an intricate machine could not form such an idea. A mouse – if mice had minds – could not form the idea of an intricate machine on its own. The cause must be at least as perfect as the effect. Isn't it possible, one might wonder, that the idea of an intricate machine should simply happen to form itself by chance in the mind of a mechanically inept person, just as the wind might scatter leaves so that by chance they spelled out a meaningful and grammatically correct sentence? Descartes would no doubt insist that while an *image* of a certain sort might form itself in a mechanically inept person's mind, she would not in that case have the idea of an intricate machine. Contrariwise, if someone does have the idea of an intricate machine, this is a significant fact about her. The idea must issue from a complex source outside herself, or she must have sufficient complexity of mind to have invented it.

Consider a related example. An image of a Japanese haiku (I don't know Japanese) is hypothesized spontaneously to form in my mind by chance. Perhaps I can even "see" the Japanese letters and lines in my mind's eye. However, I do not have the idea of a Japanese haiku because I cannot "read" my own image as a poem. Similarly, the mechanically inept person, even if a certain image were to form in her mind, could not "read" her own image as the idea of an intricate machine. Yet there is an idea in our minds that we successfully "read" as the idea of God. This implies that the image did not just get there by chance or form itself spontaneously.

Arnauld, the Fourth Objector, calls Descartes to task for suggesting that there can be materially false ideas. He finds this notion puzzling. If I represent "cold" to myself as something positive (not merely as the absence of heat), he ventures, I do not have a materially false idea of cold. Rather, I have the idea of cold that I have and I wrongly *judge* cold to be a positive quality like heat (VII:206). If Arnauld is right, Descartes's attempt to rouse suspicion that ideas of corporeal things are relatively flimsy by suggesting that our ideas of sensory qualities are fundamentally confused cannot get off the ground.

Arnauld's point is well taken, especially since Descartes himself makes clear that it is our judgments about our ideas, not our ideas themselves, that are susceptible of truth and falsity. As all too often happens when a point is well taken, Arnauld's objection occasions a lengthy and unclear reply, in which Descartes insists that, amongst the set of ideas that "do not represent anything real," some provide more "scope for error" than others. The ideas of false gods, he says, "do not provide as much scope for error as the confused ideas arriving from the senses, such as the ideas of colour and cold" (VII:234). Even more scope for error is provided by desires and appetites (VII:234). A materially false idea, it seems, can lead me to do something wrong as well as to believe something false.

CHAPTER 5

Meditation Three (II)
The Meditator finds that he can reach a perfect God in his thoughts and that this God cannot perpetrate fraud and deception and cannot be a Demon

I IS GOD MORE THAN THE MEDITATOR'S INVENTED IDEA? – COULD THE MEDITATOR BE GOD – ? CONTINUOUS CREATION – (AT VII:46–51)

The Meditator has just concluded that he could not construct or invent the idea of God by himself. God himself must be the source of the idea of God that he discovered in his mind. For the idea of God is not something that has been generated in his mind "from nothing."

> On the contrary, it is utterly clear and distinct, and contains in itself more objective reality than any other idea; hence there is no idea which is in itself truer . . . It does not matter that I do not grasp the infinite . . . for it is in the nature of the infinite not to be grasped by a finite being like myself. It is enough that I understand the infinite.
>
> (VII:46)

The idea of *substance* can be found within him and could have been constructed by him because the Meditator *is* a substance – a mental substance. The Meditator could not, however, he decides, have constructed the idea of an infinite substance by himself – or by negating his ideas of finitude. The idea of infinite substance, or God, must have "proceeded from some substance which really was infinite."

This conclusion, the Meditator realizes, might seem controversial. If he can arrive at the conception of rest by thinking of the negation of motion, and of dark by thinking of the negation of light, why can't he arrive at a conception of the infinite by considering the negation of the finite, or the perfect by considering the negation of the imperfect? Here the Causal Noninferiority Principle and the Hierarchy of Ideas (Ch. 4 Sec. 2) are intended to come jointly to the rescue. If a finite thing could produce the idea of an infinite thing, the Meditator reasons, this would violate the principle that there is more reality in a cause than in its effect, since the Idea of God is at the top of the Hierarchy of Ideas. The Meditator adds that he would not even be able to conceive himself as imperfect (with respect, for example, to his state of knowledge) unless there were already the idea of a perfect being within him. He can not have arrived at the idea of a perfect being by considering the negation of the qualities he possesses.

Unlike the flimsy ideas of sensory qualities, the idea of God, the Meditator decides, could not possibly be materially false, something unreal that we perceive or feel to be real: "For although perhaps one may imagine that such a being does not exist, it cannot be supposed that the idea of such a being represents something unreal, as I said with respect to the idea of cold." On the contrary, the Meditator thinks, the idea of the Deity "is utterly clear and distinct, and contains in itself more objective reality than any other idea; hence there is no idea which is in itself truer or less liable to be suspected of falsehood." Even if a finite being like the Meditator cannot "grasp" the infinite, the Meditator can "understand" it and can clearly perceive the other attributes of God.

The Meditator now raises a surprising possibility. Perhaps he *is* God. Perhaps he has arrived at the idea of God not by considering the negation of his own imperfections but by introspection into his own nature. Perhaps he has come to an awareness of his own potential, his own emerging but not yet actualized perfections.

How can the Meditator – the self-discovered thinking thing – know *that the Meditator is not himself God*? For the Meditator is aware that his knowledge is gradually increasing. Why shouldn't this process continue to infinity if a God's knowledge is infinite? Further, if knowledge is source of power and goodness, why shouldn't he obtain in time all the power and goodness of a God? "Further, I see no reason why I should not be able to use this increased knowledge to acquire all the other perfections of God."

The possibility that the Meditator is God is, however, dismissed. God, he decides, can contain nothing potential, emerging or unactualized, so the possibility that the Meditator is potentially God, or is an emerging God, is incoherent. The very fact that the Meditator's knowledge is increasing implies that he is not God.

The Meditator is still worried, however, by the possibility that his idea of God is self-produced. He has a bad conscience, one might suppose, about his use of the Hierarchy of Ideas and the Causal Noninferiority Principle. And he should have a bad conscience. For, from the fact that the *idea* of myself is inferior to the *idea* of God, I cannot logically conclude, via the Causal Noninferiority Principle, that I cannot cause the idea of God in myself. There is nothing in the two assumptions to exclude the possibility of a finite and imperfect *being* like myself concocting an *idea* of an infinite, perfect being that is just as fictitious as the idea of Sherlock Holmes or a chimera.

The claim that I can produce these ideas only because Sherlock Holmes and the chimera are ideas of things of lesser reality and perfection than myself does not seem convincing. The ideas of Sherlock Holmes and a chimera can be considered as ideas of things of a lower degree of reality only because those entities do not exist. (If Sherlock Holmes existed, he would not be less real and perfect than I am.) Now, if God does not exist and is only an imaginary entity, like Hermes and Athena, I would not be violating the Hierarchy of Ideas or the Causal Noninferiority Principle by producing the idea of God myself. Even if God does exist, it is not clear why I cannot produce the idea of God myself. My ability to produce the idea of God, in other words, does not seem to prove that God exists, even if we accept the Meditator's two Principles. If I were to imagine a person like myself, but without some of my various faults and failings, would I not be imagining a more perfect being than myself? No impossibility seems to be involved here.

Fortunately, a few more arguments, more intuitive, less dependent on traditional terminology and principles, occur to the Meditator. These arguments do not address the question of the origins of the Meditator's idea of God, but rather his origins as a thinking thing that has ideas.

First, the Meditator decides that only God could have produced him, because neither the Meditator, nor his parents (assuming parents exist and are not fabrications of the malevolent Demon), nor any other finite cause could have produced him. If the Meditator had had the amazing power to produce himself out of nothing, he would surely have had the power to give himself all the perfections of knowledge that he is aware that he lacks. But perhaps the Meditator has always existed and needed no cause to bring him into existence? To the contrary:

> [A] lifespan can be divided into countless parts, each completely independent of the others, so that it does not follow from the fact that I existed a little while ago that I must exist now, unless there is some cause which as it were creates me afresh at this moment – that is, which preserves me. For it is quite clear to anyone who attentively considers the nature of time that the same power and action are needed to preserve anything at each individual moment of its duration as would be required to create that thing anew if it were not yet in existence. Hence the distinction between preservation and creation is only a conceptual one. . .
>
> (VII:49)

To exist for any interval, however short, the Meditator decides, requires as much power and force as it does to be created *ex nihilo*. Think of the instants of time as a series of beads strung along a wire. Continuous existence, existence over a time interval, can be conceived as involving a passage from one bead to the next. Whence does the power to make that transition arise? If, as a mere thinking thing, the Meditator has no power to prolong his existence from instant to instant, he realizes, he must depend on some being distinct from himself.

This argument might seem incongruous: Doesn't the Meditator have the power to think? And isn't it the case that, as long as he thinks, he exists? So, by continuing to think, can't he prolong his existence indefinitely? Evidently not: the Meditator's existence, so long as he thinks, is assured, but his existence is nevertheless precarious. The Meditator has not established that he has the power to think on an ongoing basis, or that he will always continue to think.

The cause that produced me need only be at least as perfect as me, according to the Causal Noninferiority Principle, but if that cause is not God, it too requires a cause, and eventually we will be led to acknowledge a cause that derives its existence from itself and that has the power to endow itself with all perfections. As for parents (if any) – they could not have produced the Meditator as a thinking thing and do not preserve him; at best they "merely placed certain dispositions in the matter which I have always regarded as containing me," i.e., they produced the Meditator's living body (if this exists).

All things considered, it seems to the Meditator that God must be the source of the idea of God. It is the only idea that can so far be known to fall into this privileged category of ideas: ideas that cannot possibly have been invented by the Meditator using his own resources. Though it is not imaginary, the idea of God did not come in through the senses, as adventitious ideas do. It is neither invented nor adventitious, the Meditator decides, but "innate." It is simply found within the mind, though it corresponds to a being outside the mind. Since the idea is not caused by sensory experience, and yet is caused by an "external" being, it must have been stamped into the creature's mind at the first instant of its existence. His personal idea of God, the Meditator decides, is like "the mark of the craftsman stamped upon his work." Not only does the hand of the craftsman show itself in the work, but, to leave no doubt about its origins, the craftsman leaves his signature imprinted on it. Conversely, "[T]he mere fact that God made me is a very strong basis for believing that I am somehow made in his image and likeness." The Meditator can "reach" the perfect God in his thoughts, through he cannot "grasp" God's perfections.

This passage describes the discovery of a kinship between the Meditator and God that goes beyond the hierarchical relationship of creator to created. The Meditator and God are observed to be *similar*, insofar as both are understood to be possessors of truth. The Meditator aspires to the expansion of his knowledge-condition, while God's knowledge

is fully expanded. By virtue of this similarity between himself and
God, the Meditator realizes, he is able to discover and articulate the
existence of God. His ability to discover intellectual arguments for
God's existence confirms his kinship with God, and he asserts this
kinship very strongly:

> And indeed it is no surprise that God, in creating me, should have placed
> [the idea of himself] in me to be, as it were, the mark of the craftsman
> stamped on his work . . . [T]he mere fact that God created me is a very
> strong basis for believing that I am somehow made in his image and
> likeness . . . [W]hen I turn my mind's eye upon myself, I understand that
> I am a thing which is incomplete and dependent on another and which
> aspires without limit to even greater and better things; but I also under-
> stand that he on whom I depend has within him all those greater things,
> not just indefinitely and potentially, but actually and infinitely . . . The
> whole force of the argument lies in this: I recognize that it would be
> impossible for me to exist with the kind of nature I have – that is, having
> within me the idea of God – were it not the case that God really existed.
> (VII:51–2)

The Meditator's realization that he has within him potentially and
indefinitely what God has within Him actually and infinitely is at odds
with the theological doctrine that divine knowledge bears no comparison with human knowledge. The orthodox view is that humans
should not try to be knowledgeable, but only to be good, through
obedience to God's wishes. The doctrine that Original Sin has so
corrupted the epistemological faculties of humans that it is futile
for them to seek knowledge is pointedly contradicted in *Meditation
Three*. Though the Meditator does not report the traditional doctrine
of the disabling effects of Sin as one of those opinions inculcated in
childhood that have not passed through the Clarity and Distinctness
Filter, it seems right to suggest that the doctrine of epistemological
incompetence through Original Sin is now regarded by the Meditator
as untenable. The contrary proposition, that the human potential to
know facts about the world is unlimited, can correspondingly be
added to BELIEVE.

2 GOD IS VERACIOUS – THE MALEVOLENT DEMON IS AN INVENTED IDEA – THE NATURAL LIGHT – THE CONVERSION OF BELIEVE TO TRUE – ATTAINING KNOWLEDGE (VII:51–2)

God, the Meditator decides, cannot be a deceiver, since "all fraud and deception depend on some defect" and God is perfect. God is accordingly not a malevolent Deity. The malevolent Demon is a fiction on the same footing as Hermes and Athena: it was simply an idea. Contemplation of the perfections of God is accompanied with the emotions of "wonder and adoration of the beauty of this immense light so far as the eye of my darkened intellect can bear it." This contemplation "enables us to know the greatest joy of which we are capable in this life."

The acute Reader might wonder why the Meditator is now certain that only a single, perfect, benevolent God exists. Perhaps God is perfect but not good? Perhaps God is good, but the malevolent Demon exists too? These possibilities require further consideration. Meanwhile, we should return to two of the questions posed earlier in Ch. 4 Sec. 1:

2) On what basis has the Meditator determined that his belief-set contains known truths, not just opinions he is psychologically unable to doubt? Hasn't he just turned to the useless Subjective Policy discussed earlier (Ch. 2 Sec. 1)?

3) On what basis has the Meditator determined that, if certain characteristics, namely clarity and distinctness, pertain to all and only his current true beliefs, then all the truths he will come to know in the future will have the characteristics of clarity and distinctness as well?

Two definitive answers to (2), one resting on the difference between the Meditator and God, one on their similarity, are now available to the Meditator that were not available earlier. One answer is that a perfect God would not create and sustain the Meditator in such a way that he was psychologically unable to disbelieve falsehoods and compelled to assent to them. What reason could a perfect and infinite being have to deceive a poor, finite creature? Those who deceive others normally do so to acquire some benefit they lack and desire for themselves, and a supremely powerful God lacks for and desires nothing. A second answer is that a perfect being would not fashion a creature similar to Him in such a way that this creature clearly and distinctly perceived untruths to be true. Having discovered the "mark of the craftsman" stamped on himself, in the form of the idea of God, the Meditator is certain that he is not a badly flawed product.

Question (2) can also receive a new kind of answer. A perfect God that had bestowed on the Meditator the extraordinary gift of a sign of truth in clear and distinct perception would not change the sign of truth from proposition to proposition. It would be cruel and deceptive on God's part, or would indicate incompetence in His fabrication, if God had fashioned the Meditator's mind in such a way that *sometimes* clarity and distinctness were features of propositions that were signs of truth while *sometimes* entirely different features of propositions – such as their occurring in the Holy Scriptures or being asserted by authorities – were signs of truth. A good God would not arbitrarily change something as fundamental as the sign of truth from moment to moment.

On this basis, all that has been placed into the category of BELIEVE up to now can be moved directly into TRUE. Every proposition the Meditator has determined it is permissible to believe is TRUE and known to be the case, and every new proposition that is clearly and

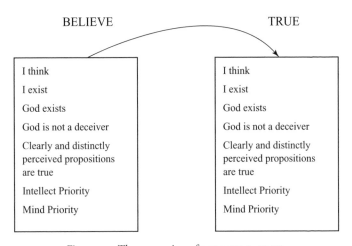

Figure 19   The conversion of BELIEVE to TRUE

distinctly perceived will also be TRUE and known to be the case. (Since it is true that false propositions are false, the Meditator can also compile a list of propositions known to be FALSE.)

There are a number of references appearing for the first time in *Meditation Three* to the "natural light," a kind of inner illuminator. The natural light seems to reveal intellectual truths when we turn our attention to them and concentrate on them in the same way that a torch reveals objects that were there all along but invisible in a dark room when it is turned on and aimed. It is the natural light that is said to have revealed to the Meditator in *Meditation Two* that, from the fact that he is doubting, it follows that he exists. The natural light also revealed in *Meditation Three* that: (a) causes must have as much or more reality than effects; (b) ideas of non-things must arise from the Meditator's own nature; (c) creation and preservation are not really distinct actions; and (d) since all fraud and deception proceed from some defect, God is not a deceiver. The natural light was described as the most trustworthy faculty the Meditator possessed. Without the natural light, the argument of *Meditation Three* would not be able to *move*.

How, though, does the Meditator know that he possesses such a trustworthy faculty and that the metaphysical principles revealed by the natural light, and the inferences he makes from these principles, are true? For, presumably, the Meditator believed before he began to meditate that he had a natural light. It would have been procedurally correct, one might think, to have put that faculty, or its reliability, in doubt, along with the Meditator's other spontaneous and natural beliefs. The objection that the Meditator is "reasoning in a circle," or relying on unproved assumptions, is advanced by Arnauld in the *Fourth Set of Objections* and is discussed, along with Descartes's response to it, below in Sec. 4.

The situation meanwhile is as follows: the various metaphysical principles (a)–(d) revealed by the natural light can be added to the Meditator's knowledge-set. They can be collected under the heading "Various metaphysical principles." Even with the hypothesis of the malevolent Demon refuted, however, and the pretense that the Demon exists set aside, much remains doubtful. The Meditator cannot simply decide to believe again all the long-held opinions that he came to doubt when he decided to entertain the hypothesis of the malevolent Demon. For the opinions remaining in DOUBT have not all been examined for their clarity and distinctness; they have not been put through the filter. Nevertheless, the Meditator can now distinguish between propositions still subject to doubt and those that can be decisively rejected.

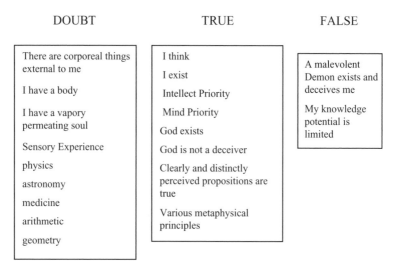

Figure 20　The Meditator's knowledge-set at the end of *Meditation Three*

3 OBJECTIONS TO *MEDITATION THREE* (II)

Recall Caterus's objection (VII:92), cited in the previous chapter, that ideas do not need to be assigned causes and Descartes's riposte, that there must be as much "objective intricacy" in the cause of an idea of an intricate machine in someone's mind as in the idea. The analogy between the idea of a complex machine and the idea of God should make the further argument of *Meditation Three* clearer. There is something in the Meditator's mind that he is able to "read" as the idea of an infinite and perfect being. The idea cannot have got there spontaneously or by chance. The Meditator must be competent to form that idea. One way to develop knowledge with respect to intricate machinery is to come into causal interaction with intricate machinery by operating it or at least watching it being operated. By being in the presence of a machine, one comes into causal contact with it, even if one never actually touches it. Analogously, one way to come to be knowledgeable about God and competent to form the idea of God is to come into causal interaction with God. This indicates, one might think, that there is something – God – that causally acts upon us to give us the idea of God.

However, one can come to be competent to form the idea of an intricate machine even if no intricate machines exist or have ever existed. Perhaps ideas for intricate machines that have never been built exist in human minds. They might be imaginative elaborations upon much simpler machines. The analogous possibility – that the idea of God is a mental fabrication built up from simpler elements of experience – is raised by several of the later commentators.

Caterus further objects that Descartes's causal arguments are not very original. Aristotle had argued (*Physics* 8, 251ff., *Metaphysics A* 1072ff.) that everything, except a thing that causes itself, needs an extrinsic cause, and St. Thomas repeats this argument (*Summa Theologia*, Pt. I question 2 article 3). A typical "First Cause" argument runs as follows: my parents produced me, and their parents produced them, and perhaps some nonhuman ancestor produced one of my earlier ancestors, but eventually we must admit an infinite regress of causes, which is impossible, or come to a self-causing First Cause.

Descartes says that he did not intend to advance a conventional First Cause argument that depends on the existence of corporeal things, including human bodies. The Meditator is represented only as trying to find the cause of his existence as a thinking thing, the cause of his continuing in existence, and the cause of his being able to formulate an idea of God.

Caterus now insists that we do not have a clear and distinct idea of an infinite being. Thinking of God is like thinking of a thousand-sided figure – a chiliagon – that we can represent to ourselves only vaguely (VII:96). Therefore, the implication is, no particularly grand cause is required. Descartes replies that looking at two sides of a chiliagon is nevertheless looking at a chiliagon. Conceiving God is accordingly like looking at the sea. We do not see its entirety. Still, it is the sea that we see (VII:113).

Mersenne, the Second Objector, again raises the possibility that the Meditator has fabricated the idea of God himself and cannot infer from the existence of an idea of God to God as the cause of that idea: "We can find simply within ourselves a sufficient basis for our ability to form [the idea of a supreme being] even supposing that the supreme being did not exist." I can think of an object with some degree of perfection, mentally add one more degree of perfection to it, and think of myself as continuing that process indefinitely to arrive at the idea of an infinitely perfect being (VII:123). Descartes insists that his argument is meant to show that it is this "sufficient basis" that needs explaining. *I* would not have the power (cf. the "intricate machine" argument above) to form the idea of God unless I were created by God.

Mersenne, citing the "spontaneous generation" of insects and plants in the earth in the presence of heat and moisture, also disputes the Causal Noninferiority Principle:

> You say . . . that an effect cannot possess any degree of reality or perfection that was not previously present in the cause. But we see that flies and other animals, and also plants, are produced from sun and rain and earth, which lack life. Now life is something nobler than any merely corporeal grade of being; and hence it does happen that an effect may derive from its cause some reality which is nevertheless not present in the cause.
> (VII:123)

Descartes replies that this is not a refutation of his Principle. Mersenne's argument depends on inferences drawn from the sensory observation of corporeal things. The existence of corporeal things (as well as the "science" allegedly pertaining to them) has meanwhile been shown to be doubtful. At this stage of the argument, they cannot be assumed to exist, so Mersenne's argument is, strictly speaking, not available. The other animals, lacking reason, Descartes goes on to say, going along for the moment with the assumption that animals exist, have no perfection that is not present in inanimate bodies. It would not be a violation of the Causal Noninferiority Principle were they to come into being by "spontaneous generation" from earth, water, and warmth. Only an animal that has reason must derive its reason from somewhere other than earth, rain, and sun. Humans, therefore, cannot be spontaneously generated.

Mersenne raises the further objection that the idea of God might never have occurred to Descartes had his upbringing been different:

> [I]f you had not grown up among educated people, but had spent your entire life alone in some deserted spot, how do you know that the idea would have come to you? You derived this idea from earlier preconceptions, or from books or from discussion with friends and so on, and not simply from your mind or from an existing supreme being . . . [T]he fact that the natives of Canada, the Hurons and other primitive peoples, have no awareness of any idea of this sort seems to establish that the idea does come from previously held notions.
>
> (vii:124)

Descartes insists that there is "no force in this suggestion." If the idea of God were a "mere figment," it would not be conceived by everyone in the same way as, he implies, it manifestly is. The metaphysicians would not agree more about the properties of God – His omniscience, omnipotence, and infinite benevolence – than the "philosophers" (natural scientists) agree concerning the properties of corporeal things. Descartes does not discuss Mersenne's assertion that there are human beings with no innate idea of God (vii:136). To Gassendi, however, he remarks that someone who says that he has no idea of God might as well say that nothing exists, "thus remaining in the abyss of impiety and the depths of ignorance" (ix a:210). Again, Descartes avoids confronting the question how there can be natural atheists if the idea of God is innate.

To Mersenne's insistence that "the idea of a perfect being is no more than a conceptual entity, which has no more nobility than your own mind, which is thinking" (vii:123–4), Descartes makes an unexpected and provocative reply. There is a sense, he says, in which everything is a conceptual entity: "[I]ndeed this entire universe can be said to be an entity originating in God's thought, that is, an entity created by a single act of the divine mind" (vii:134).

Hobbes, the Third Objector, insists that we have "no idea or image corresponding to the sacred name of God." "God" is merely a name or a label given to a thing believed in or acknowledged to exist (VII:180). Nor, for that matter, do we have ideas of the soul, or of substance, and it is unclear how there can be "degrees" of reality (VII:185). To these points, Descartes can only insist that one can have an idea without having an image, that it is manifest that we do have ideas of God and of the soul (VII:183), and that there are degrees of reality: substance is "more of a thing" than are modes; infinite, independent substance is "more of a thing" than are finite and dependent substances.

Arnauld insists that it is incorrect to say that God derives His existence from Himself. An infinite being must be indivisible, permanent, and exist all at once, without there being a time before and after it existed (VII:211). Descartes should take care not to imply that God causes Himself to exist, since nearly all theologians will object (VII:214). God, they will say, does not need an efficient cause of His existence because His essence is not distinct from His existence. Descartes shows himself deferential on this point: "I am extremely anxious to prevent anything at all being found in my writings which could justifiably give offence to the theologians" (VII:245). All he meant to say, he pleads, was that God does not need any other efficient cause to exist, so that He is, "in a sense," His own cause (VII:236ff.).

Finally, Arnauld raises the problem of the so-called "Cartesian circle."

I have one further worry, namely how the author avoids reasoning in a circle when he says that we are sure that what we clearly and distinctly perceive is true only because God exists.

But we can be sure that God exists only because we clearly and distinctly perceive this. Hence, before we can be sure that God exists, we ought to be able to be sure that whatever we perceive clearly and evidently is true. (VII:214)

Descartes claims to have answered this objection already (In fact, he has not. It has not been raised.) He has, however, already made two points in reply to Mersenne earlier that are relevant to it.

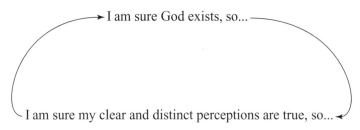

Figure 21　The "Cartesian Circle"

First, Descartes claims that, where knowledge of first principles is concerned, one can recognize them as self-evidently true "by a simple intuition of the mind" (VII:140). Presumably, it is the "natural light" that has this capability. Knowledge of the existence of God is *not* necessary for us to have confidence in the natural light. This point is consistent with the structure of the argument of *Meditation Two*, in which metaphysical principles known by the natural light are used to infer the existence of God. One might suppose that the existence and reliability of a natural light ought to have been doubted from the start. Shouldn't the Meditator have supposed that the malevolent Demon had endowed him with a faculty that revealed false, deceptive propositions? (The inner light might resemble a slide-projector rather than a torch.)

If there is no natural light or if the natural light projects false images and does not reliably illuminate truths, then, even if the Meditator, the target of the malevolent Demon, exists and thinks, God may not exist. All the Meditator's clever reasonings may have made him "see," with his intellectual vision, not truths illuminated by this inner torch, but something more akin to pictures cast onto a wall by an inner projector. The Meditator may be a victim of the Demon, who has induced in him the cognitive illusion that he has sound proofs for the existence of a veracious God, and who now mocks him for accepting the delusory belief that his clear and distinct perceptions are true. For it seems that before the Meditator has proved that God exists and is benevolent and veracious, he has no basis for trusting his own reason and insight.

However, unless the Meditator can trust his own reason and insight *to some extent*, he cannot construct any proofs or indeed any arguments, sound or unsound, at all. Fortunately, he does not need to trust his reasoning powers very far in order to reason to the existence of God. He does not need to be able to trust his own ability to make arithmetical calculations, or even to count the sides of a square in order to do so. Nor does he need to trust his own ability to distinguish valid from invalid syllogisms in formal logic. (Perhaps a malevolent Demon could have made it seem to the Meditator that valid syllogisms seemed invalid and that invalid ones "looked right." I can imagine looking at the following syllogism under the influence of the malevolent Demon and thinking it is a sound argument: *Some cats are striped. All tigers are striped. So all tigers are cats.*) The supposition in force is nevertheless that the Demon could not have made it seem to the Meditator that his power to think was not working adequately when it was, or that it was working adequately when it was not. Clear and distinct perception, the Meditator suggests, is a criterion of truth *for us* whether or not God exists and whether or not God or some superior being perceives things otherwise. Whatever we cannot doubt, we are not only inclined to accept as true, we ought to accept as true, because there is no other criterion besides indubitability – clear and distinct perception – that could possibly serve as a criterion of truth.

If [a] conviction is so firm that it is impossible for us ever to have any reason for doubting what we are convinced of, then there are no further questions for us to ask: we have everything that we could reasonably want. What is it to us that someone may make out that the perception whose truth we are so firmly convinced of may appear false to God or an angel, so that it is, absolutely speaking, false? Why should this alleged "absolute falsity" bother us, since we neither believe in it nor have even the smallest suspicion of it?

(VII:144–5)

In other words, it *was* always the case that clear and distinct perceptions signaled the truth, though the Meditator did not realize that this was so until after he had entertained the supposition of a malevolent Demon and refuted it.

Objector 5, Gassendi, raises the problem of relativism. Perceptions differ amongst different animals and in different states of health of the same animal. I may clearly and distinctly perceive the taste of a melon, but it need not be true that a taste of this kind exists in the melon. Moreover, "Everyone thinks that he clearly and distinctly perceives the truth which he champions" (VII:278), and many great thinkers have become skeptics, concluding that "the truth of things is hidden either in God or in a deep well" (VII:277).

Descartes's reply is that Gassendi is (as usual, he might have added) failing to attend to the terms of Descartes's own argument by introducing references to the great minds of the past, other people and animals, melons, etc., the existence of which is still in doubt at the close of *Meditation Three*. Skepticism based on the variety of opinions held by past philosophers is, he says dismissively, "a standard move and not a bad one" but it does not invalidate the proposed criterion. "Nor is anything proved by the fact that some people face death to defend opinions that are in fact false; for it can never be proved that they clearly and distinctly perceive what they so stubbornly affirm" (VII:361). This reply raises the question whether *I* can ever be certain that I clearly and distinctly perceive what I think I clearly and distinctly perceive, but Descartes's implicit position is that I *can* be certain of this in my own case.

Gassendi suggests – elaborating Mersenne's point – that it is "absolutely true" that the attributes Descartes understands to be in God "did not originate from you alone."

[Y]ou did not acquire your understanding of them from yourself or through your own efforts. But this is because they in fact originated and were derived from things, parents, teachers, professors and from the human society in which you have moved . . . [T]ell me in good faith whether you do not in fact derive all the language which you use of God from the human society in which you live." And if this is true of the words, is it not also true of the underlying notions which these words express?

(VII:294)

For a change, Gassendi anticipates Descartes's reply: Descartes will say that this rival hypothesis concerning the origin of his idea of God is simply not available to the Meditator, whose case, not Descartes's own, is under consideration. Gassendi's riposte is that in discussing these matters and presenting his own views, Descartes is admitting something outside of himself – other people, their conversations and influence.

Gassendi's next point is astute. The Meditator, he says, possesses the idea of an infinite substance only verbally (VII:295); it has been "constructed by the process of composition and amplification." Certain early philosophers amplified their ideas to arrive at the ideas of an infinite universe, an infinite number of worlds, and infinite principles [i.e., atoms]: "Do you then propose to say that they did not form such ideas by their own mental powers, but that it was an infinite universe, infinite worlds, and infinite principles that made these ideas come into their minds?" (VII:295). Accordingly, "the attributes that we do know prove nothing about God which they do not also prove of the infinite set of worlds mentioned in the above example. Indeed, these infinite worlds can be understood from our clear perception of this one world very much more clearly than God, or an infinite being, can be understood from your perception of your substance, whose nature you have not yet established" (VII:297).

Gassendi is referring to the "Epicurean" hypothesis that there exists a multiplicity of self-created *cosmoi* assembled by chance from the motion of atoms without the direction of a supervisory God. It is provocative on his part to suggest that the Epicurean hypothesis is on the same footing as the Meditator's argument for a creator God. Descartes avoids any direct response, claiming that he has already answered this objection, though it is not clear that he has.

Gassendi further insists that the claim that creation and preservation are not really distinct is too strong. Some effects need to have their efficient cause continuously present. The sun must keep giving off light for there to be light, but procreation and manufacture do not require continuous application. No created thing has a power to guarantee its future existence but it has to be supposed that the Meditator has "a power sufficient to ensure that you will continue unless some destructive cause intervenes" (VII:302). Descartes replies that to posit such a power of self-continuation is to ascribe to the created thing a perfection appropriate to the Creator. To bring our existence to an end, God need perform no positive action, He needs only to cease to perform His customary preserving action (vii:370).

Finally, with respect to the Meditator's notion that the idea of God is "stamped" in him, like the craftsman's mark, Gassendi takes strong exception to the Meditator's claim that that there is a resemblance between him and God: "[Y]ou cannot say that you resemble him any more than a house resembles a bricklayer" (vii:306). Gassendi asks whether the Meditator might not be merely an idea of God's: "Are you nothing else but a mode of thought?" he asks. (Cf. Descartes's remark that the universe is, in a sense, an entity originating in God's thought [vii:134]).

A few remarks on Cartesian theology are in order. While the Meditator refers to God as "He," suggesting that the Meditator thinks of God as resembling a male person, he did not try to show that God was anything like a male person. Nor did the Meditator argue for the existence of a God who spoke to Moses, sent plagues, fathered Jesus, punished various people, and did all the other things ascribed to God in the Scriptures. The idea of God is simply the idea of a being with the divine attributes of omnipotence, omniscience, benevolence, perfection, eternality, and immutability. Any images attached by custom to this idea are, it might be said, cultural additions. To that extent, Descartes's theology, as it is presented through the Meditator, is consistent with the view that the idea of God that most of his contemporaries possess is largely though not wholly a human invention.

Has the Meditator really established that the God he thinks of is not just extremely powerful, but actually omnipotent, or infinitely powerful, so powerful that He must be the unique Deity? Has he established that this God is *good*, as opposed to simply powerful? If so, how was God's ethical perfection established? Earlier in *Meditation Three*, the Meditator characterized God as "a substance that is infinite, eternal, immutable, independent, supremely intelligent, supremely powerful, and which created both myself and everything else (if anything else there be) that exists" (vii:45). His idea of God did not seem to incorporate goodness along with the other predicates and he has advanced no considerations helping to establish God's overall goodness. Perhaps God is not malevolent or cunningly deceptive – since these personality features indicate weakness and are incompatible with His creative power – but simply indifferent and ethically neutral. Or, perhaps the malevolent Demon co-exists with a (possibly good, possibly indifferent) God.

The Reader may well agree that the Meditator does not really know at this stage that God is good, or is the unique Deity, or in what sense God can be said to be perfect, or even that God is perfect. Perhaps the Meditator can be thought of as having discovered that the idea of the Demon is a materially false idea. For the idea of total deceptiveness, like the ideas of hell and evil, is perhaps only a confused representation of a pure negation – the absence of truth and goodness. Perhaps "veracity" is the only real quality of the pair *veracity–deceptiveness*, just as "heat" is the only real quality of the pair *heat–cold*, and "light," the only real quality of the pair *light–dark*, though subjectively all these terms seem to name equally real qualities. If an idea is materially false, one might reason, its corresponding idea must be materially true. So, if the idea of a malevolent, deceptive, extremely powerful being is materially false, not merely a fiction like Sherlock Holmes, its counterpart idea – the idea of a good and veracious extremely powerful being – must be materially true.

Unfortunately, there is no textual basis for supposing that *Descartes* thought that the idea of the malevolent Demon was materially false, and the Meditator was silent on this subject. The Meditator will, however, take up the question of God's goodness explicitly in *Meditation Four* and God's perfection – a perfection that must exclude co-existence with rival gods – in *Meditation Five*, as though dissatisfied with what he has managed to learn about these matters so far in *Meditation Three*. To give a preview of what lies ahead, the Meditator will come to understand *in what way* God can be said to be good and the nature of God's perfections only as he continues to advance in knowledge. God's goodness, let it be noted, will turn out to have nothing to do with God's special care for individuals, or his ability to rescue those He favors or to punish evildoers.

With respect to the promotion of BELIEVE to TRUE undertaken in *Meditation Three*, one might wonder finally whether the Clarity and Distinctness Filter really does provide a criterion of truth. Isn't it too lax in being hopelessly subjective? If not, and if the Meditator's reasons for accepting *all* clearly and distinctly perceived propositions as true are sound, has he really shown that he should accept *only* clearly and distinctly perceived propositions? Just as it is somewhat uncertain whether the Meditator has good reason to think that there is *only* one God, it is somewhat uncertain whether he has good reason to think that *only* clearly and distinctly perceived propositions are true.

No direct argument for accepting only clearly and distinctly perceived propositions has actually been given. If God, and not a malevolent Demon exists, why shouldn't I now feel free to accept my former opinions, vague and unsubstantiated as they may be, as true, since I know that I am not radically deceived? *Meditation Four* is intended to plug this conceptual gap: Descartes's Meditator will discover there that the source of his errors is his propensity to assent to propositions he has not scrutinized sufficiently.

One might nevertheless wonder whether the criterion is too stringent in excluding some perfectly good sources of knowledge just because what they tell us is not always clear and distinct. To see the merits of the proposed criterion, consider the following rival criteria for truth:

Whatever I clearly and distinctly perceive is true vs.

Whatever my elders tell me is true
Whatever is to be found in books published by university presses is true
Whatever computational result is generated by this computer is true
Whatever the oracle says is true
Whatever the priest or the Bible tells me is true
Whatever this statistical analysis will tell me is true

Why is the criterion of clear and distinction perception preferable? Well, the Meditator does not know whether there are any parents, books, computers, oracles, priests, Bibles, statistical analyses, or anything of the sort. The Clarity and Distinctness Filter can be put to use in the absence of any knowledge about the existence of any of these things. Setting aside this consideration for the moment, are these sources really worthy of complete trust and confidence?

Older relatives are normally wise and experienced, and often give excellent advice, but they can make mistakes, even serious mistakes. University presses depend on the competence and veracity of their authors and on that of fact-checkers and critical readers. Yet all these persons may overlook errors or project false images. Religious authorities have been known to make mistakes of fact and errors of judgment. Reliance on computers or statistical analysis might avoid the problem of human, personal bias, but these machines and processes are designed and operated by fallible humans.

If my own clear and distinct perceptions are the touchstone, I can make some use of these external sources of opinions. I need not ignore them or deny that they are sometimes correct in what they maintain. So long as I myself perceive clearly and distinctly what they tell me, I should accept it as true . . . but not otherwise. If I can clearly and distinctly perceive that my mother's or the priest's perceptions are clear and distinct, I can confidently accept what they say as true. If I am unsure whether my mother's or the priest's perceptions are clear and distinct, I should not have complete confidence in their opinions.

Given the alternatives, the Meditator's decision to rely on his own clear and distinct perceptions does not seem unreasonable. It would be a fine thing if we could decide that some sources of opinions external to ourselves are perfectly trustworthy and employ the Authority Principle (Ch. 1 Sec. 2) to formulate and reformulate our own belief-sets. To do so, however, we would have to perceive clearly and distinctly that all the existing opinions of a given Authority are true and clearly and distinctly to perceive that there is an underlying good reason why all future opinions of the Authority will continue to be true. None of the sources of opinions above produces opinions that we can be certain will always pass through the Clarity and Distinctness Filter. There are nevertheless sources of knowledge that we *deem*, often with good reason, to be free or relatively free of mistakes, misjudgments, and biases, such as trustworthy newspapers, independent laboratory reports, friends whose predictions have come true in the past. In cases where practical action is called for, I may have no choice but to believe certain opinions when perfect clarity and distinctness are lacking and to accept certain sources as reliable, even when I cannot be certain that they are fully reliable.

Are there perhaps important truths – poetic truths, or hard to articulate truths – that can only be perceived vaguely and indistinctly? This possibility seems to be excluded. Though we must sometimes act on the basis of vague and indistinct perception, precipitate judgments involve a degree of risk, as the Meditator now discovers.

CHAPTER 6

Meditation Four (1)
The Meditator broods on her epistemological and moral errors and deficiencies and discovers the true power of her will and its spontaneous attraction to truth and goodness

I TRUE AND FALSE JUDGMENT – DIVINE AND HUMAN WILL – THE USE OF FREE WILL (AT VII:52–8)

Meditation Four begins with the Meditator's recapitulation of the contents of her knowledge-set. She has determined that God exists and is veracious. Although deceit is a manifestation of power, which God has in abundance, it is also a manifestation of malice and weakness that cannot be ascribed to a perfect being. The malevolent Demon can only be a fiction. Moreover, because her mind bears the image of God within it, like the mark of the craftsman stamped on his work, she must possess some of the excellence of her creator. Encouraged by this result, the Meditator describes her intimation that "from this contemplation of the true God, in whom all the treasures of wisdom and the sciences lie hidden, I think I can see a way forward to the knowledge of other things." The initial, risky choice of the Withholding Policy continues to vindicate itself as further propositions are added to the Meditator's knowledge-set.

This is the first mention of the sciences since the beginning of *Meditation One* when the Meditator first announced her desire to discover something in the sciences that was firm and lasting. Led through knowledge of herself to a knowledge of God, the first thing whose existence outside herself she was able to establish securely, the Meditator is about to be led onward and outward to "knowledge of other things."

A nondeceiving God is the creator and preserver of the mind that the Meditator knows herself to be: "Every single moment of my entire existence depends on him." Therefore, a nondeceiving God must be the creator and preserver of the Meditator's faculty of judgment, her capacity for distinguishing between true and false opinions. This deduction raises a problem. If God is not a deceiver, why is the Meditator ever wrong about any factual or any practical matter?

The Meditator doesn't *know* that she is ever wrong! the astute Reader might protest. She has no idea what is really true in any of the sciences, so what basis does she have for believing that she was ever mistaken in the past? And how does she know that she has ever been morally remiss? For if she and God exist but there are no other people in her world, she has had no opportunities to harm anyone else. Well, one might respond, it is true that she does not know that the objects she has beliefs about actually exist, and even if they do exist, she does not know which of her former beliefs were false. Nevertheless, it is possible that there are other entities in the world besides herself and God, and it is possible that her doubts about her own capacities are justified. *Many of my beliefs are false* was, after all, the point of departure of her inquiry in *Meditation One*.

While the Meditator does not know whether she has ever harmed another person, she has certainly *seen₁* instances of moral harm, some of them involving her own decisions and her own "actions," and it is at least possible that she has *seen₂* instances of moral harm and that some of those instances involved her decisions and actions. Yet the Reader is right to note that, technically, the claim that the Meditator is sometimes wrong is assumed by her without proof, merely on the basis of her subjective impression of a long past history of confusion and error. We can concede that her epistemological and moral frailty is assumed by the Meditator in *Meditation Four*, and continue with her train of thought.

The weakness of her sensory organs and the finite storage capacity of her brain cannot be cited as the causes of her intellectual weakness; for the Meditator still doubts that she really has a body and brain. Nor is the Biblical story of Adam's Fall and the corruption of our faculties an acceptable explanation for her deficiencies. According to the theologians, Adam brought confusion and ignorance, along with moral error – the refusal to shun evil when one knows the difference between good and evil – upon himself, his consort, and all his descendants, by yielding to temptation and aspiring to unholy knowledge. The explanation of the Meditator's error-proneness cannot, however, be referred to theology; the existence of the historical Adam is doubtful. Her aim is to discover reasons for her fallibility which are intrinsic to the constitution of her own mind.

It now occurs to the Meditator that she must be a finite creature intermediate between God, the infinite substance, and the opposite of God, the absence of all perfections, which is Nothingness. In *Meditation Two*, she discovered that she was not nothing and the fact that she is not God was established, after careful consideration, in *Meditation Three* (Ch. 5 Sec.1). Her error-proneness perhaps indicates no more than her status as an intermediate substance, for, as a finite creature, she might be thought to "participate in nothingness," as well as sharing in some of the attributes of God:

> I realize that I am, as it were, something intermediate between God and nothingness, or between supreme being and non-being: my nature is such that in so far as I was created by the supreme being, there is nothing in me to enable me to go wrong or lead me astray; but in so far as I participate in nothingness or non-being, that is, in so far as I am not myself the supreme being and am lacking in countless respects, it is no wonder that I make mistakes . . . Hence my going wrong does not require me to have a faculty specially bestowed on me by God; it simply happens as a result of the fact that the faculty of true judgement which I have received from God is in my case not infinite.
>
> (VII:54)

The Meditator decides on reflection that this explanation is not entirely satisfactory. It is not clear what it is to "participate in nothingness" and one might wonder whether *nothingness* is not a materially false idea, in which case there is nothing to participate in. Moreover, God seemingly could have created a much better version of the Meditator without making her another infinite substance. The existence of a finite creature that never falls into moral error and that has no false beliefs and a vast multitude of true beliefs does not seem to be an impossibility. If God could have created me as a perfect finite creature, why didn't He? "The more skilled the craftsman, the more perfect the work produced by him . . . [H]ow can anything produced by the supreme creator of all things not be complete and perfect in all respects?"

Recourse to the hypothesis of divine inscrutability is one possible solution to the dilemma. God is capable of "countless things whose causes are beyond my knowledge." Perhaps the solution to the question why God has made the Meditator less perfect than He could have lies in her relationship to the whole of which she is a small part. Bitter chocolate is unpleasant to the palate and pure sugar is repulsively sweet, but, mixed together, these two imperfect substances create a perfect ambrosia. Though a mouse is an imperfect creature, short-lived, and virtually defenseless, it has a place in the overall ecology. It multiplies quickly and serves as food for the hawk. The imperfections of each creature sustain a functioning whole that is overall good, and perhaps God intends the good of the whole. Although the Meditator still does not know anything to exist outside herself, she states that "many other things have been made by [God] or at least could have been made, and hence . . . I may have a place in the universal scheme of things."

At the same time, as a finite and defective creature, the Meditator has little or no insight into the organization of the whole. She cannot determine why it might be conducive to God's purposes that she suffer from weakness of judgment. Indeed, she states forthrightly that "the customary search for final causes [is] totally useless in physics."

This claim requires some explanation. A final cause is a concept that explains for what purpose something is constituted as it is, or was made to happen as it did. By citing a final cause, we answer such questions as: "What is it for?" "What role does it play?" "Why do we/they have it?" "What is the reason for such things to be?" or "What is the intention behind this?" To the question "What does this button marked REW on the VCR do?" one might reply that it rewinds the tape; the reason the VCR has such a button, the final cause of the button, is *in order that* tapes can be rewound. To the question "Why do badgers have snouts?" the answer might be that they *use them for* digging for grubs. To the question "Why do I have to get this vaccination?" the answer might be that *the point is* to protect me against the dreaded disease, cholera. Where such "Why" questions are answerable, they make reference to needs, to biological functions, and to intentions and goals. Tapes need rewinding and manufacturers know this; therefore, there is a button for this purpose. Badgers need to eat and have evolved to be able to capture their insect prey in their habitats. People try to avoid getting cholera and letting others get cholera and vaccinations make this possible.

A worthwhile end, such as preventing cholera, can require a painful injection. People commonly reason backwards, assuming that, if a painful event has occurred, there must be a worthwhile end for which it occurred. They may ask *why*, a lovely child "had to" die young, as though some good must necessarily have been intended through the death of the child, and they may even try to find some good consequence of the child's death. Or they may describe such sad events as "senseless," indicating that most other sad events, if not this particular one, can be explained in terms of overall purpose. They may refuse to accept accounts that mention only "efficient" and not "final" causes – such as explanations that cite infection with a rare virus or medical incompetence – as fully adequate explanations.

The Meditator is convinced, however, that the search for final causes is "totally useless in physics." This implies that the notion of a final cause is also totally useless in medicine, a physical science. On this view, there is normally no answer in terms of final causes to the question why a particular individual had to die, since normally no one intends for individuals to die, God included. One might wonder how the Meditator can know that God does not have particular purposes in mind in killing off, or allowing to die, certain individuals, or how she can know God does not send messages or seek to influence some people by killing off others or allowing to them to die. She is not making a positive assertion in this respect, merely pointing out that we have no epistemological access to the intentions of God. Therefore, we should not assume that events such as the death of a lovely child are part of an intentional divine plan. Maybe they happen for a reason, maybe not, but we can never discover what these reasons might be and it is presumptuous to try: "there is considerable rashness in thinking myself capable of investigating the impenetrable purposes of God."

The Meditator decides that she cannot sensibly ask what purpose her ignorance might serve, what it might be for. There is no point in trying to speculate about what God must have intended in creating her as a fallible creature and subjecting her to misfortune. The metaphysical explanation in terms of her participation in nothingness being dubious, the ecological explanation in terms of her fitting into the whole, unavailable, and the explanation in terms of final causes, presumptuous, the Meditator has no satisfactory explanation for her liability to error, whether moral wrongdoing or epistemological misjudgment. Yet all is not lost, she realizes. Just as one can learn how a lovely young person came to die of some disease, though not why, she can come to know how errors are made, though not why. Indeed, it may be better to know how rather than why, since one can then perhaps avoid making them. If errors and deficiencies do not have any knowable purpose, have no positive ecological significance, and are not metaphysically inevitable, there is good reason to try to avoid them and a proper diagnosis of their sources will be valuable.

The Meditator reasons that her judgments, which are subject to error, depend on two faculties: knowledge and will. Intellect, the knowledge-faculty, enables the Meditator to perceive ideas. Ideas, however, as the Reader will recall from *Meditation Three*, are neither true nor false. Furthermore – the Meditator's insight here is extremely acute – propositions that are merely thought are neither true nor false. The will is required for us to be able to go beyond mere thinking to the making of true and false judgments.

Suppose I imagine an angel: a woman with wings growing from her shoulderblades. There is nothing true or false in my perception of this idea. For my mere idea of a woman with wings to become a judgment expressing what I believe about what is / was / might be the case, something, it seems, has to be added to the idea – something that makes it expressible as a proposition.

Now suppose I have one of the following thoughts expressed as a proposition:

A woman with wings growing from her shoulderblades exists (Ontological thought)

A woman has in the past grown wings from her shoulderblades (Historical thought)

A woman could possibly grow wings from her shoulderblades (Modal thought)

Even though I "have" one of the propositional thoughts expressed in one of the three declarative sentences above, I do not have a belief and I have not made a judgment. For I can entertain each proposition neutrally, thinking about *what it would be like* for it to be true, without being in the least inclined to believe or disbelieve it. For a propositional thought about what is the case to be more than idly contemplated, for it to become a judgment, something further, has to be added, something that we might be tempted to express by putting the words YES! or NO! in front of a particular sentence, for example as follows:

NO! *A woman has in the past grown wings from her shoulderblades*

We might suppose that the above formula captures a particular historical judgment, the judgment that it is false that a woman has ever in the past grown wings from her shoulderblades. The formula above expresses, one might say, what it is to "think the proposition negatively."

A moment's reflection, however, will show that this theory is wrong. A judgment requires a person who makes the judgment. And *whose* judgment might the above formula's be? The formula is just another propositional thought that somebody could have, not a judgment after all. *I*, for example, can think the above thought negatively or positively. I can think that it is true or that it is false. Imagine yourself *denying* the thought: NO! *A woman has in the past grown wings from her shoulderblades*. You would in that case be judging that a woman has in the past grown wings from her shoulderblades or at least that this cannot be ruled out.

The upshot is that believing and disbelieving, judging to be true and judging to be false, cannot be conceived as the mere having in mind of a propositional thought. A judgment of truth or falsity requires not simply a thought, but something like a movement of the will by someone, something analogous to picking the judgment up and keeping it, or else throwing it away. For me to come to believe a proposition requires me to step out of an attitude of detached neutrality and open-mindedness with respect to it. I must accept it, embrace it, and welcome the judgement as it were into my belief-set.

An image often accompanies a thought, and a thought is a precondition of a judgment. To make a judgment as to whether angels exist, we usually form an image of a person with a sweet face, curly hair, and wings growing from her shoulderblades. We may go on to entertain the historical thought that such a creature has appeared in some place at some time. Yet to make the judgment that there are angels we have to do more. We might interpret the Meditator's thoughts about error as follows: some errors are errors of *omission* – some thoughts, perceptual thoughts amongst them – are not even entertained by us because we do not have the corresponding perceptual ideas and we cannot form the corresponding thoughts. Other errors are errors of *commission*; some thoughts, perceptual thoughts amongst them, are entertained *and* they are wrongly embraced or pushed away by the will.

Some of the Meditator's error in this case arises from the fact that there are many perceptual thoughts, as well as many abstract thoughts, that she does not have, so that there are many true judgments she cannot make. An omniscient being would know what it feels like to a snail to be trodden on and whether a person ejected from a spacecraft in orbit would have a sensation of cold and vertigo, but I have no idea. Nor do I know what the inside of a computer looks like, whether the parts inside are colorful or relatively colorless. I do not have a clear idea where various organs, such as the spleen and the pancreas, are located in the human body. I have never had the perceptual thoughts that would allow me to entertain numerous propositions. There is a perhaps infinite number of mathematical equations that are true or false that I can not possibly think of or represent in any way in my mind. They correspond to undecided propositions that have never occurred to me.

The imperfection of my knowledge is, then, partly a function of the limited representational capacity of my finite mind. I can not complain that God has not given me all possible thoughts any more than I can complain that a craftsman has not put every function into every one of his machines. I am not "deprived" of beliefs about what it is like to fall out of a spacecraft. I merely lack them. Not possessing the associated perceptual ideas is not a form of punishment.

The remainder of her error, the Meditator realizes, arises from the way in which she employs her will with respect to the thoughts that she does have. For she sometimes assents to propositions in a rash and ill-considered fashion, where assent involves something analogous to a movement or an embrace.

This overactive tendency on the part of the will cannot be considered an intrinsic defect. The will's very capaciousness can be considered another mark of the divine craftsman left on His product. Indeed, the Meditator decides, while she has to admit that her knowledge – the set of true beliefs by which she represents the world – is pitifully incomplete compared to God's knowledge, it is "above all in virtue of the will that I understand myself to bear in some way the image and likeness of God . . . God's will . . . does not seem any greater than mine when considered as will in the essential and strict sense."

What gives the Meditator the impression that her will bears comparison with the divine will? It is that the experiences of deciding, willing, and choosing seem to be entirely different from the experience of being compelled to do something or pushed in some direction by an external force. The will presents itself as an internal power that can act against internal inclination and resist external coercion. Of course, it is not the case that, simply by willing it, I can do anything I want to, or that simply by deciding that I shall hold my ground, I can always hold my ground. Willing alone will not enable me to win an arm-wrestling contest against a stronger opponent, or leap twenty feet into the air, or build a skyscraper with my bare hands. Nor does the will always preserve me from temptation. One makes an impulsive, ill-considered purchase or eats or drinks too greedily, aware that this is a form of discreditable weakness. Nevertheless, even if I fail to hold my ground because the forces acting on me are too strong for my frail organism or because my inclinations are too powerful, it can remain true of me that I did not will what happened to me, that I did not assent or consent. The will, in a sense, cannot be coerced, though it cannot make anything at all happen either. Threatened by gangsters, I might have to give up my billfold. Tempted by some delicacy, I might be unable to do otherwise than consume it. There is still a difference, however, between submitting willingly and submitting unwillingly. If the Meditator's comparison between the human will and the divine will has any plausibility, it lies in this: the human will is such that no external power on earth and no internal urge can compel *me* to submit willingly to it if I do not want to.

This might seem controversial: Couldn't my brain be wired up and stimulated electrically by mad scientists so that, when ordered by them to do something I antecedently did not want to do, such as harm a favored animal, I was compelled to do so willingly? Couldn't they make me *want* to harm the favoured animal and accordingly will to do so? If the Meditator is right, though, this is impossible. The scientists could induce certain feelings in me, such as a feeling of enthusiasm for harming the animal, a sadistic impulse, by stimulating my cortex appropriately. But this would not be the same as making me want to harm it willingly. Similarly, I can get myself into a condition – drug addiction, for example – in which certain temptations are irresistible. The pleasure of the drug is too intense to forgo, the pain of deprivation too excruciating to endure. If I am an addict, I can not help but take the drug. Suppose, though, I do not want to be an addict. Then I have not submitted willingly to the urge.

If I do not want to be an addict, I must, one might think, feel some disgust at and anger with myself when I take the drug. Yet suppose the same mad scientists were able to suppress my self-directed anger and disgust at being an addict by stimulating parts of my cortex, so that I did not care? Still, it would not be right to say that now I had been compelled to submit willingly. (One might even employ a version of the malevolent Demon argument. A malevolent Demon can make me do many things I do not want to do. The Demon can give me sadistic impulses or turn me into a guiltless addict, but the Demon can never bring it about that I will to inflict pain and will to be an addict if I do not want to.)

If this interpretation of the thesis of the perfection of the will is correct, the quasi-divinity of the Meditator's will can not be understood in terms of the power to make things happen or fail to happen in the external world. Our creative and transformative *agency* with respect to material things has to be considered just as paltry with respect to God's agency as our representational capacity is with respect to God's omniscience. Our agency is limited by our size and strength, as well as our restriction to certain times and places. Our will, however, the Meditator thinks, is not limited in the same way.

At the same time, God's will, though it can not be constrained by anything either external or internal to God, seems to be characterized by a certain steadiness. It is "firm and efficacious." How is this to be explained and what consequences does this steadiness have for the human will that mirrors it? Recall that God not only creates, but sustains created things from moment to moment, according to *Meditation Two*. Of course, we are still not entitled, in the terms of

Meditation Four, to look outward at the regularities of the natural world and to observe and comment on the effects of that steadiness. For now, though, we can observe that if God's will were not steady, I, who am preserved by God's agency, might flicker in and out of existence like a bad television image, my thoughts an incoherent collage of chaotic ideas. The freedom and power of the divine will manifests itself in patterning, not in chaos. The freedom and power of the human will also manifest themselves in patterning and not in chaos, namely in my spontaneous attraction to truth and goodness.

Her will, according to the Meditator, is attracted by "reasons of truth and goodness." It is inclined towards some propositions and away from others on the basis of their appeal to reason:

> In order to be free, there is no need for me to be inclined both ways; on the contrary, the more I incline in one direction – either because I clearly understand that reasons of truth and goodness point that way, or because of a divinely produced disposition of my inmost thoughts – the freer is my choice.
>
> (VII:57–8)

This inclination to assent to the reasonable is present even when I am not in the least indifferent between two propositions. To illustrate, suppose I contemplate the following pair of propositions with an eye to determining which of them is true:

1) *A woman has in the past grown wings from her shoulderblades and flown away*
2) *A woman has never in the past grown wings from her shoulderblades and flown away*

My experience might be like that of someone trying to decide whether to go to a movie or stay home, to have chocolate ice-cream or have vanilla, in circumstances in which I am genuinely indecisive and alternate between the two prospects, trying to determine which pleases me more. Often, however, I am able to choose between alternatives decisively. One alternative strikes me immediately as right or correct. I embrace (2) in this case without reserve. In a sense I "can't help" but believe (2) and disbelieve (1). I do not feel constrained by an external force that compels me to pick (2). I freely endorse alternative (2). Might I be reproached in that case with having weakly given in to an alluring *temptation* to assent to (2)? After all, I should not just believe (2) precipitately, without making a careful historical investigation.

Perhaps I do not clearly and distinctly perceive the truth of (2) and should not believe it. A sense of conviction and an accompanying lack of indecision is not, however, always a symptom of prejudice and precipitate judgment. My lack of indecision will be even more pronounced when faced with "self-evident truths" such as the truth that *I exist*. I assent because "I clearly understand that reasons of truth point that way."

At other times, my experience in evaluating alternative propositions is like that of an irresolute person trying to decide whether to go out or stay home. In such cases, I am torn between the two alternatives at the start of my deliberation. I may be unable to decide, or feel I can only guess at which of two claims is true. Consider the following two sentences:

1) *A woman could possibly be made to grow wings in place of arms and fly away*

2) *A woman could never possibly be made to grow wings in place of arms and fly away*

I do not know which of the pair is true; I am genuinely undecided. For one thing, the proposition expressed by each of the two sentences is not clear. This is in part because the sentences are vague and the terms they contain are ambiguous. It is not clear whether the "possibility" referred to is logical possibility or biological possibility, constrained by the laws of nature existing in our universe and conditions on our planet. Is it logically possible even if it is not biologically possible for a woman to grow wings? It is not clear what definition of "woman" would make (1) true under the specification that we are considering logical possibilities. Is it biologically possible? The theory of evolution tells me that some creatures gradually evolved wings in place of arms, so, if we are considering biological possibility, maybe this could happen all at once in a human being, or be made to happen by powerful scientists with perfect mastery of DNA splicing techniques. Maybe a human somehow growing wings is consistent with the laws of nature in our universe and conditions in our world. Where both logical and biological possibility are concerned, I have no overwhelming tendency to believe either (1) or (2). In this respect I seem to be free to assent to either proposition, in case someone insists "Well, just tell me what you *think*."

This freedom, resulting from "the indifference I feel when there is no reason pushing me in one direction rather than in another" is, however, according to the Meditator, "the lowest grade of freedom." It is evidence of a defect in my knowledge. My ability to choose either alternative – as I seemingly can when someone asks me whether I believe there is intelligent life elsewhere in the universe – follows from my limited understanding. If I never experienced that low grade of freedom, but only a complete disinclination or an irresistible inclination to believe, I would be a more perfect creature. A more perfect creature would be able to decide between (1) and (2) straight off, once the relevant definitions and presuppositions were introduced. (She would know exactly what these were.) If I were a more perfect creature, I would never be indecisive or indifferent with respect to courses of action. I would not experience moral dilemmas because I would immediately see what it was right to do: "For if I always saw what was true and good, I should never have to deliberate about the right judgement or choice."

CHAPTER 7

Meditation Four (II)
The Meditator diagnoses the cause of her epistemological and moral errors, adds an error-prevention rule to her knowledge-set, and confirms that God is truly benevolent

I ERROR – THE DENIAL OF FINAL CAUSES – DIVINE GOODNESS (AT VII:58–62)

Error results, the Meditator decides, when I opt to believe a proposition . . . but not because I clearly understand that reasons of truth point that way, or when I opt to act in a certain manner . . . but not because I clearly understand that reasons of goodness point that way. In such cases, I am merely exercising my low-grade freedom:

> So what then is the source of my mistakes? It must simply be this: the scope of the will is wider than that of the intellect; but instead of restricting it within the same limits, I extend its use to matters which I do not understand. Since the will is indifferent in such cases, it easily turns aside from what is true and good, and this is the source of my error and sin. (VII:58)

If I make an epistemological error, it follows that I employed my will improperly, embracing a proposition without having sufficient grounds for doing so. If I make a moral error ("sin" in the Meditator's terms), I engaged my will to perform some action despite my knowledge that it was wrong, or because I failed to perceive its wrongness. Does it follow, though, that whenever I embrace a proposition without having sufficient grounds for doing so, or act spontaneously without much consideration, I make a mistake?

The position that we *always* make errors when exercising our low-grade freedom seems overstated. Often, we come to believe a proposition on very slender evidence, on the basis of little more than guesswork, or we act in some way without being convinced that reasons of goodness support performing the action. As it happens, we are often correct or turn out to have done the right thing. I can catch a bus that I hope will take me to my destination across the city without being sure that it is the right bus, and, as it happens, my hopes are fulfilled. I have been epistemologically and practically "lucky." While exercising our low-grade freedom may be a necessary condition of our making errors of judgment and performance, it does not seem to be a sufficient condition, thanks to the operations of luck.

The Meditator recognizes that we can be epistemologically or morally lucky. She insists, however, that as-it-happens-true beliefs that are arrived at by guesswork are an indication of fault, since "the perception of the intellect should always precede the determination of the will." I can commit a methodological fault even when an outcome is favorable for me. And I should try, one might suppose, to avoid committing these faults of precipitate judgment because I am just as likely to be unlucky as to be lucky. (I suppose it is intrinsic to the concept of luck that good and bad luck are exactly equal over the long haul for all creatures, even if not for smallish person-intervals.) It is a separate question whether we could function well without guesswork; and this question is given an airing in the *Objections* below.

The Meditator's new theory of the origins of error may still seem puzzling. For, if I feel indifferent about a proposition, I am not very likely to fall into error by embracing it. It is easy to be agnostic on the question whether men can grow wings. My stance can be this: I do not know! Ask me again in ten years when the biological manipulation of organisms will probably have become more common. Then I may have a better idea. Why do I have to tell you one way or the other right now? Conversely, I often make errors by feeling quite certain about things and not at all indifferent. In such cases, it *seems* to me as though "reasons of truth . . . point that way" and I am wholly inclined to one proposition and not at all towards its contrary. If it never happened that I felt irresistibly impelled to believe anything false, it would be comparatively easy to avoid error by submitting to all and only feelings of overwhelming subjective inclination.

Indeed it is unclear how the Meditator proposes to explain errors that result when I am *not* indifferent between the alternatives and do not merely guess precipitately that one or the other is right. The fixed delusions of the psychiatric patient, the stubbornness of bigots and dogmatists are accompanied by feelings of great clarity and conviction. How is the error of the madman or the fanatic to be understood?

The Meditator might well answer as follows: when you suffer from a fixed epistemological or moral delusion, it is admittedly not the case that your low-grade freedom has been employed to guess at an alternative. Either you are an unwilling victim whose normal capacity for judgment has been eroded by an illness, or you have your normal capacity but you have employed your low-grade freedom in guessing that you did not need to investigate further before believing a proposition. Neither the madman nor the fanatic is exactly careless, adopting one belief in preference to the other on a whim. The bigot, by contrast, is careless in thinking that he does not need to investigate further before insisting on his prejudiced claim about how things are or ought to be.

Analogously, if I spontaneously come to believe in the existence of corporeal things, or the truths of geometry and arithmetic, without having established a proper warrant, I am not exercising proper caution; a certain carelessness is involved. It is not that I carelessly believe on a mere whim that material objects exist without having a powerful and forceful inclination to do so. Rather, it is somewhat careless to believe everything that I have a powerful and forceful inclination to believe. In spontaneously continuing to believe what she had been taught in childhood, the Meditator did not realize that she was employing her low-grade freedom and, in effect, just guessing. The malevolent Demon hypothesis enabled her to see that she could be considered careless and insufficiently cautious and critical in believing without further ado in an external world.

A second analogy might be helpful. Suppose I have a large stock portfolio. Every morning, my broker telephones and instructs me what to buy and what to sell and I follow her instructions to the letter. My low-grade freedom is not being employed with respect to deciding what stocks to buy and sell; it cannot be said of me that I am "just guessing" what to buy and sell. That description would apply to me if I made my decisions by closing my eyes and pointing to a line in the financial pages. My low-grade freedom has been employed, however, in deciding to follow the instructions of the broker to the letter. If I reflect more widely, I ought to realize that there is always some reason to wonder whether the advice of stockbrokers in general and this stockbroker in particular is any good. Moreover, while no one would say that I have succumbed to a wicked temptation or a dreadful vice in talking to my broker on the telephone every morning, if I do not think over my participation in the stock market and arrive at satisfactory answers to the ethical questions involved in the generation and distribution of wealth, I can be said to be ethically careless and in danger of moral error.

If the Meditator's theory of error is correct, I am at fault and insufficiently defended against error in two contexts. In one context, I adopt a belief or perform an action recognizing that there is much to be said against adopting it or performing it and that my reasons for adoption or performance are somewhat weak. I take a risk that I can perceive, or make a gamble, hoping to be vindicated. In another context, I adopt a belief or perform an action with great conviction or out of fixed habit, unaware that I am taking a risk. Here I should have been critical of my feeling of conviction and my fixed habits. Whenever I take my powerful, spontaneous inclination to believe something *as* a sign of my being inclined by "reasons of truth," I need always to consider whether I *should* withhold judgment for lack of proper evidence, rather than believing. In the same way, whenever I am thoroughly convinced that I am acting properly, inclined by "reasons of goodness," I need always to consider whether I have sufficient reason to believe that I am inclined by just those reasons, and am not confused or self-serving.

Regardless of my known susceptibility to error and tendency to self-indulgence, skepticism about my competence to know and to act rightly must come to an end at some point. I have to accept clarity and distinctness as signs of truth and goodness. Otherwise, I will find myself in the position of the Total Skeptic, so paralyzed that I cannot assent to any propositions or perform any action. It is impossible for her to go wrong, the Meditator decides, if she restrains her will whenever she is called upon to make a judgment "so that it extends [only] to what the intellect clearly and distinctly reveals . . . I shall unquestionably reach the truth, if only I give sufficient attention to all the things which I perfectly understand, and separate these from all the other cases where my apprehension is more confused and obscure."

To her expanding knowledge-set, then, the Meditator can add a *normative* rule. She not only knows certain facts and principles, including the principle that what is clearly and distinctly perceived is true, she now knows that if she is to add more propositions to her knowledge-set, there is something she must do, a rule she must follow. As this rule is a practical rule – a command or instruction what to do – it should be represented as an imperative (Do this!), not as a declarative (This is so). The instruction to keep the will within bounds is represented below as "Restrain the Will!" It is TRUE that she ought to do this.

DOUBT	TRUE	FALSE
There are corporeal things external to me I have a body I have a vapory soul Sensory Experience physics astronomy medicine arithmetic geometry	I exist I think God exists God is not a deceiver Clearly and distinctly perceived propositions are true Restrain the will! Various metaphysical principles	A malevolent Demon exists and deceives me God is a mere idea My knowledge potential is limited

Figure 22   The Meditator's knowledge-set at the end of *Meditation Four*

The Meditator reflects in a passage shortly before the end of *Meditation Four* that she ought to be grateful for the epistemological capacities that she has, not resentful of their limitations: "I have reason to give thanks to him [God] who has never owed me anything for the great bounty he has shown me, rather than thinking myself deprived or robbed of any of the gifts he did not bestow." The Meditator has no reason to complain about the expansiveness of her will, her inborn and difficult-to-repress tendency to embrace propositions without having thoroughly investigated her warrant for doing so. For, if she were not powerfully impelled to embrace propositions that appeared clear and distinct to her, if there were not an automatic connection between the truth-appearance of a proposition and her acceptance of it, she could not be said to have a strong orientation towards the truth. God's benevolence is revealed in the manner in which our errors arise from our capacious will and in our love of and attraction to truth and goodness.

An analogy from the practical realm – one suggested by some of Descartes's own writings on the emotions–will make this point clearer. Our affectionate dispositions often lead us to love creatures who are not really good and therefore truly lovable. We may overreach ourselves in this respect, being moved by the mere appearance of goodness and not taking time to determine whether the goodness is real. Nevertheless, if we did not have the disposition to love those who appear lovable to us, we would have no spontaneous disposition to love the truly lovable and good either. The attraction truth has for our minds entails, unfortunately, that the *appearance* of truth has a similar attraction for our minds, and our disposition to love good people entails (unfortunately) that we love those who only appear good. Like emotional impulsiveness, epistemological and moral impulsiveness is both a liability and a condition of attaining what we want by way of truth and goodness.

Would not God have done better, one might wonder, to create a more discriminating creature that was forcefully impelled towards truth and goodness – but only towards actual truth and real goodness not towards the appearance of truth and goodness?

> God could easily have brought it about that . . . I should . . . never make a mistake. He could, for example, have endowed my intellect with a clear and distinct perception of everything about which I was ever likely to deliberate; or he could simply have impressed it unforgettably on my memory that I should never make a judgment about anything which I did not clearly and distinctly understand. Had God made me this way,

> then I can easily understand that, [if there were only myself in the world]
> I would have been more perfect than I am now. But I cannot deny that
> there may in some way be more perfection in the universe as a whole
> because some of its parts are not immune from error . . . And I have no
> right to complain that the role God wished me to undertake . . . is not
> the principal one or the most perfect of all.
>
> (VII:61)

Again, the prospect of an ecological answer to the question of our
failures is raised. The Meditator speculates that perhaps the perfection
of the wider universe requires that the parts be less than perfect. Insight
into final causes rejected, however, the hypothesis that the Meditator's
deficiencies contribute to an overall perfection cannot be proved.

2 OBJECTIONS TO *MEDITATION FOUR*

Mersenne thinks it overhasty to conclude that God is veracious and
cannot deceive us. Does not the Bible relate that God hardened
Pharaoh's heart, thereby causing him to make wrong judgments, and
caused his prophets to lie? Can't God employ beneficial deception,
like a doctor or a father (VII:126)?

Descartes replies that there are two distinct ways of speaking about
God: a popular style "for ordinary understanding" – which is the
style of the Holy Scriptures – and a philosophical style. The second
way of speaking "comes closer to expressing the naked truth – truth
which is not relative to human beings." This is the style that Descartes
says he had a "special obligation" to use in the *Meditations*, and it is
the one that everyone ought to use while philosophizing (VII:142).
In any case, the Meditator does not have access to reliable books
truthfully narrating events; indeed, the Meditator does not know
that there are books, let alone that a world exists outside her. The
philosophical architecture of the *Meditations* is such that counter-
arguments referring to books, kings, prophets, and historical events
are not to the point.

Stepping outside the framework of the *Meditations*, Descartes admits that God may issue threats or tell lies when these have a good

purpose. God also allows us to be deceived by our natural instincts – those for whom too much water is dangerous to their health can experience a powerful urge to drink. However, God cannot deceive us in making our "clearest and most careful judgments" false. There is no possibility that God could have mired us in incorrigible error and, if our clearest and most careful judgments were false, our error would be incorrigible (VII:144).

But, Mersenne persists, even if God is not a deceiver, we may be constantly wrong:

> The cause of this deception could lie in you, though you are wholly unaware of it. Why should it not be in your nature to be subject to constant – or at least very frequent – deception? How can you establish with certainty that you are not deceived, or capable of being deceived, in matters which you think you know clearly and distinctly? Have we not often seen people turn out to have been deceived in matters where they thought their knowledge was as clear as the sunlight?
> (VII:126)

Descartes insists that God's goodness and his relation to God as Creator is such that he must have been created with a capacity to know the truth and to distinguish it from falsehood, a tendency to believe the truth, and a means of avoiding error. The implication for the reader is this: I could not have been created as a hopeless, irredeemable, epistemological incompetent. (For one thing, if I were a hopeless, irredeemable epistemological incompetent, I could not come to know the truth that God exists. I should then be uncertain whether my belief in God was true.) It is worth repeating Descartes's statement quoted in Ch. 4 Sec. 3:

> If [a] conviction is so firm that it is impossible for us ever to have any reason for doubting what we are convinced of, then there are no further questions for us to ask: we have everything that we could reasonably want. What is it to us that someone may make out that the perception whose truth we are so firmly convinced of may appear false to God or an angel,

so that it is, absolutely speaking, false? Why should this alleged "absolute falsity" bother us, since we neither believe in it nor have even the smallest suspicion of it?

(VII:144–5)

Do we ever, though, have a sufficiently firm conviction to be confident that what we believe cannot be false? We do, Descartes assures us, though never in connection with mere sensory experience, such as the perception of color. Many people have indeed been deceived on these matters, but no one, he maintains, has ever been deceived when he thought his knowledge was as clear as sunlight and when that person relied solely on his intellect (VII:145–6).

A problematic case of knowledge is presented by conclusions that are deduced from a long chain of reasonings. These lack the immediate certainty, Descartes realizes, of *I exist so long as I am thinking* or *What is done cannot be undone*.

Imagine, for example, that I have a long "proof" written out on a series of pages before me and that I am looking at the conclusion on the last page. The conclusion is not self-evident. In fact, it is quite unexpected and surprising. I am aware of having written this proof myself and I now recollect that I began by writing down some self-evident principles whose truth I perceived clearly. I further recollect that I made and wrote down inferences from them that were self-evident in a step-by-step way.

Do I clearly and distinctly perceive the truth of the conclusion written on the last page? The question is important for Descartes to answer, since the *Meditations* might be said to exhibit exactly this structure: a long chain of reasonings at the end of which are to be found some unexpected conclusions. On one hand, we are tempted to say "No!" The conclusion looks improbable and surprising and its truth cannot therefore be clearly and distinctly perceived. On the other hand, we want to say "Yes!" The step-wise method of moving from one line to another described above always gives true conclusions. If the deduction on each line is correct, the conclusion to the whole series of deductions must be true. If I know that the step-wise method was employed properly, I can clearly and distinctly perceive *that* the conclusion must be true. A malevolent Demon cannot make it the case that there exists a document such that, while the deduction on each line is correct, the whole proof is invalid and the conclusion is false.

However, a malevolent Demon could make it the case that I believe of some document that the deduction on each line is correct when it is not. Given that this is possible, how can I know that the step-wise method was employed properly?

Demons aside, my senses and my memory may be fallacious. Perhaps I think these pages in front of me are a step-wise proof because I recollect writing such a proof over the last half-hour. But perhaps the pages are covered with total nonsense, disguised by my bad handwriting. I recollect beginning with self-evident propositions, but perhaps I have misremembered. Maybe I began with an assumption that was in fact arbitrary and that I knew at the time to be arbitrary, or an assumption I planned to undermine by deriving a contradiction from it before I got confused. Indeed, we need not suppose that the proof is very long to generate the skeptical conclusion. Perhaps the proof covers only half the page and is still garbled nonsense. Perhaps it is only a few lines long and is still garbled nonsense. Perhaps the meaning I was attaching to a given symbol changed from the first line to the second and I did not realize this.

Descartes claims that if *I* know that God exists and that the malevolent Demon does not, I can be confident of my step-wise proofs. Unfortunately, the problem of the Cartesian Circle raised by Arnauld in connection with *Meditation Three* resurfaces here. If I could not trust stepwise proofs but only immediate insights and these only at the moment when I had them, I *would be* an epistemological incompetent and this would be incompatible with the existence of a good God. "So what?" an opponent might venture. "You may be an epistemological incompetent, and God may not exist. The step-wise proof of God's existence you 'remember' just having constructed may be a piece of garbled nonsense. Prove it isn't so!"

Now, Descartes might have replied as follows: my ability to prove the existence of God step-wise shows that I am not an epistemological incompetent. For, if I am an epistemological incompetent, it could only be with respect to an angelic "absolute truth." This angelic truth would have nothing to do with ordinary standards of argument, according to which my proof was a good one. This, however, presupposes some standard of argument possessed by some great, authoritative truth-possessing power, in which case God must exist. So whether my proof is good or not, God exists, which is what I was trying to prove in the first place.

Unfortunately the reply is not quite adequate. Perhaps there is an absolute truth but no entity at all has any knowledge of reality. Alternatively, perhaps the malevolent Demon is in possession of the truth and withholds it from me out of a cruel impulse. It can still be the case that my knowledge is hopelessly defective and that a benevolent God does not exist.

Mersenne worries further that Descartes's injunction to limit the exercise of the will can encourage the unbelief of the atheist and perhaps lead to moral skepticism: "Indeed if this rule of yours is true, there is almost nothing that the will is going to be allowed to embrace, since there is almost nothing we know with the clarity and distinctness which you require for certainty which is beyond any doubt." He argues that it follows from what Descartes says that a Turk – that is to say a Muslim – is not in moral error if he does not embrace Christianity, lacking clear and distinct knowledge of its truth. (By implication, any unbeliever who sincerely reported that he failed to perceive clearly and distinctly that God existed would not be in a state of error.)

Descartes replies that his doctrine is not dangerous. "I made a careful distinction," he says, referring to the earlier *Discourse on Method*, "between the conduct of life and the contemplation of truth."

As far as the conduct of life is concerned, I am very far from thinking that we should assent only to what is clearly perceived. On the contrary, I do not think that we should always wait even for probable truths; from time to time we will have to choose one of many alternatives about which we have no knowledge, and once we have made our choice, so long as no reasons against it can be produced, we must stick to it as firmly as if it had been chosen for transparently clear reasons.

(VII:149)

In practical matters, then, in deciding what to do – how to live, what aims to pursue, whom to befriend, what religious group to affiliate oneself with, whether to obey all the laws of the state – our low-grade freedom has to be and should be employed. We have to make practical decisions on the basis of inadequate knowledge and to refuse to make a decision is to have made a decision by default. Descartes's other writings suggest that the Authority Principle and the Conformity Policy may be appropriate in the moral, political, and theological realms, at least provisionally, even though they are not in the epistemological and scientific realms.

To decide to participate in a certain religion is a practical decision, according to Descartes. The decision does not require knowledge about transcendental matters. It does not even require us to judge that the doctrines of the chosen religion (in the case of Christianity, the identification of Christ through the miracles performed by the historical Jesus of Nazareth and the redemption of the sinful world by Christ's self-sacrifice) are more probable than the doctrines of other religions (in the case of Islam, the role of the prophet Mohammad in receiving and communicating the word of God), or that any existing religion is composed of truths. According to Descartes, the clear and distinct knowledge we have of the existence of God does not imply that we have clear and distinct knowledge of the specific doctrines of any particular religion.

Descartes even characterizes the truth of Christianity, which contains numerous special doctrines in addition to the doctrine of an omnipotent, omniscient, and benevolent God, as "obscure."

> The sin that Turks and other infidels commit by refusing to embrace the Christian religion does not arise from their unwillingness to assent to obscure matters (for obscure they indeed are), but from their resistance to the impulses of divine grace within them . . .
> (VII:148)

Descartes notes that many of the special features of Christianity that differentiate it from other monotheistic religions such as Islam and Judaism (the doctrines of Original Sin, transubstantiation, the resurrection, and the Trinitarian nature of God) are believed by Christians to have been revealed by God (VII:148). However, the belief that these doctrines are true and that God has revealed their truth can only arise legitimately from "the impulses of divine grace" that create faith. These beliefs, he implies, cannot arise through reason and attention to rational argument. Accordingly, a Turk who subscribed to Christian doctrine on the basis of arguments ("fallacious arguments") would be committing a sin by not using his reason correctly. Only if he is converted by experiencing the divine impulse that creates faith in the doctrines is he exempt from blame. Descartes claims to acknowledge the existence of a "supernatural light" in us that is distinct from the natural light that reveals self-evident truths of reason (VII:148).

Objector 3, Hobbes, thinks that our error-proneness cannot be explained as a mere privation or lack. If it were a mere lack, stones could be said to be ignorant, which is absurd. There must be a "positive faculty" in us that stones lack that creates error (VII:190). Descartes replies that we do not call stones "blind" either. Nevertheless, blindness is simply privation of sight and does not need to be explained by any positive capacity of *not seeing* that the blind possess and the sighted lack (VII:191). Hobbes goes on to say that Descartes asserts without proof what the Calvinists deny, namely that we have free will (VII:190). Descartes replies:

> I [make] no assumptions beyond what we all experience within ourselves. Our freedom is very evident by the natural light.
> (VII:191)

Objector 4, Arnauld, expresses some of the same worries as Mersenne, namely that readers may think that Descartes is applying hypercritical standards that encourage skepticism about morals and religion. Since "those many people who in our age are prone to impiety may distort his words in order to subvert the faith" (VII:217), Descartes should make it clearer, he insists, that it is intellectual or scientific error that results from a too hasty acceptance of what we have not held up for examination by reason, not moral error pertaining to matters of faith and conduct (VII:215). St. Augustine himself warned, Arnauld points out, that "absolutely nothing in human society will be safe if we decide to believe only what we can regard as having been clearly perceived." So Descartes seems to be flatly contradicting the opinion of a founding Father of the Early Church and exposing human society to the risk of collapse (VII:216).

Arnauld also thinks that Descartes's emerging theory of substance and qualities is likely to give offence to theologians because it is incompatible with the mystery of the Eucharist, the transformation of the Communion bread and wine into the body and blood of Christ during the Catholic Mass. If Descartes does not fix this part of his doctrine, there could be dire consequences: "Even though his intention was to defend the cause of God against the impious, he may appear to have endangered the very faith, founded by divine authority, which he hopes will enable him to obtain that eternal life of which he has undertaken to convince mankind" (VII:218). This loaded passage requires some explanation.

On the prevailing Aristotelian theory of qualities adopted by theologians, there are "substances" composed of "matter" and "form." "Accidents," qualities such as whiteness, flatness, crispness, "inhere" in substances. According to the doctrine of transubstantiation, the "substance" of the bread is removed during Holy Communion and replaced with the "substance" of the body of Christ. Yet the "accidents" of the bread remain behind, now inhering in the body of Christ, so that we still seem to see and taste ordinary bread – white, flat, and crispy.

Descartes, according to Arnauld, is committed to the view that "there are no sensible qualities, but merely various motions in the bodies that surround us which enable us to perceive the various impressions which we subsequently call 'colour,' 'taste' and 'smell.' Hence only shape, extension, and mobility remain." For Descartes claims that he has a "complete understanding of what a body is when I think that it is merely something having extension, shape and motion" (VII:121). (Since the Meditator has not advanced the theory that color, taste, and smell result from motions in bodies possessing only shape, extension, and mobility, it seems that Arnauld is drawing on his background knowledge of Descartes's psycho-physical theory.) This view makes it difficult to understand how the collection of corpuscles with the extension, shape, and motion that cause us to perceive something flat, white, and crispy (bread) can be replaced by something utterly different in nature (the Body of Christ) that causes us to have exactly the same perceptions.

Descartes strenuously defends his "reductionistic" theory of qualities, without, however, really being able to offer an account of transubstantiation consistent with it. The old theologians, he says, used to think that accidents were something "real and distinct," that could exist independently of the substance from which they were removed. They should have recognized that sensation can occur only through contact:

> Nor can anything be more in accordance with reason or more widely accepted among philosophers than the general statement that not just all sense-perception but, in general, all action between bodies occurs through contact, and that this contact can take place only at the surface.
> (VII:255)

Throwing the accusation of advancing dangerous doctrines back at Arnauld, Descartes says that he thought it right to state his psychophysical premise openly, "in order to forestall, as far as I could, the slanders of those who want to seem more learned than others and are thus never more annoyed than when some new proposal is made in the sciences which they cannot pretend they knew about already . . . To try to use the authority of the Church in order to subvert the truth . . . is surely the height of impiety" (VII:255–6):

> So if I may speak the truth here without fear of causing offence, I venture to hope that a time will come when the theory of real accidents will be rejected by theologians as irrational, incomprehensible and hazardous for the faith, while my theory will be accepted in its place as certain and indubitable.
> (VII:255)

Objector 5, Gassendi, thinks that Descartes's rejection of final causes is problematic. For, he argues, a contemplation of the purposes that natural things fulfill, for which they must have been designed, is the best route to knowledge of God's existence: "Leaving aside the entire world, the heavens and its other main parts, how or where will you be able to get any better evidence for the existence of such a God than from the function of the various parts in plants, animals, man and yourself" (VII:309)?

The Argument from Design is an extraordinarily popular argument with a lengthy pedigree. It was employed by the Stoic philosopher Cicero in ancient times and is still cited by devout persons. The regularity of the heavens, the motion of the sun around the zodiac, the waxing and waning of the moon, and the scheduled appearances of the planets suggest a great machine created and maintained by God. The adaptation of living creatures to their environments, their possession of useful limbs and organs of great complexity, according to the Design Argument, are not features of the world that could have arisen by chance or simply from the motion of matter. They imply the existence of an intelligent and benevolent designer who foresaw the needs of individual animals, the way they might fit together into a balanced system with nourishment for all and the means to procure it. Though the Argument was shown by Hume to be philosophically quite complex, it was earlier regarded as particularly suitable for instructing the simple, unsophisticated person. For even an illiterate peasant could appreciate the order and harmony of the natural world, whereas only a small elite could understand abstract arguments based on metaphysical principles and propounded in scholarly Latin books.

Gassendi thinks, moreover, that we can only admire the works of God; they surpass our puny understandings:

> You will say that it is the physical causes of this organization and arrangement which we should investigate, and that it is foolish to have recourse to purposes rather than to active causes or materials. But no mortal can possibly understand or explain the active principle that produces the observed form and arrangement of the valves which serve as the openings to the vessels in the chambers of the heart . . . Since, I say, no physicist

is able to discern and explain these and similar structures, why should he not at least admire their superb functioning and the ineffable Providence which has so appositely designed the valves for this function? (VII:309)

Descartes replies that we ought to glorify the craftsmanship of plants and animals "but we cannot guess from this what purpose God had in creating any given thing. In ethics . . . where we may often legitimately employ conjectures, it may admittedly be pious on occasion to try to guess what purpose God may have had in mind in his direction of the universe; but in physics, where everything must be backed up by the strongest arguments, such conjectures are futile" (VII:375).

This is an interesting claim but it is not very precise: Descartes could mean that it is acceptable to speculate in an ethical context on what God wants us to do and how God expects us to behave. Alternatively, Descartes could mean that we can speculate about what ethical message God might be communicating in permitting certain natural disasters, or in saving the life of one sick peson and allowing another to die. On either interpretation, we cannot, according to Descartes, ask: What are earthquakes for? Why does God permit painful illness and death? Why are there humans or animals anyway? What purpose did God have in creating a creature with free will? All God's purposes are "equally hidden in the inscrutable abyss of his wisdom" (VII:375).

Descartes makes the further point that we can understand how things work better than Gassendi implies. Human anatomy, far from serving as an example of an impenetrable mystery, is precisely the kind of subject about which people do acquire knowledge (VII:375).

Gassendi insists that there is still a tension between the goodness of God and our propensity to error as it is laid out by Descartes. Surely, a universe in which all parts are perfect is better than one in which only some are (VII:311). Descartes says that wishing that there were no creatures in the world that were liable to error is like wishing the whole body to be covered with eyes, on the grounds that the eyes are the most beautiful part of the body (VII:376).

The Sixth Set of Objectors – miscellaneous philosophers and theologians – take issue with Descartes's suggestion that liberty of indifference is only low-grade liberty and that the highest degree of freedom is expressed when we are overwhelmingly inclined to assent to a proposition by a clear and distinct perception of its truth. Since God has only clear and distinct perceptions, this seems to take away all God's liberty of indifference, compelling him to judge and to act in particular ways. "It is an article of faith," they remind Descartes, that God was originally indifferent whether to create no world, one world, or innumerable worlds (VII:417).

Descartes's reply is quite startling. It is that God neither deliberates between alternatives nor is compelled by a clear and distinct perception of the best. Rather, whatever God, in His truly radical freedom, wills to create is what is true and good:

> [T]here is not even any priority of order, or nature, or "rationally determined reason" as they call it, such that God's idea of the good impelled him to choose one thing rather than another. For example, God did not will the creation of the world in time because he saw that it would be better this way than if he had created it from eternity; nor did he will that the three angles of a triangle should be equal to two right angles because he recognized that it could not be otherwise, and so on. On the contrary, it is because he willed to create the world in time that it is better this way than if he had created it from eternity; and it is because he willed that the three angles of a triangle should necessarily equal two right angles that this is true and cannot be otherwise . . .
>
> (VII:432)

God, in other words, does not *respond* to any independently existing truth or goodness; this would be inconsistent with His power. He is not even moved or compelled to reward the merit of the saints (VII:432). Their merit is simply part of an order etablished at the Creation according to which they are meritorious and rewarded.

Modern experimental epistemology has taken up the question of final causes in epistemology, reviving Descartes's question as to the significance of our errors. The best answers given so far seem to involve the stability and economy of systems. Psychologists studying human judgment have reinforced Descartes's suggestion that error results from haste: it is too time-consuming to make full investigations. Our survival may depend on our relying on our instincts and using guess-work, avoiding lengthy, considered judgments a good proportion of the time. If our guesswork produces mostly harmless errors and brings real benefits where our survival is concerned, our error-proneness will become entrenched.

Descartes would perhaps reject this "naturalistic" answer. On his theory of the animal machine, reason, free will, and conscious judg-ment were bestowed on us by God, subsequent to the natural forma-tion of a machine geared to survival. Again, though, it is worth asking whether Descartes in *Meditation Four* has his Meditator draw certain inferences from the already-established goodness of God or whether the Meditator is still in the process of establishing the goodness of God. On the latter interpretation, God, for all the Meditator knew in *Meditation Three*, though omnipotent and veracious, was ethically neutral and indifferent to His creature. Now she is gradually discov-ering, by her own unaided reason, that, contrary to the teachings of the theologians, there is no reason to believe in any residue from Eve's act of temptation and Adam's disobedience. Our errors do not indicate that we are being punished or that God bears us any ill-will. Further, the way in which our minds have been constructed so as to be spontaneously attracted to truth and goodness, and only liable to epistemological errors that we can in principle control, suggests that God is not merely ethically neutral, but benevolent.

CHAPTER 8

Meditation Five
The Meditator reflects on his experiences of mathematical and abstract concepts and arrives at a proof of God's existence

I THE ESSENTIAL NATURE OF CORPOREAL SUBSTANCE –
CATEGORY 1 AND CATEGORY 2 PROPERTIES –
MATHEMATICAL OBJECTS AND MATHEMATICAL TRUTHS –
TRIANGLES, UNICORNS, AND GOD – REALISM AND
PSYCHOLOGISM (AT VII:63–5)

The Meditator's task is to reconsider the items remaining under DOUBT. The hypothesis of the malevolent Demon has been refuted and the Meditator's potential to expand his knowledge-set indefinitely has been established. *Meditation Three* revealed that clarity and distinctness were the signs of truth and that they were the only signs of truth.

Recall that the Meditator also determined in *Meditation Three* that his ideas of material objects with sensory qualities – qualities such as heat, cold, color, warmth, and so on – were characterized by a certain flimsiness. The following proposition:

There exist corporeal things external to me

was not clearly and distinctly perceived. At the start of *Meditation Five*, the Meditator has not even determined that one particularly significant corporeal thing exists, namely, his own body. Earlier, in *Meditation Two*, the Meditator assumed that his "body" was a hallucination induced by the Demon. While he is now certain that he is not deceived by a Demon, the feeling that he is an embodied creature that moves himself around with some effort, needs to eat, and suffers various aches and pains, may nevertheless be a kind of illusion, involving only a kind of *perception₁* (see above, Ch. 3 Sec. 2) of bodily sensations. Just as a person who has lost an arm may continue to feel pain in her non-existent "phantom" arm, the Meditator may experience a variety of sensations in what is only a phantom body.

The Meditator's knowledge-condition is as follows:

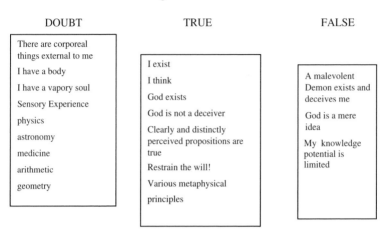

DOUBT

There are corporeal things external to me

I have a body

I have a vapory soul

Sensory Experience

physics

astronomy

medicine

arithmetic

geometry

TRUE

I exist

I think

God exists

God is not a deceiver

Clearly and distinctly perceived propositions are true

Restrain the will!

Various metaphysical principles

FALSE

A malevolent Demon exists and deceives me

God is a mere idea

My knowledge potential is limited

Figure 23   The Meditator's knowledge-set at the beginning of *Meditation Five*

Before going on to tackle the question whether there are any objects external to his mind other than God, the Meditator picks up the thread of his reflections on the idea of a corporeal thing as it is understood by the intellect, returning to the theme of the "piece of wax" in *Meditation Two*. His aim is to try to determine what can be clearly and distinctly understood about the things that he formerly considered to exist external to his mind and to be the causes of his sensory ideas of material objects.

The idea of "continuous quantity," corporeal substance in the abstract – insofar as it is "distinctly imagined" by the Meditator – comprises the following:
1) *Extension* in length, breadth, and depth
2) *Division* of what is extended into parts possessing various sizes, shapes, and positions
3) *Motion* of these parts, of various intensities and durations
Corporeal substance is understood to be extended (literally, "stretched out") in three dimensions, divisible into parts or composed of parts, and able to move in various directions at various speeds. The idea

of corporeal substance does not represent it as colored in a particular way, or as hard or soft, warm or cool to the touch, or as having certain tastes, or scents.

Yet even if corporeal substance, as it is considered by the intellect, does not possess any of these qualities, material objects do seem, by and large, to possess them. This suggests the following division of *qualities* or *properties* of material objects and their parts:

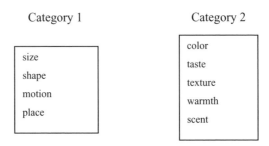

Figure 24   Category 1 and Category 2 properties

The distinction between the two categories was already foreshadowed in *Meditation Two*, when the Meditator decided that the wax he *saw₁* dripping from his candle was better known through the intellect, as a substance extended, flexible, and changeable, than through the senses, as a substance fragrant, colored, and soft. The Meditator earlier found color, warmth, and cold, and other such Category 2 properties, flimsy by comparison with the Category 1 properties of shape, size and motion, which he claims to perceive "distinctly." In *Meditation Three*, he suspected that some or all of his ideas of sensory qualities might be "materially false" (Ch. 4. Sec. 2). The Meditator does surprisingly little to justify the distinction between Category 1 and Category 2 properties or qualities. Is there nevertheless a principled way to understand the basis for the distinction? Can we "rationally reconstruct" his thoughts in this connection?

Recall that if I clearly and distinctly perceive a proposition to be true, not even an omnipotent Demon can cause the proposition to be false. So perhaps Category 1 properties are such that I cannot be deceived about them. We might ask (retaining the Demon "test," even though the hypothesis that the Demon exists has been discarded) whether an omnipotent and malevolent Demon could make a material object appear to be colored, flavored, or warm or cold, when it was not.

This eventuality seems easily conceivable. The Demon could make yellow lemons appear blue to me, sweet honey taste bitter, and a cold ice cube applied to my forehead feel warm.

Category 1 properties are, however, just as subject to Demonic manipulation as Category 2 properties. The Demon could make a small mouse appear to me to be the size of an elephant, a moving car appear to me to be stationary, or a square look to me like a triangle. The Demon could even make it seem to me that there are many objects before me when there is only one. So it might seem that there is little basis for saying that Category 1 properties are more distinctly known than Category 2 properties. While the Principle of Intellect Priority advanced in *Meditation Two* stated that material objects, if any existed, would be better known by the mind than by the body, the Principle of Mind Priority stated that knowledge of corporeal things was harder to achieve than knowledge of the mind. Here the Principle of Mind Priority trumps the Principle of Intellect Priority. Apparently, I can be deceived about *any* qualities or properties of a material object. Indeed, experience suggests that we just as often experience "deception" by the senses with respect to size (recall the "little sun" of *Meditation Three*) and shape as with respect to color.

However, it is a remarkable fact that, while the Demon can make me hallucinate any sort of object that is not there at all, the Demon cannot make me *see₁* a material object without making me *see₁* it as having a certain size, shape, location, and as being in motion or at rest. One cannot *see₁* an object that has no apparent size, or no apparent shape, or no apparent place relative to the observer and that appears to be neither moving nor at rest. By contrast, one can see a colorless object (a piece of wavy glass); touch an object that is neither warm nor cold, smooth nor rough, and neither hard nor soft; sniff an object that has no scent; and so on. So something could *be* a material object while being colorless, odourless, neither warm nor cool, and untextured.

Whether or not there exist corporeal things outside of his mind, the Meditator now has an understanding of the essential nature of the corporeal substance of which they must be made if they do exist.

Essentially, corporeal things have Category 1 properties; these properties alone cannot be removed even in thought from the notion of a corporeal thing. The idea of a material object – the lowest category in the Hierarchy of Ideas – has become a little less flimsy.

The Meditator now abruptly shifts his focus from the essence of corporeal things to the essences of things more broadly. He goes on to consider the entire class of ideas that can be seen to have "their own true and immutable natures," whether or not they correspond to anything external to the Meditator.

What is peculiar and puzzling about ideas that seem to have their own true and immutable natures, he realizes, is that one can make discoveries about them and acquire certain knowledge with respect to them merely by thinking and reasoning. Mathematical ideas are of this sort:

> [E]ven before, when I was completely preoccupied with the objects of the senses, I always held that the most certain truths of all were the kind which I recognized clearly in connection with shapes, or numbers or other items relating to arithmetic or geometry, or in general to pure and abstract mathematics.
>
> (VII:65)

By contrast, it seems, there are many ideas that do not lend themselves to rewarding investigation. Ideas of many imaginary objects are like this. For example, I can invent the idea of a creature with the body of a cat and the head of an eagle. I can even think about this creature and ask myself questions like "What would such a creature eat?" But it is hard to see how I could make discoveries about this creature. The properties it has – should I spin out a myth about the cat-eagle – will only be the properties with which I invest it. For the same reason, even if there is a collective myth in our minds about unicorns, according to which they live deep in the forest and can only be tamed by virgins, it seems we cannot make any new discoveries about unicorns. We cannot investigate them and learn about them as we investigate and learn about antelopes or sheep. So it is tempting to divide the entities about which we think into the following two exclusive types:

Type 1 Object: exists outside the mind (extramentally) and new
  discoveries can be made about it.

Type 2 Object: exists in the mind (intramentally) only and new
  discoveries cannot be made about it.

Mathematical objects, however, seem to defy this categorization.
Objects such as "the Triangle," "the Circle," "the Number 7," seem to
be intramental. Like Type 2 Objects, they cannot be captured and investigated, or even observed from a distance like antelopes. Like Type
1 Objects, however, one can make genuine new discoveries about
them:

> When, for example, I imagine a triangle, even if perhaps no such figure
> exists, or has ever existed, anywhere outside my thought, there is still a
> determinate nature, or essence, or form of the triangle which is immutable
> and eternal, and not invented by me or dependent on my mind. This
> is clear from the fact that various properties can be demonstrated of the
> triangle, for example that its three angles equal two right angles . . . These
> properties are ones which I now clearly recognize whether I want to or
> not, even if I never thought of them at all when I previously imagined
> the triangle.
>
> (VII:64)

So perhaps it is wrong to think of mathematical objects as intramental. Perhaps circles, numbers, and triangles are extramental Type 1
Objects, like antelopes, stars, and crystals.

The Meditator insists that he can make discoveries about the Triangle "even if no such figure exists or has ever existed outside my
thought." By this locution, the Meditator seems to mean "even if
there are no triangular physical objects," such as triangular pieces of
cloth, triangular tiles, or the plastic triangles set up on the roadway
by stalled vehicles. Even if no one, including the Meditator, had ever
drawn a triangle on paper, or scratched one in the sand with a stick,
it seems that there would still be truths about triangles, for example
the truth that the sum of the angles of a triangle is equal to 180°.

The Meditator is evidently thinking of the Triangle as an extramental object that would exist even if there were no triangular pieces

of cloth, tiles, etc. For the truths that can be discovered about triangles do not depend on the features the Meditator *ascribed* to them in the course of his "inventing" the Triangle. The Meditator can't invent a triangle whose angles sum to 190° (though if the Meditator were to form an idea of a "spherical triangle" he could discover that the angles of a triangle sum to 240°). Someone who said, "The triangle *I* am thinking of does not have the property of having the sum of its angles equal to 180°" would not be thinking of a (Euclidean or plane) triangle at all. Yet our lack of freedom to characterize the Triangle any way we like does not establish its extramental existence. Suppose someone tells us: "The unicorn *I* am thinking of has no horn in the middle of its forehead – it is not that it has lost it, it is just a hornless kind of unicorn." We will respond that she is not thinking of a unicorn at all. This does not imply the extramental existence of unicorns.

Both the Unicorn and the Triangle have "true and immutable natures." We know – more or less – when someone has overstepped the boundaries in claiming to think about them. One can think about a feathered unicorn, a spotted unicorn, and so on, but perhaps not about a unicorn that looks just like a zebra. Furthermore, contrary to the suggestion earlier that rewarding investigation of unicorns is impossible, it now appears that, merely by considering the definition of a unicorn as a horselike animal with one horn, we can discover many new truths about unicorns, e.g., that they are not stones, not bicycles, and so on.

Nevertheless, there is a major difference between the new truths we can discover by thinking about the true and immutable nature of the Unicorn and by thinking about the true and immutable nature of the Triangle. We cannot discover any *interesting* new truths about the Unicorn by thinking about its nature. By contrast, when we consider the definition of the Triangle, we seem to be able to extract an indefinite number of interesting truths. In this respect, what we can learn about triangles is as rich and complex as what we can learn about extramental objects such as antelopes, stars, and crystals.

Perhaps, then, we should revise the ontology above and introduce a third object-type to accommodate the differences and similarities noted so far, giving us:

Type 1 Object: exists extramentally and interesting new discoveries can be made about it (e.g. the Antelope).

Type 2 Object: exists intramentally only and interesting new
discoveries cannot be made about it (e.g., the Unicorn).

Type 3 Object: exists intramentally only and interesting new
discoveries can be made about it.

(Readers who naturally think in symmetrical terms might wonder
whether we should also recognize a Type 4 Object: exists extramentally
and interesting new discoveries cannot be made about it. Recent
advances in physics might suggest that this category is not empty.)

The upshot is that, although we can be sure that the Triangle is
not a Type 2 Object, since we know that we can make interesting
discoveries about triangles, we cannot be sure whether it is a Type 1
Object that exists in the world or a Type 3 Object that exists only in
the mind. One of the following theories of the Triangle must be true,
but which?

REALISM: The Triangle is extramental. As it is a Type 1 Object,
we can make interesting discoveries about it, albeit by studying
its true and immutable nature, not by empirical inquiry.

PSYCHOLOGISM: The Triangle is purely intramental. We may
nevertheless be able to make interesting discoveries about it by
reflecting on its true and immutable nature as a thought-object.

In a moment, the Meditator will try to make an interesting discovery about God by considering God's true and immutable nature.
The question his attempt will raise is this: which Theory of God is
the right one – realism or psychologism?

REALISM: God is extramental. As a Type 1 Object, we can make
interesting discoveries about Him, albeit by studying God's true
and immutable nature, not by empirical inquiry.

PSYCHOLOGISM: God is purely intramental. We may nevertheless be able to make interesting discoveries about God by
reflecting on God's true and immutable nature as a thought-
object.

If psychologism is the correct theory of the Triangle, we can make
interesting discoveries about the Triangle, provided it is not a Type 2
Object like the Unicorn. And if psychologism (and not realism) is
also the correct theory of God, we may be able to make interesting

discoveries about God, provided God is not a Type 2 Object like the Unicorn either. If God is *more like* the Triangle than the Unicorn the probability of making interesting discoveries about God is much greater.

Note that one may hold that psychologism is the right theory of the Triangle while still believing that triangles are important objects, and that one ought to believe in, and learn about, triangles. Only a few persons are committed to psychologism as the appropriate theory of the Triangle whilst maintaining that, because triangles are merely intramental entities, acquiring knowledge of the properties of the Triangle is an utter waste of time. We might distinguish in this respect between the Respectful Atheist and the Disrespectful Atheist. Both believe that psychologism is the correct theory of God: God does not exist outside of minds. The Respectful Atheist, however, holds the view that God is a Type 3 purely intramental object, an important one, about which it is possible to make interesting discoveries. The Disrepectful Atheist holds the view that God is a Type 2 purely intramental object, a fairy-tale entity like the Unicorn, of no great importance. According to the Disrespectful Atheist, no interesting truths beyond what is already contained in the mythology of this object – which, like the unicorn mythology, involves a virgin – can be discovered. Both the Respectful and Disrespectful Atheist are to be distinguished from the Realist, who insists that God has an extramental existence and that interesting truths about God can be discovered on that account.

Meanwhile, the Meditator has added geometrical and arithmetical truths to his knowledge-set:

> I can think up countless other shapes which there can be no suspicion of my having encountered through the senses, and yet I can demonstrate various properties of these shapes, just as I can with the triangle . . . and therefore they are something, and not merely nothing . . . [T]he nature of my mind is such that I cannot but assent to these things, at least so long as I clearly perceive them.
>
> (VII:65)

2 THE ONTOLOGICAL ARGUMENT – COULD GOD (STILL) BE A FICTIONAL ENTITY? – NECESSARY EXISTENCE (AT VII:65–71)

It should now be clear why, after reflecting on the Triangle, the Meditator asks himself whether the discovery that he can acquire knowledge of mathematical and geometrical objects might be a possible basis for another proof of the existence of God: "Certainly, the idea of God, or a supremely perfect being is one which I find within me just as surely as the idea of any shape or number. And my understanding that it belongs to his nature that he always exists is no less clear and distinct than is the case when I prove of any shape or number that some property belongs to its nature."

Why another argument? one might wonder. Wasn't the existence of God already demonstrated by a number of different arguments in *Meditation Three*? One such argument relied on the Causal Noninferiority Principle and the Hierarchy of Ideas. Others relied on the impossibility of the Meditator's creating himself and of his maintaining himself in existence. The first argument, however, relied on two rather obscure metaphysical principles and was less than straightforward. The latter two arguments had their own weaknesses. (Recall the numerous criticisms of the Objectors in Ch. 4 Sec. 3 and Ch. 5 Sec. 3.) A cleaner argument for the existence of God – one depending on fewer assumptions – is desirable, and the Meditator now produces one.

Arguments that rely on few assumptions can be short, elegant, and valid: proofs; or they can be short, elegant, and invalid: sophisms. There is considerable debate as to the status of the argument worked out by the Meditator: Is it a proof or a sophism?

Contemplating his idea of God, much as he might contemplate his idea of the Triangle, the Meditator decides that it would be a contradiction to think of God, who is perfect, as lacking the perfection of existence. One can no more think of God as lacking existence than one can think of a mountain without a valley. Therefore – it might seem reasonable to conclude – God must exist. This argument-pattern is known as the Ontological Argument.

> [W]hen I concentrate more carefully, it is quite evident that existence can no more be separated from the essence of God than the fact that its three angles equal two right angles can be separated from the essence of a triangle, or that the idea of a mountain can be separated from the idea of a valley. Hence it is just as much of a contradiction to think of God (that is, a supremely perfect being) lacking existence (that is, lacking a perfection), as it is to think of a mountain without a valley.
> (vii:66)

The Meditator now raises an objection to this reasoning: once one has made the supposition that God has all perfections, one must conclude that God exists. Perhaps, though, the original supposition *All perfections are possessed by God* is false.

By analogy, if I make the supposition that *All quadrilaterals can be inscribed in a circle* I have to conclude that a rhombus can be inscribed in a circle, as well as a square, a rectangle, and a diamond. But a rhombus cannot be inscribed in a circle, so the original supposition is false. Perhaps the supposition that *All perfections are possessed by God* is false. Perhaps the perfection of existence is not possessed by Him.

The Meditator's answer to his own objection is that the analogy is misleading. I simply do not find within myself the idea of a set of all quadrilaterals, each of which can be inscribed in a circle. But I do find within myself an idea of a perfect God: I "bring forth the idea of God from the treasure house of my mind, as it were."

Still, a sophism seems to be involved. It is true that the idea of a mountain is such that there cannot be a mountain without a valley. Nevertheless, the following is not a valid argument:

Argument 1
A mountain cannot exist without a valley
So, there is a mountain with a valley

For it is possible that there are no mountains at all. The argument is invalid: the premise can be true and the conclusion false. The premise of Argument 1 *presupposes* the existence of mountains; it does not *imply* the existence of mountains.

Nor, it seems, is the following analogous argument valid:

Argument 2
A God cannot exist without having the perfection of existence
So, there is a God with the perfection of existence

Yet the Meditator seems to accept Argument 2 while agreeing that Argument 1 is invalid: "[F]rom the fact that I cannot think of God except as existing, it follows that existence is inseparable from God, and hence that he really exists." The Meditator claims that the idea of God is "not something fictitious which depends upon my thought but an image of a true and immutable nature."

Why does the Meditator so readily accept (2) while so definitely rejecting (1)? Perhaps the key to this puzzle is that he implicitly accepts another argument:

Argument 3
A triangle cannot exist without having the sum of its angles equal to 180°
So, there is a triangle whose angles equal 180°

This argument seems valid: at least, we cannot so easily bring against it a similar objection to the one brought against Argument 1, for it does not seem possible that the conclusion is false. As we saw earlier, however, to say that the Triangle exists, or that there are triangles, is not necessarily to say that there exists an *extramental* triangle, or that there are some extramental triangles.

Whether the Triangle is intramental or extramental depends on which theory of the Triangle – or perhaps of mathematical entities generally – realism or psychologism, is correct. Whether an argument could show that God exists outside our minds depends on whether realism or psychologism is true of God – and perhaps of divinities generally. If psychologism is true of God, then God is purely intramental. However, if God is a Type 3 rather than a Type 2 object, we can discover interesting truths about God. The upshot is this: we cannot use Argument (2) to prove that realism is the right Theory of God. But couldn't one argue as follows?

God is by definition perfect
Extramentality is a perfection
So, God is extramental

Unfortunately, this argument still fails to show that realism is the right Theory of God. There is further discussion of this point in section 3. Meanwhile, compare the argument above with the following:

> *TRI is a perfect three-sided figure*
> *Extramentality is a perfection*
> *So, TRI is extramental*

Though he does not acknowledge any flaws in his reasoning, it is not surprising that the Meditator seems uncertain whether he has really produced a short, clean proof for the existence of God and not a sophism. He decides, however, that the only problem with the argument concerns the role of memory. The propositions of arithmetic and geometry can be known to be true as long as I am clearly and distinctly perceiving them. Yet I cannot constantly hold them in my mind. Do they cease to be true and become doubtful when I am not considering them and approving them as true?

[M]y nature is such that . . . I cannot fix my mental vision continually on the same thing, so as to keep perceiving it clearly; . . . And so other arguments can now occur to me which might easily undermine my opinion, if I were unaware of God: and I should thus never have true and certain knowledge about anything, but only shifting and changeable opinions. (VII:69)

As long as the Meditator attends to the proof of the proposition that the three angles of a triangle are equal to two right angles, he knows that this is true: "But as soon as I turn my mind's eye away from the proof, then in spite of still remembering that I perceived it very clearly, I can easily fall into doubt about its truth if I am unaware of God." The Ontological Argument, by implication, suffers from the same defect. If the Meditator loses his awareness of God, he can easily fall into doubt about whether the Ontological Argument works to prove the existence of an extramental God.

Here, the Meditator seems to be conceding what some of his critics urged earlier. I can change my mind about whether I clearly and distinctly perceived something in the past and the false impression of clarity and distinctness is insufficient for truth. Moreover, my own memory, of whose fallibility I have ample evidence, may deceive me even if the Demon does not. Perhaps I remember perceiving the truth of some proposition clearly and distinctly but I have never done so. Is a clear and distinct memory of formerly having clearly and distinctly perceived some proposition sufficient to establish its truth?

The Meditator's reaction to these doubts recalls the argument of the previous chapter. If it is possible that my memory is so deceptive that what I recollect to have been clearly and distinctly perceived, or formerly proved with arguments that progressed step-wise in a clear and distinct fashion, is false, I am a seriously defective epistemological creature. For, in that case, all my knowledge is merely momentary. I can know that I think and I exist as long as I entertain the proposition *I think*. Unfortunately, however, I cannot establish further results and build on them, for I cannot hold the established results in my mind while I work out their implications. It is as though someone began to read through a geometrical proof and, while she was satisfied that each line followed from the last, she immediately forgot whether the line before that had followed from the line before it. At the end of the proof, she would not know whether the QED proposition was true. A moment later, she would forget the whole thing.

If I can know that I am a creature of God, I cannot be in the pathetic state of having such a poor or deceptive memory that I cannot be convinced of my own arguments. Knowing that God exists and created me, and that there cannot be an omnipotent God *and* another God of lesser power, or two omnipotent Gods, I cannot raise the objection that a malevolent Demon could distort my memory and my clear and distinct perception. Even if I have no proof that God is specially predisposed in my favor, I have no reason to doubt my own reasoning powers and the operation of the natural light within me. For I know that God is not a deceiver and is in fact good, and that (unless I am a madman) all my errors arise, directly or indirectly, from my own will and its inclination to hasty, careless judgment and action.

Can the possibility that I am now dreaming render the conclusion that God exists doubtful? Evidently not: even if the Meditator is dreaming, his knowledge-set will have the same composition. The possibility that he was dreaming did not provide a reason for the Meditator ever to doubt the truths of mathematics and he does not place the Ontological Argument in question on this basis either. As we know from considering the problem of the Cartesian Circle (Ch. 5 Sec. 3), however, the Meditator needs to be assured that the following scenario is impossible: he is *not* a creature of God *and* all the proofs of God's existence that he has thought out are delusory. This assurance can only arise from confidence in his own reasoning powers.

The Meditator's knowledge-set is now that shown in Figure 25. God's existence has been shown (to the Meditator's satisfaction) to be implied by his essence. God does not simply exist (as an intramental or extramental object), He exists necessarily.

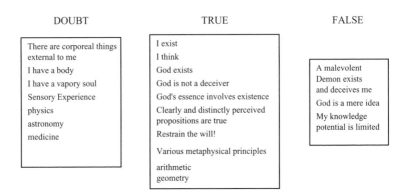

DOUBT

There are corporeal things external to me
I have a body
I have a vapory soul
Sensory Experience
physics
astronomy
medicine

TRUE

I exist
I think
God exists
God is not a deceiver
God's essence involves existence
Clearly and distinctly perceived propositions are true
Restrain the will!

Various metaphysical principles
arithmetic
geometry

FALSE

A malevolent Demon exists and deceives me
God is a mere idea
My knowledge potential is limited

Figure 25   The Meditator's knowledge-set at the end of *Meditation Five*

The set of propositions remaining in DOUBT continues to shrink as the Meditator prepares to investigate the status of the remaining opinions that he still takes to be doubtful – that there are extramental corporeal things; that he has a vapory, material soul; that his sensory experiences furnish him with knowledge; and that the sciences, including physics, astronomy, and medicine, are repositories of knowledge. He is already confident that he understands the true and immutable nature of corporeal substance, but he has not yet proved that material objects exist extramentally.

> Thus I see plainly that the certainty and truth of all knowledge depends uniquely on my awareness of the true God . . . And now it is possible for me to achieve full and certain knowledge of countless matters, both concerning God himself and other things whose nature is intellectual, and also concerning the whole of that corporeal nature which is the subject-matter of pure mathematics.
>
> (VII:71)

3 OBJECTIONS TO *MEDITATION FIVE*

Descartes's objectors spend little time discussing the Meditator's new-found proof for the existence of God. For one thing, they know it is not very original, and they are familiar with the argument and with the objections made to it already in the fourteenth century. Objector 1, Caterus, points out that it is the same as the Ontological Argument for the existence of God given by St. Anselm but criticized by St. Thomas (*Summa Theologia*, Part I, Question II, Article I). For Thomas realized that "It does not follow that . . . what is signified by this word [God] exists in the real world. All that follows is that it exists in the apprehension of the intellect." The *concept* of existence is linked to the *concept* of a supreme being and that is all that can be said (VII:99). The Ontological Argument, in other words, presupposes realism about God and does not prove that psychologism is the wrong Theory of God.

Descartes concedes that we do not know immediately whether God's essence is "a fiction of the intellect . . . immutable and true, or merely invented by us" (VII:116). He suggests, however, that there is a way to tell: ideas invented by us, he maintains, can always be split up – e.g. a winged horse can be split into a horse and a pair of wings. By contrast, a triangle and the size of the square superscribed around it cannot be split up; given the triangle, the relative size of the square around it is determined. He admits that the idea of a supremely perfect *body* could be split up from the idea of its existence – such a body might or might not exist. But the idea of a supremely perfect *thing* cannot, he claims, be split up from its existence. A supremely perfect *body* would not necessarily have the power to bring itself into existence and remain in existence, but a supremely perfect *thing* must have that power (VII:119).

Descartes says that when we think of some being and try to decide whether existence pertains to it, we must first decide whether possible existence pertains to it. (In trying to decide whether [a] a round square and [b] an immortal golden pelican exist, I will realize that a round square is not possible, though an immortal golden pelican is. The latter can exist in some possible world, the former cannot.) Now, if God is even possible, then, given God's immense power, God must be able to exist by His own power, so God's existence cannot be merely possible (like the immortal golden pelican's existence) (VII:118). Necessary existence is contained in the idea "not by any fiction of the intellect, but because it belongs to the true and immutable nature of such a being that it exists" (VII:119).

Objector 2, Mersenne, points out that God's existence has not been shown to be possible. The Meditator's argument only works if there is no contradiction in God's existing, and some people think the idea of God is impossible or contradictory. How can Descartes have made a sufficiently profound investigation of God to be sure of having a clear and distinct apprehension of His possibility (VII:127)?

Descartes replies that impossibility resides in our thought when we join together mutually inconsistent ideas. But "as far as our concepts are concerned there is no impossibility in the nature of God; on the contrary, all the attributes which we include in the concept of the divine nature are so interconnected that it seems to us to be self-contradictory that any one of them should not belong to God" (VII:151). If we deny that God is possible, Descartes goes on to say, in what can only be described as an emotional fit of exasperation, we might as well deny that someone who is thinking exists, and that anything we perceive by means of the senses is true: "The upshot will be that all human knowledge will be destroyed, though for no good reason" (VII:151).

Gassendi, Objector 5, claims that existence is not a perfection. It is that without which no perfections can be present (VII:323). Further, the Meditator's claim that there could not be two Gods (VII:68) is unsupported, and Descartes has given no reason to suppose that God has existed from eternity and will abide for eternity (VII:326). Descartes (wrongly, I think) claims in his *Reply* that he has already discussed these matters. Finally, Gassendi says, no one will believe that you are more certain about geometrical proofs after proving the existence of God than before. Though it is true that God exists and is not a deceiver, the proofs that establish this seem less certain than geometrical proofs. Many people dispute the existence of God; no one disputes the truths of geometry (VII:328). Descartes claims that this is empirically false: there have been those who disputed the truths of geometry and they must have been atheists (VII:384).

The Reader may still be perturbed by the Ontological Argument. There is good reason to be so. If the Argument does not establish the extramental existence of God but only His necessary intramental existence, God cannot act on the world, except after the fashion of other intramental entities who, like fictional characters, may provoke fear and love, and even inspire us to act in certain imitative ways. For if we can fear and fall in love with fictional characters, or model our behavior on theirs, why shouldn't we have an emotional and emulative relationship with God as well? The Respectful Atheist will allow all these possibilities, while the Disrespectful Atheist maintains that, although we can tell stories about God or the Unicorn, our knowledge of both is limited to a few trivial implications of the definition of each.

Suppose now that psychologism is true of mathematical objects and of divinities as well. Is it paradoxical to suggest that we can make the following (interesting or uninteresting) discovery: *The intramental object God is an extramental object?*

This discovery seems well within our grasp. Consider the following analogy. I might have both of the following two purely intramental ideas. The first is the idea of a large, active spider the size of a tank that really exists and that terrorizes the population of a city. The second is the idea of a large, active spider the size of a tank that does not exist but that is believed by the population of a city to exist and that is believed by them to be terrorizing them. The former intramental object is an extramental object; the latter intramental object is an intramental object. There is no paradox. It may be true of the intramental object God that He is an extramental object. For this reason, even if extramentality is a perfection, we cannot use a variant of the Ontological Argument to prove that realism is the right Theory of God.

CHAPTER 9

Meditation Six (1)
The Meditator determines that he is apparently attached to a particular human body. His mind and this putative body are nevertheless distinct and separable, so that immortality is possible even if bodies in general are perishable

I VISUAL IMAGINATION – THE MEDITATOR'S PUTATIVE BODY (AT VII:72–8)

> It remains for me to examine whether material things exist . . . I now know they are capable of existing, in so far as they are the subject matter of pure mathematics, since I perceive them clearly and distinctly.
> (VII:71)

Anything could exist, could be created by God, the Meditator decides, so long as there is no contradiction involved in the supposition that it is perceived distinctly. The notion of a material object that is regarded as the subject matter of pure mathematics is not self-contradictory, for there is no contradiction involved in my perceiving a geometrical object such as a triangle or a cube or a sphere distinctly. What is it, though, for a body to be regarded mathematically, to be "the subject matter of pure mathematics?"

Recall that the Meditator decided in *Meditation Five* that what was distinctly imagined in bodies was their "continuous quantity." A body and its parts are characterized by the following attributes:

Extension in length, breadth, and depth

Division or divisibility into parts possessing various sizes, shapes, and positions

Motion of these parts, of various intensities and durations

Mathematics treats of objects of certain dimensions, certain sizes, shapes, and relative positions. A formula such as $x + y = 2$ can be represented as a line on a graph, and we can write the formula for a circle. We can measure extended substances and compare their lengths; we can use the measure πr^3 to calculate the volume of a sphere. Mathematics can also treat motions, since the velocity of bodies, and even their acceleration, can be quantified. The pathways through space traced by a cannonball, a planet, or a pendulum can all be described geometrically. What is more, there is no contradiction involved in supposing that the extended, divisible, moving substance, to which mathematical reasoning can be applied, exists extramentally. Therefore, God may have created it as something extramental: for God has the power to do anything possible.

The Meditator observes that it is the visual imagination, not the intellectual understanding, that makes him aware of corporeal things. When he thinks of a triangle, he does not merely understand what a triangle is – a figure bounded by three lines. The Meditator sees in his "mind's eye" the three lines "as if they were present before me." A pentagon too can be both understood through its definition as a five-sided regular polygon and visualized in the imagination. Some objects, however, can be understood through their definitions but not imagined – a chiliagon, for example, a thousand-sided figure. An additional effort of the mind beyond that required in order to understand their intellectual concepts is required in order for us visually to imagine objects.

The power of visual imagination is not, the Meditator decides, "a necessary constituent of my own essence, that is, of the essence of my mind." I would not cease to be myself if I only understood the definitions of geometrical objects and could not bring their images to mind. I could still contemplate certain of my ideas. So the fact that I *can* imagine many of these figures – any time at all – suggests, without making it a necessary inference, that something exists in addition to my mind that is a nonessential part of me, i.e., a body, to which my mind is joined:

> I can easily understand that, if there does exist some body to which the mind is so joined that it can apply itself to contemplate it, as it were, whenever it pleases, then it may possibly be this very body that enables me to imagine corporeal things. So the difference between this mode of thinking and pure understanding may simply be this: when the mind understands, it in some way turns towards itself and inspects one of the ideas which are within it; but when it imagines, it turns towards the body and looks at something in the body which conforms to an idea understood by the mind or perceived by the senses . . . But this is only a probability.
>
> (VII:73)

The fact that I can visually imagine triangles, pentagons, and other such figures does not imply that triangles, pentagons, and other such figures exist as extramental objects, as realists maintain, but only that there exists *something* apart from my mind that enables me to experience mathematical imagery.

Further, I experience sensory imagery – colors, sounds, tastes, pain, and so on. Do these images as well suggest the existence of something apart from my mind? To answer this question, the Meditator has to review the basis that he originally took as adequate for doubting that there was anything external to him except the malevolent Demon.

Before resolving to doubt, in the old days when he was accustomed to taking his senses as providing reliable information, the Meditator used to suppose that he had "a head, hands, feet, and other limbs making up the body which I regarded as part of myself." One might say: he perceived, from time to time, certain hands, and he regarded those hands as *his* hands; with his hands, he touched a head from time to time that he regarded as *his* head. He believed that he had a whole human body:

> I also perceived by my senses that this body was situated among many other bodies which could affect it in various favourable or unfavourable ways; and I gauged the favourable effects by a sensation of pleasure, and the unfavourable ones by a sensation of pain. In addition to pain and

> pleasure, I also had sensations within me of hunger, thirst, and other
> such appetites, and also of physical propensities towards cheerfulness,
> sadness, anger and similar emotions.
>
> (VII:74)

The Meditator now notices that he seems to be subject to harmful
and beneficial interaction with other bodies and that he seems to
have appetites directed towards other bodies. He also seems to react
with emotion to perceived configurations of bodies and changes in
configurations perceived as outside himself – to situations and events.
Besides these "visceral" feelings that he experiences as "in" his own
body, he has impressions and sensations of things external to his
body and of qualities that apparently enable him to distinguish and
recognize those bodies:

> [B]esides the extension, shapes and movements of bodies, I also had
> sensations of their hardness and heat, and of the other tactile qualities.
> In addition, I had sensations of light, colours, smells, tastes and sounds,
> the variety of which enabled me to distinguish the sky, the earth, the seas,
> and all other bodies, one from another.
>
> (VII:75)

Whether or not there are any bodies external to his mind, the having
of these experiences is constitutive of what it is like to have a body,
the "phenomenology" of being conscious, embodied, and aware of
one's body.

A certain theme is emerging in these paragraphs. Inner sensations,
emotions, and outer sensations of qualities seem to function as signs of
favorable and unfavorable conditions. Inner sensations and emotions
appear to tell me what is harmful and helpful for "my" body (the
body I may have), or simply for me. Hunger seems to inform me
that eating will be good for me; pain, that I should get away from
some noxious object; cheerfulness, that a certain experience or state
is worthwhile. Other sensations and perceptions seem to enable me
usefully to distinguish objects in the environment one from another

and to tell what they are. The senses do not only seem to *represent* an external world to me; they also seem to provide instruction and guidance concerning what I ought to do.

The Meditator notes that it was "not unreasonable" for him to think that the objects he seemed to perceive – the sky, the earth, and so on, were distinct from his thought. He took there to be external-to-himself "bodies which produced the ideas." For there was something involuntary about the flow of his sensory ideas that at least suggested that the Meditator had not generated these ideas on his own. I cannot simply choose to see a familiar face whenever I want to; and some sensory ideas, for example, the idea of pain, come unbidden and are unwelcome. Accordingly, there seemed to the Meditator to be two kinds of sensory experience. The ideas he experienced in memory and imagination, which seemed to be to some extent under his own control, were less vivid, while the ideas of perception, which seemed to be out of his control, were more vivid.

> [M]y experience was that these ideas came to me quite without my consent, so that I could not have sensory awareness of any object, even if I wanted to, unless it was present to my sense organs; and I could not avoid having sensory awareness of it when it was present. And since the ideas perceived by the senses were much more lively and vivid and even, in their own way, more distinct than any of those which I deliberately formed through meditating or which I found impressed on my memory, it seemed impossible that they should have come from within me; so the only alternative was that they came from other things.
>
> (VII:75)

Before he began to put beliefs acquired in childhood to the test, the Meditator believed not only that his sensory ideas were caused by material objects outside him, but also that "the things resembled the ideas." He also now remembers that:

1) He seemed to have the use of his senses before he developed reason.

2) The ideas he formed for himself in his imagination were made up of involuntary sensory ideas.

At the time, the Meditator confesses, "I easily convinced myself that I had nothing at all in the intellect which I had not previously had in sensation." Finally, amongst all the seeming objects-of-an-extramental-world, there seemed to be one particular object to which he stood in a privileged relation:

> As for the body which by some special right I called "mine," my belief that this body, more than any other, belonged to me had some justification. For I could never be separated from it, as I could from other bodies; and I felt all my appetites and emotions in, and on account of, this body; and finally, I was aware of pain and pleasurable ticklings in parts of this body, but not in other bodies external to it.
>
> (VII:76)

"Later on, however," the Meditator recollects, "I had many experiences which gradually undermined all the faith I had had in the senses."

The Meditator gives here a detailed and specific itemization of the sensory beliefs that he decided to assume were false in *Meditation Two*. He now recalls that he gradually amassed reasons for doubt, such as his occasional deception by optical illusions. He remembers that even the internal senses, such as pain, can be deceptive, not with respect to whether we are suffering, but with respect to what we are suffering: "I had heard that those who had a leg or an arm amputated sometimes still seemed to feel pain intermittently in the missing part of the body." He concludes that feeling pain in his leg is not sufficient evidence to warrant the conclusion that his leg is hurt: he may not have a leg. Finally, he recalls the dream argument and the malevolent Demon hypothesis that he was able to frame.

The opinions in the box below, regarded as false under the supposition of the Demon, are still doubtful. Although he has rejected the malevolent Demon hypothesis as false, he must continue to employ the Clarity and Distinctness Filter that has demonstrated its serviceability thus far. For the Meditator knows, having established this in *Meditation Four*, that his capacious will can easily overreach his understanding and that many of his spontaneous beliefs are false. The set of propositions below still requires filtering:

DOUBT

I have a vapory soul

There is a body that specially belongs to me

I could never be separated from this body

All my ideas come from my senses

Objects resemble my ideas of them

The senses instruct me as to the real characteristics of corporeal things

physics

astronomy

medicine

Figure 26　The set of propositions that are still doubtful at the beginning of *Meditation Six*

2 MORTALISM – DISTINCT EXISTENCE – SEPARABILITY OF MIND AND BODY – PERCEPTION AND IMAGINATION ARE NOT ESSENTIAL TO THE MEDITATOR (AT VII:78)

The Meditator tackles his still doubtful erstwhile beliefs one by one. Before trying to decide definitively whether there *are* extramental bodies, he brings up for consideration his old belief that there was a body that accompanied him everywhere, from which he was never for a moment apart. This belief led him formerly to suspect that he could not exist without his body and to worry that the death of this body would mean his total annihilation as a creature.

There is a wide range of beliefs concerning the fate of the soul after death. Most religions teach that what we call death is only a moment of transition to another form of existence in which we retain our consciousness and some of our personal qualities. In Islamic and Christian theology, the immortality of the soul is associated with a theory of divine reward and punishment. We are said to remain responsible after death, as persons, for deeds committed in this life. Further, many religions, including Christianity, teach some form of reincarnation doctrine. On the Christian view, the souls of the dead are eventually reunited with their bodies, restored to functioning, animal life, on the day of the Resurrection and those condemned to hell are made to suffer endless physical torments. Other schools of thought teach that souls are united, not with the bodies to which they were formerly attached, but with the bodies of newly born humans or animals.

Still other philosophical sects teach that consciousness, though not individual consciousness, persists after the body dies. On a view deriving from Aristotle, each individual mind loses self-consciousness and is absorbed into the Divine Mind or what Aristotle called the Active Intellect. Only the Epicureans taught that death is the end of the person and individual consciousness. According to their account, the vapory soul, composed of rarefied, fast-moving atoms (Gassendi's "flower of matter"), dissipates into the atmosphere before the body crumbles into dust. The doctrine that the self perishes at the clinical death of the body is known as "Mortalism," the denial of the immortality of the soul.

Though most religions deny Mortalism, it is easy to be skeptical about their tenets. We have no experience of disembodied existence. We have good reason to wonder whether it is possible for a thinking, experiencing thing to exist without a brain and a body.

The Meditator does not actually take a position on whether Mortalism is false. He does, however, determine that the mind, as a separate substance, can be shown conceptually to be entirely distinct from the body. A conceptual argument is appropriate, for the Meditator at this stage knows only that material objects are possible and that the idea of a material object is not self-contradictory, not that any exist extramentally. He now determines that there is no reason why the death or destruction of the body should *entail* the death or destruction of the mind.

I know that everything which I clearly and distinctly understand is capable of being created by God so as to correspond exactly with my understanding of it. Hence the fact that I can clearly and distinctly understand one thing apart from another is enough to make me certain that the two things are distinct . . . On the one hand I have a clear and distinct idea of myself, in so far as I am simply a thinking, non-extended thing; and on the other hand I have a distinct idea of body, in so far as this is simply an extended, non-thinking thing. And accordingly, it is certain that I am really distinct from my body, and can exist without it.

(VII:78)

Interpreted as an argument for the logical possibility of the survival of the individual mind after the death of the body, the Argument from Conceivability looks like this:

The Main Argument
Phase One
Premise 1: If I *can* clearly and distinctly understand A apart from B and B apart from A, then God *could* have created one without the other, and A cannot depend on B for its existence, or B on A.
Premise 2: I can clearly and distinctly understand myself as a thinking thing apart from body, and body as an extended thing apart from thought.
Preliminary Conclusion: God could have created my mind in such a way that it does not depend on any body.

Phase Two
Premise 3: God could have created my mind in such a way that it does not depend on any body.
Premise 4: If A could have been created to be independent of B, A can exist when B no longer exists.
Premise 5: When I am dead, my body (as such) will no longer exist.
Conclusion: I can exist when my body is dead.

Note that the Argument from Conceivability has two phases. The Preliminary Conclusion derived in Phase One serves as Premise 3 in Phase Two. As for the other Premises, 1, 2, and 4 are evident truths, the kinds of principle the Meditator described earlier as known by the "light of nature." Premise 5 is not easily disputed.

Because the Meditator still has not shown that he *has* a body, i.e., that there is some material object to which he is specially related, or indeed that any external corporeal thing exists, one might wonder why he is already turning over in his mind the possibility of his survival after death. Indeed, the Meditator confesses that he is anticipating. His anticipation is perhaps explained by the fact that a version of the same Argument from Conceivability can be fashioned to test the opinion that the Meditator has a vapory, material, and, therefore, perishable soul. The vapory soul – something like a wind, or a flame whose presence makes the animal body warm, lively, and sentient – was one of the original spontaneous beliefs the Meditator resolved to doubt in *Meditation Two*. Consider Variant Two of the Argument from Conceivability:

Variant Two
Phase One
Premise 1: If I *can* clearly and distinctly understand A apart from B and B apart from A, then God *could* have created one without the other, and A cannot depend on B for its existence, or B on A.

Premise 2': I can clearly and distinctly understand myself as a thinking thing apart from a vapor.

Preliminary Conclusion': God could have created my mind in such a way that it does not depend on a vapory soul to think and experience.

Phase Two
Premise 3': God could have created my mind in such a way that it does not depend on a vapory soul to think and experience.

Premise 4': If A could have been created to be independent of B, A does not depend on B.

Conclusion': So, I do not depend on a vapory soul to think and experience.

The reader will observe that the first version of the Argument from Conceivability is not convincing as an argument *for* the immortality of the soul. At best, it can be taken to show that the proposition *I cannot possibly survive the death of my body* is false. This is a useful result, but it is not equivalent to a proof of the immortality of the soul. Consider Variant Three of the Argument from Conceivability:

Variant Three

Phase One

Premise 1: If I *can* clearly and distinctly understand A apart from B and B apart from A, then God *could* have created one without the other, and A cannot depend on B for its existence, or B on A.

Premise 2'': I can clearly and distinctly understand trees as plants of a certain type apart from soil and soil as matter of a certain type apart from trees.

Preliminary Conclusion'': God could have created trees in such a way that they did not depend on soil.

Phase Two

Premise 3'': God could have created trees in such a way that they did not depend on soil.

Premise 4'': If A could have been created to be independent of B, A can exist without B.

Final Conclusion'': So, trees can exist without soil.

This argument is sound and the conclusion is perfectly acceptable. Premise 2'' is obviously true, for I can clearly and distinctly conceive of a tree existing without soil and soil without a tree. In the former case, I simply imagine a tree with its roots in the air, or a tree with its roots embedded in rock, or drifting in the ocean. Soil without trees rooted in it is equally easy to conceive. So the Preliminary Conclusion'' that God could have created trees that do not depend on soil is in order, and Phase Two of the argument is unproblematic.

In fact, though, trees by and large *do* depend on soil and if there were no soil in the universe we should have different sorts of trees or possibly no trees at all.

Am I justified in concluding that, because a tree *can* exist without soil, the tree in my garden *will* continue to exist if I remove all the soil from its roots? Clearly not. Nor am I justified in concluding that, because I *can* exist without my body, if my body is destroyed, I *will* continue to exist. God could have created minds without bodies and bodies without minds – perhaps God has even created some. But – one might protest – in fact minds by and large *do* depend on bodies, and if there were no bodies we should have very different kinds of minds in the universe or possibly no minds at all. In any event, I cannot conclude that *I* shall outlast my body.

To this attempt to show that the Main Argument from Conceivability really establishes nothing of great importance, the following response might be made.

Variant Three, unlike the Main Argument, contains a false premise, namely Premise 2''. I cannot clearly and distinctly understand trees as plants of a certain type apart from soil. To have a thorough knowledge of trees – the kind of knowledge of trees possessed by the arborist – is to appreciate that trees need soil. I can have a clear mental image of a tree existing without soil, but, as the Meditator often reminds us, imagination is not understanding. I cannot therefore reach either the Preliminary or the Final Conclusion in Variant Three. There is no basis, however, for comparing Variant Three with the Main Argument. For Premise 2, unlike Premise 2'', is simply true. The argument is sound and the mind can exist in a world like ours without an associated body, though trees by and large in this world cannot exist without soil.

However, the claim that Premise 2'' is false of trees as the well-informed person knows them to be can be turned back against the Meditator. Perhaps (as Arnauld intimated in response to *Meditation Two*), I cannot clearly and distinctly understand a mind existing without a body. My vague idea of what it is like to be a mind that is not attached to or located in a body may be on the same footing as my fleeting image of a tree floating in air unattached to the ground. In both cases, my imagination may be at work, but my understanding may have been temporarily shut down.

Still, one has to admit that the claim that specialist knowledge of trees or minds can show us that trees need soil and that minds need bodies is inconclusive. Ask a specialist why a tree needs soil and she will tell you that the soil provides nutrients for the tree to grow and produce seeds and that it stabilizes the tree, allowing it to stand upright and receive light from all sides. Ask a cognitive scientist why minds need bodies and you will not get such a satisfying answer. The expert might give a compelling answer to the question why minds need bodies in order to see, or to experience inner sensations, or even to have emotions. He might point out that a physical mechanism for collecting and focusing light waves and particular cells that respond to the presence of light are necessary for us to be able to see. Why minds need bodies simply in order to think is not, however, so clear. The Meditator comes to believe, to be sure, that the ability to employ the imagination – seeing in one's "mind's eye" – suggests the presence of a body. So perhaps a body is needed to imagine. Nevertheless, if there can be thought without imagination, as the Meditator seems to believe there can be, perhaps there can be thought without a body.

The Meditator decides that imagination and sensory perception are not essential to him, as thinking is. If the mind survives the death of the body, this implies, its subsequent immortality will not involve imagination and perception but only intellectual understanding. Accordingly, even if intellectual understanding has a personal, in-dividual dimension (contrary to the Aristotelian hypothesis that the individual mind is absorbed into the Active Intellect or the Divine Mind after the death of the body), the Meditator has no basis for inferring that God will reward and punish him after death for deeds performed during his terrestrial life. Subsequent reunification with a body for this purpose is not excluded, but the Meditator does not speculate in this direction. To prove or disprove God's retribution or reward is quite beyond the scope of the Meditator's methods. It is hard to think of a topic on which our ideas are less clear and distinct than the topic of what happens after death.

3 OBJECTIONS TO *MEDITATION SIX* (I)

Gassendi takes up the Meditator's conjecture that the existence of corporeal things is merely probable at the start of *Meditation Six* and that the faculty of imagination provides some evidence in their favor. The Meditator had decided that his ability, not merely to understand the term "triangle" intellectually, but actually to see a triangle in his mind's eye rendered it quite probable that his mind was joined to a body. For, when imagining the triangle, the mind seemed not to be turning its attention to itself, but to something other than itself. Images "in" the mind seem to be produced by interaction between the mind and something "outside" it.

Gassendi suggests that the distinction between understanding and imagining is not sharp. It is not clear that we understand what it is to be a figure with a thousand sides, a chiliagon, when we fail to visualize it. As the number of sides of a figure is increased, we lose the ability both to imagine it and to understand it (VII:330). Gassendi suggests that the additional effort we put into visualization does not show that there are two faculties, intellect and imagination: "it will not follow that you have the basis for setting up more than one type of internal cognition, since it is purely a contingent matter, and a question of degree, whether you contemplate any given figure distinctly or confusedly, and with or without a concentrated effort" (VII:331).

According to Gassendi, the mind never turns to anything but a corporeal object in thinking. Every aspect of our mentality, in his view, renders it overwhelmingly probable that something material in our bodies thinks by generating corporeal images. In keeping with his overall skepticism about abstraction and conceptual argumentation, Gassendi expresses his doubts that corporeal nature can be the subject of pure mathematics. On his view and that of his followers, only qualitative physics "dealing with the things created by God" can constitute a real science. Mathematical statements regarding extended bodies in motion are abstract rather than concrete and are accordingly "only imaginings and fictions of our mind which cannot have any subsistence" (IXA:212). Descartes summarizes the views of his Gassendist critics with respect to mathematical physics as follows:

> They say that many people of great intelligence think they clearly see that mathematical extension, which I lay down as the fundamental principle of my physics, is nothing other than my thought, and hence that it does not and cannot have any subsistence outside my mind, being merely an abstraction which I form from physical bodies. And they conclude that the whole of my physics "must be imaginary and fictitious, as indeed the whole of pure mathematics is, whereas real physics dealing with the things created by God requires the kind of matter that is real, solid and not imaginary."
> (IXA:212)

Descartes is contemptuous of the view that physics and mathematics are separate disciplines, and that, to the extent that physics is mathematical, it deals with imaginary objects and cannot be applied to real ones. This view implies, he charges, that "we must entirely close the door to reason and content ourselves with being monkeys or parrots rather than men." For, if all abstract truths concern fictions and are to that extent false, we cannot pursue truth at all. Our discourse will simply consist in the copying of other texts (a slur on Gassendi's own unoriginal approach to scholarship), or in mindless chattering without real understanding (IXA:212). Mathematical physics, by contrast, allows us to make genuinely new discoveries about the extramental material world, just as a purely conceptual argument enables us to make a significant discovery about the God outside our minds.

> [W]hen it understands, the mind cannot attend to [triangles, pentagons, chiliagons] except as corporeal or quasi-corporeal objects. As for the ideas of allegedly immaterial things, such as those of God and an angel and the human soul or mind, it is clear that even the ideas we have of these things are corporeal or quasi-corporeal, since . . . the ideas are derived from the human form and from other things which are very rarefied and simple and very hard to perceive with the senses, such as air or ether.
> (VII:332)

Other objectors attack the Meditator's distinctness proof directly. Caterus points out that the Medieval philosopher Duns Scotus had asserted that some predicates can be conceived apart from one another but cannot exist apart from one another. Scotus's example of two such predicates was divine justice and divine mercy. We have distinct ideas of these two qualities: they are "formally" distinct. Yet it is impossible that God should be just but not merciful, or merciful but not just. Accordingly, says Caterus, the fact that mind and body can be conceived apart from one another does not show that they can exist apart from one another (VII:100).

Descartes's reply is that it is indeed true of many features of the world or entities in the world that, even if they can be conceived in abstraction from other features or entities, they depend on them.

Motion and shape, for example, can be understood as distinct from one another and as distinct from "body." There cannot, however, be motion without there being a moving body, or shape without there being a shaped thing. Nor can there be divine justice without God, or God without divine mercy and vice-versa. If someone were to insist that this was possible, this could only mean that he did not have a complete understanding of the entities and features involved. When we have a complete understanding of a feature or an entity, then all its dependencies are evident to us. Descartes maintains emphatically that we do have a complete understanding of mind on one hand and body on the other:

> I have a complete understanding of what a body is when I think that it is merely something having extension, shape and motion, and I deny that it has anything which belongs to the nature of a mind. Conversely, I understand the mind to be a complete thing, which doubts, understands, wills, and so on, even though I deny that it has any of the attributes which are contained in the idea of a body. This would be quite impossible if there were not a real distinction between the mind and the body.
>
> (VII:121)

Descartes asserts that, for it to be the case that we can understand two things distinctly and separately, they must really be entities in their own right. On the *assumption* that we do have a complete understanding of each of mind and body as distinct, it follows that they are really distinct. But what reason is there to accept this assumption? Perhaps my thought can "reach" my mind but cannot "grasp" its true and immutable nature (cf. Ch. 5 Sec. 2). The very idea of a distinct and separable soul may be only a fiction.

Objector 4, Arnauld, takes up Caterus's point that some distinctions that exist in thought (e.g., motion and shape, divine justice and divine mercy) obscure underlying dependencies and entailments. Though motion and shape can be conceived distinctly, there cannot be either without body. It is possible that the Meditator failed to conceive himself adequately in conceiving himself as a non-extended thing. "[T]hose who maintain that our mind is corporeal," Arnauld says, "do not on that account suppose that every body is a mind" (VII:201). Body might be to mind as genus to species. That is, some bodies might be minded; others not. In the same way, some animals are cats, others are not: *animal* and *cat* are distinct concepts, but there are underlying dependencies. Being a cat *entails* being an animal. Specially constituted bodies might be minded, just as specially constituted animals are cats.

Descartes's answer is that all the attributes attributable to body can be denied of mind (VII:227). He does not, however, really address Arnauld's point. If some bodies are minded, as some animals are cats, we should be able to see some mind-features in those bodies as we see cat-features in some animals. Arguably we do. We see mind-features in human bodies, but not in stones. Nor does Descartes try to strengthen his argument for the immortality of the soul in response to Arnauld's claim that both animals and humans may have perishable minds.

Arnauld insists that the Meditator has not proved that he is not a body. The Meditator's argument, which he represents as follows, proves too little:

> *I know that I exist and think*
> *I doubt that there are bodies*
> *I know that I am not a body*

This argument, Arnauld points out, is invalid. Consider the following variant:

> I know that T is a right-angled triangle
> I doubt that the square of the hypotenuse of a right-angled triangle is equal to the sum of the squares of the other two sides
> I know that it does not belong to the essence of T that its hypotenuse squared is equal to the sum of the squares of the other two sides (VII:202)

Even if I can remove "in thought" the property of the hypotenuse squared's having a determinate relationship to the sides of the triangle, it is a property of the triangle under consideration. It is unclear that God could have created a triangle without this property. Perhaps the fact that I am an extended, corporeal thing belongs, along with thought, to my nature, though I wrongly doubt it. Perhaps God could not have created me otherwise. After all, "the power of thought appears to be attached to bodily organs, since it can be regarded as dormant in infants and extinguished in the case of madmen" (VII:204). Arnauld does not press his objections to the Argument from Conceivability in a spirit of materialism. Like Descartes's other theological critics – Caterus and Mersenne – he is worried about the foothold materialism has achieved. The theologians are concerned that Descartes's arguments should be decisive enough to silence, in Arnauld's words, "those impious people who try to do away with the soul" (VII:204).

To the claim that he has proved too little, Descartes replies that the triangle argument furnishes a poor analogy. For, to understand clearly that T is a right-angled triangle is to understand, he claims, that its hypotenuse squared is equal to the squares of the other two sides. While God could have made the ratio different, He could not have created a triangle with no relationship between the hypotenuse and the sides. If I understand clearly that I exist and think, by contrast, I need not have any particular thoughts about my body.

The Sixth Set of Objectors ask how, when the intellect makes a distinction between two things, we can know that the distinction arises from the things, not from the intellect (VII:418)? They put their objection with great force:

> [W]e cannot go so far as to assert that what we call thought cannot in any way belong to a body subject to some sort of motion. For since we see that there are some bodies that do not think, and others, namely human bodies and perhaps those of the brutes, which do think, will not you yourself convict us of sophistry and of making rash judgments if we infer from this that there are no bodies that think? . . . [Y]ou seem to be so preoccupied and prepossessed by this method that you seem to have dulled your mind with it, so that you are no longer free to see that the individual properties or operations of the soul which you find in yourself depend upon corporeal motions.
> (VII:420)

They insist that Descartes would have torn the Argument from Conceivability to shreds had someone other than himself proposed it.

They are convinced, they say, of many self-evident truths, such as that two and three make five and that equals taken from equals leave equals, but they do not find Descartes's meditative method for discerning the distinctness of the soul and the existence of God adequate to the task: "we have read what you have written seven times, and have lifted up our minds, as best we could, to the level of the angels, but we still are not convinced" (VII:421).

[S]ince we do not know what can be done by bodies and their motions, and since you confess that without a divine revelation no one can know everything which God has imparted . . . how can you possibly have known that God has not implanted in certain bodies a power or property enabling them to doubt, think etc.?

(VII:421)

Note that there is a pattern to the objections of Gassendi and the philosophers composing the Sixth Set. The Objector proposes a counter-hypothesis that is materialistic or semi-materialistic in ascribing to bodies or to matter the power to think. Gassendi, for example, insists that "you may be a rarefied body infused into this solid one or occupying some part of it. At all events you have not yet convinced us that you are something wholly incorporeal" (VII:336). The Objector then asserts that Descartes has not ruled out this counter-hypothesis by showing why it is incoherent or self-contradictory to suppose that matter can think, or why God could not have made it so.

Descartes's standard retort is that the counter-hypothesis falls outside the scope of his argument. He has constructed his case carefully, over six *Meditations*, arriving at the conclusion that what thinks is an immaterial and separable substance, capable of independent existence. If he has made an error in his reasoning along the way, it should be pointed out. His critics, however, "cannot point to any flaw whatsoever in these arguments of mine."

Descartes's response can be best understood through a comparison with mathematical argumentation. If I propound a geometrical thesis T, for example, that the sum of the angles of a triangle is equal to two right angles, there are many counter-theses incompatible with T; e.g., that the sum of the angles of a triangle is equal to three right angles, or one right angle, and so on. It would be a waste of time for me to pursue all these counter-theses and prove that each is false. To establish T, all I need to do is to show that my proof is correctly done with conclusions rightly extracted step-wise from acceptable premises.

> [T]he only possible reason that I can see why neither these critics, nor, as far as I know, any others, have so far been able to fault my arguments is that they possess complete truth and certainty; in particular, they are deduced step by step, not from principles which are obscure and unknown, but in the first place, from total doubt about all things, and, in the second place, from principles which appear to be utterly evident and certain to the mind, once it has been set free from preconceived opinions. It follows from this that there cannot be any mistakes in my arguments which would not be noticed without difficulty by anyone of even moderate intelligence. (VII:446–7)

Yet, there is reason not to be entirely satisfied with Descartes's posture. One might agree that a philosopher does not need to demonstrate all incompatible theses to be false in order to establish his thesis as true. Nevertheless, in the empirical sciences that deal with the external world, certain relevant alternatives often need to be excluded to establish a given theory. The materialistic hypothesis that it is the body that thinks is perhaps a relevant alternative in the metaphysical realm. Further, Descartes does not consider the possibility, later raised by Kant, that, where metaphysical proofs concerning God, the soul, and the nature of substance are concerned, equally good proofs can be given for two incompatible theses. Kant thought that this feature distinguished metaphysics from mathematics.

Several critics point out that Descartes's intention to prove the immortality of the soul cannot be fulfilled merely by his showing that the soul is distinct from the body. Since Descartes had written in his Dedicatory Letter to the Sorbonne that serves as the Preface to the *Meditations* that one of the most important aims of his work was to prove the immortality of the human soul, the absence of such a proof in the *Meditations* indicates egregious failure. Arnauld lodges the following complaint:

[S]ince our distinguished author has undertaken to demonstrate the immortality of the soul, it may rightly be asked whether this evidently follows from the fact that the soul is distinct from the body. According to the principles of commonly accepted philosophy this by no means follows, since people ordinarily take it that the souls of brute animals are distinct from their bodies, but nevertheless perish along with them.
(VII:204)

If animals have distinct souls, and if all that is required for immortality is a distinct soul, then animals too must be immortal, an unpalatable consequence. Arnauld realizes that Descartes denies that animals have any souls or any conscious awareness at all, but he doubts that this view will ever come to be widely accepted. He finds incredible Descartes's claim that light can mechanically move the fibers of the optic nerves of a sheep to initiate hydraulic currents that make it run mechanically from a predator (VII:205).

Descartes continues to press his view that animals cannot be immortal since they are merely machines. Once this is properly understood, he implies, the difference between men and animals will be sufficiently plain to rebut the objection that if humans have immortal souls, so must animals, as well as the objection that, since it is unlikely that animals have immortal souls, it is unlikely that humans do either.

[B]oth in our bodies and those of the brutes, no movements can occur without the presence of all the organs or instruments which would enable the same movements to be produced in a machine . . . [A] very large number of the motions occurring inside us do not depend in any way on the mind. These include heartbeat, digestion, nutrition, respiration when we are asleep, and also such waking actions as walking, singing and the like, when these occur without the mind attending to them. When people take a fall, and stick out their hands so as to protect their head, it is not reason that instructs them to do this; it is simply that the sight of the impending fall reaches the brain and sends the animal spirits into the nerves in the manner necessary to produce this movement even without

> any mental volition, just as it would be produced in a machine . . . [A]ll
> the actions of the brutes resemble only those which occur in us without
> any assistance from the mind.
> (VII:229–30)

Mersenne, Objector 2, points out that the Meditator not only failed to prove the immortality of the soul, he did not even address the question:

> [Y]ou say not one word about the immortality of the human mind. Yet this
> is something you should have taken special care to prove and demonstrate,
> to counter those people, themselves unworthy of immortality, who utterly
> deny and perhaps even despise it . . . [I]t does not seem to follow from
> the fact that the mind is distinct from the body that it is incorruptible
> or immortal. What if its nature were limited by the duration of the life
> of the body, and God had endowed it with just so much strength and
> existence as to ensure that it came to an end with the death of the body?
> (VII:127–8)

Descartes concedes the point: "I admit that I cannot refute what you say. For I do not take it upon myself to try to use the power of human reason to settle any of those matters which depend on the free will of God" (VII:153). He goes on to say that if the question is about the absolute power of God, then, indeed, God "may have decreed that human souls cease to exist precisely when the bodies which he joined to them are destroyed." God has, however, revealed to us (in the New Testament's promise of eternal life) that He has not made this decree and has in fact ordained that human souls will survive the death of their bodies (VII:154).

Descartes falls back on faith and Revelation as well in reply to the Sixth Set of Objectors. These critics complain that Descartes's sharp division between animals and humans is inconsistent with Scripture. According to the Book of Ecclesiastes, they note, "a man hath no preeminence above a beast," and we do not know whether the soul goes "upwards or downwards" after death (VII:416). Descartes responds that it is not his job to comment on Scriptural texts: "I have never become involved in theological studies" (VII:429). He concedes to his critics that we cannot know by the power of reason anything about the soul's ultimate fate: "I have certainly tried to prove by natural reason that the human soul is not corporeal, but I grant that only faith can enable us to know whether it will ascend above" (VII:431).

Despite this concession, Descartes does supply a philosophical reason for believing in the immortality of the soul. The difference between the human body and other bodies consists, he says, merely in the arrangement of limbs and other accidents of this sort:

> [T]he final death of the body depends solely on a division or change of shape. Now we have no convincing evidence or precedent to suggest that the death or annihilation of a substance like the mind must result from such a trivial cause as a change in shape . . . Indeed, we do not even have any convincing evidence or precedent to suggest that any substance can perish. And this entitles us to conclude that the mind, in so far as it can be known by natural philosophy, is immortal.
>
> (VII:153)

Now, on one hand, even trivial causes can have massive effects. A single spark can blow up a house, and one tiny breach in a blood vessel can render a person blind or unable to speak. On the other hand, if B is independent of A, whatever happens to A, even if it is far from trivial, should have no effect on B, and vice-versa.

What reason might there be to think that any and all substances are imperishable? In theological terms, finite substances have existed since God created them and will cease to exist only if and when God decides to annihilate them. Perhaps God cannot possibly be ascribed any motive to annihilate corporeal or mental substance or to annihilate Himself, for that matter. Clearly, if we think of an orange, a piece of chalk, or a temple as a "substance," the principle of substance-imperishability is false. Each of these things decays over time and is resolved into its elements. Astronomers tell us that we are all made of fragments of exploded stars, and that matter in the universe is constantly recycled into various forms. Accordingly, one might think that corporeal substance as such is eternal or at least imperishable. The forms of animals, plants, molecules, planets, and other such objects are transitory and fleeting by astronomical time-scales, but the substance underlying them all, one might think, has always existed and always will exist.

The view that corporeal substance has always existed may be wrong. Perhaps corporeal substance came into existence *ex nihilo* from "fluctuations in the quantum vacuum" or some such nonsubstantial thing and will cease to exist, through a collapse into the vacuum. These are matters for speculation by physicists and philosophers of physics. Suppose, however, it is true that corporeal substance is imperishable. Perhaps there are numerous forces in the universe able to reduce ordinary physical objects to their constituent "parts" or "particles": forces of grinding, smashing, eroding, scattering, drifting, and decaying. It may yet be the case that there is no force in the universe powerful enough to reduce the ultimate "parts" or "particles" of things to nothing. Why shouldn't mental substance be imperishable as well?

When a human body dies, corporeal substance is not annihilated. It is simply resolved into smaller particles and these eventually become part of other living and nonliving bodies, whether the corpse is eaten by wild animals, nourishes the daisies, or merely crumbles into dust. Descartes is surely right to say that there is no reason to think that the death and disintegration of the body can cause the deterioration of the mind, if the mind is a separate substance. However, if human bodies disintegrate into the parts of which they are composed after a certain number of years, why shouldn't human minds as well? Why should I suppose that *I* will remain a coherent bundle of memories, thoughts, etc.? Perhaps these thoughts will scatter and recombine to make another human soul. Mental substance might be imperishable without my individual mind and all its contents being so.

Descartes would reject this suggestion. On his view, perceptions, thoughts, and memories are not constituents or parts of mental substances, i.e. of the individual minds, but modes that inhere in mental substance. It seems that Descartes is conceiving *each mind* as equivalent to *all of* extended substance. Matter can assume various forms without ever being annihilated, and so, in his view, can each mind.

Descartes has proved too little, Arnauld charges, but if his Argument from Conceivability can be made to work, Arnauld implies, he will then have proved too much. For he seems to be taking his readers back to the unacceptable Platonic view that "nothing corporeal belongs to our essence, so that man is merely a rational soul and the body merely a vehicle for the soul" (VII:203). The Platonic view was not acceptable to most theologians. For it was orthodoxy that human beings were intrinsically sinful, that sin was transmitted (by mothers, beginning with Eve) to their offspring, and that sin manifested itself in concupiscence, or bodily desire. If a human being is essentially a rational mind, and if his body is "merely a vehicle," it is hard to see how humans can be considered intrinsically sinful and how they can be understood to transmit sin to their offspring through their concupiscence.

Descartes denies that he has proved too much. Though he does not seem interested here or elsewhere in providing metaphysical foundations for the transmission of Original Sin, he insists that our souls do not merely "make use of" our bodies (VII:228). His reasons for insisting that he has shown in *Meditation Six* that the mind is "substantially united" to the body will become clear in the following two chapters.

CHAPTER 10

Meditation Six (11)
The Meditator establishes that extramental corporeal things definitely exist, confirms that she has a personal body to which she is united, and learns that neither her sensations nor her perceptions resemble their causes in the external world

I THE ACTIVE CAUSE OF IDEAS – CORPOREAL THINGS EXIST (AT VII:78–80)

Though perception and imagination have been deemed faculties that are not essential to the Meditator, the operation of those faculties implies the existence of a thinking substance: "I can clearly and distinctly understand myself as a whole without those faculties; but I cannot, conversely, understand those faculties without me, that is, without an intellectual substance to inhere in." Wherever there is conscious awareness of objects, there is a mind; no mere body, the Meditator is convinced, can perceive, imagine, or feel. What can she now conclude about the source of her perceptions and sensory experiences?

The Meditator knows that *some* ideas do not come from the senses. The non-pictorial ideas of the self and of God were not passively received by the senses. They were found within the mind after a search during which she ignored the sensory impressions that might have been only demonic interference. At the same time, the Meditator seems to have a faculty, albeit a nonessential faculty, that is independent of her will, for "receiving and recognizing" the ideas of corporeal things.

From her knowledge that the malevolent Demon does not exist and the observation that she seems to receive and recognize ideas of corporeal things, can the Meditator conclude that extramental corporeal things exist? This inference would be overhasty. Given that I receive and recognize sensory ideas, I can conclude that some active faculty of *producing and delivering ideas of distinct sorts* exists in addition to my passive faculty of receiving and recognizing. There are still three possible sources of my ideas.

1) The active faculty resides in me (mental substance).
2) The active faculty resides in God (divine substance) or something "noble."
3) The active faculty resides in material objects (corporeal substance).

The idealist rejects Option (3). According to the idealist, there are only minds and experiences. Our experiences are either formed in our own minds, or we acquire them through participation in, or communication with, the mind of an incorporeal divine substance. Option (3) does not, however, entail materialism. It posits material objects as the causes of our experiences without implying that there are only material objects.

The Meditator begins by considering idealism, only to reject it. She reasons as follows: perhaps I myself have both the active power to produce ideas of corporeal things and give them to myself, and the passive ability to receive and recognize them. If I can find the idea of God within myself and recognize it, why can I not find the ideas of all other things, including so-called "material objects," within me and recognize them as being of different types?

On reflection, however, Option (1) seems unlikely. The Meditator returns to the idea that the involuntary appearance of sensory ideas suggests that they originate outside her from a different source: "the ideas in question are produced without my co-operation and often even against my will." Of course, this does not prove that I am not the source of these involuntary ideas. Think of an angry person experiencing involuntary but self-generated revenge fantasies. However, the quality of our usual sensory experience is quite unlike the quality of these intrusive, self-produced thoughts. Our experience changes, for example, merely as we feel our eyes moving around the room.

"[T]he only alternative," the Meditator decides, is that the faculty of producing ideas resides "in another substance distinct from me." This leaves Options (2) and (3):

> This substance is either a body, that is, a corporeal nature, in which case it will contain formally <and in fact> everything which is to be found objectively <or representatively> in the ideas; or else it is God, or some creature more noble than a body.
>
> (VII:79)

Consider Option (2), the supposition that the mind of God is the active power that produces all my experiences. If the supposition were true, God would be, contrary to what was shown earlier, a malevolent deceiver. For, according to the Meditator, He has also given her a "great propensity to believe" that her ideas are produced by corporeal things, i.e. to believe in Option (3). God would still be a deceiver even if He had offloaded the power of idea-production to some "noble" (unlike the malevolent Demon), but still non-corporeal, substance – perhaps a bevy of angels. If Options (1) and (2) can be rejected, idealism is false and only Option (3) is viable. There must actually be corporeal things external to me that possess the power to produce ideas in my mind.

Any causal source for my ideas is deceptive, according to the Meditator, if it does not contain *formally* what is to be found in the idea *objectively*. This claim can be unpacked as follows: an angel with the power to produce in me the experience of seeing a stone is on a different footing from a stone with the power to produce in me the experience of seeing a stone. The actual stone formally contains "stoneness," while the angel does not. The Meditator expresses this by saying that the angel contains "stoneness" only eminently. God can be said to contain all things within Himself eminently, including stones, hair, mud, etc. By contrast, God does not contain stones, hair, and mud within Himself formally, but only the attributes of divinity.

> It follows that corporeal things exist. They may not all exist in a way that exactly corresponds with my sensory grasp of them, for in many cases the grasp of the senses is very obscure and confused. But at least they possess all the properties which I clearly and distinctly understand, that

> is, all those which, viewed in general terms, are comprised within the subject-matter of pure mathematics.
> (vii:80)

To pause and take stock, note how the Meditator's set of still-doubtful beliefs is shrinking: the existence of corporeal things outside her own mind is now established. Yet what these objects are like, beyond providing a subject matter for pure mathematics, has not been determined. Nor has it been determined that the Meditator is specially related to any particular material object, i.e., a personal body.

DOUBT

> There is a body that specially belongs to me
>
> Objects resemble my ideas of them
>
> The senses instruct me as to the real characteristics of corporeal things
>
> physics
>
> astronomy
>
> medicine

Figure 27　The set of propositions that are still doubtful in the middle of *Meditation Six*

2 THE RESEMBLANCE THEORY OF SENSATION REFUTED – GOD–NATURE AS AN ORDERLY SYSTEM – THE UNITY OF MIND AND BODY – SENSATIONS ARE CONFUSED (AT VII:80–8)

The material objects that are now known to produce her ideas contain "formally" the *content* or "objective reality" of those ideas. So, why isn't the way clear for the Meditator to conclude that her ideas do after all *resemble* their causing objects, just as she used to suppose? In that case, the propositions *Objects resemble my ideas of them* and

The senses instruct me as to the real characteristics of corporeal things are no longer doubtful and can be known to be true. This question is addressed later in *Meditation Six*. Meanwhile, the Meditator adduces a few considerations relevant to the problem of sensory representation.

A little earlier, the Meditator noted that it is difficult to explain why certain sensations seem to "mean" or "inform us of" certain things:

> [W]hy should that curious tugging in the stomach which I call hunger tell me that I should eat, or a dryness of the throat tell me to drink, and so on? I was not able to give any explanation of all this, except that nature taught me so. For there is absolutely no connection (at least that I can understand) between the tugging sensation and the decision to take food, or between the sensation of something causing pain and the mental apprehension of distress that arises from that sensation.
> (VII:76)

Our sensations of hunger, pain, cold, thirst, and so on are ideas that we suppose to be caused by objects in the world and states of the world external to our minds. The condition of my stomach, and the levels of glucose in my blood and brain are the causes of the feelings of hunger that assail me every six hours or so. On reflection, however, it is apparent that the feeling of hunger does not resemble the causes of hunger. The connection between the tugging sensation and the deprived state of the hungry body, is as arbitrary as the connection that we can be taught to make between the word P-F-E-R-D, considered as a set of black marks on paper, and a horse.

P-F-E-R-D means "horse" in German. That is to say (very roughly) that some people, German speakers, are so constituted in virtue of their past experiences and current neural wiring that they think of a horse when they see this configuration on paper. Often, when thinking of a horse, or wishing others to think of a horse, these same people make these "shapes" on paper or utter the sounds conventionally associated with these shapes aloud. Yet there is no resemblance between a horse and the configuration P-F-E-R-D. Other people are related to the configuration C-H-E-V-A-L in the same way the first group are related to P-F-E-R-D. But the two configurations do not resemble each other and C-H-E-V-A-L does not resemble a horse any more than P-F-E-R-D.

Analogously, the tugging in my stomach means "I should eat." Nature has constituted me in virtue of my past experience and current internal organization in such a way that, whenever I experience the tugging sensation, I am inclined to think *that* I should eat, just as, if I am German I cannot help thinking *of* a horse if I see the configuration P-F-E-R-D.

To convince yourself that, even if we read our sensations "automatically" and follow the directions they give us, the Meditator is right in claiming that there is "absolutely no [intelligible] connection" between a sensation and what it indicates I should do, suppose that Nature communicated with me in a different language and that I understood this alternative language. Whenever I felt a tugging sensation in my stomach, I thought I should look for a glass of water and drink it, and whenever I had a dry throat sensation, I thought I should get something to eat. If I followed these prompts, I immediately felt better and the annoying sensations went away. Suppose further that a certain irritating pink light occasionally lit up my visual field, generally late in the evening. I could make it stop bothering me by falling asleep and remaining asleep for a while. This would usually keep the pink light from reappearing for 12–16 hours.

Suppose I were suddenly switched over to one of these alternative signaling systems. It would not feel natural at first. I might continue for some days or hours to eat when I felt the tugging in my stomach and to drink when my throat felt dry, before realizing that I felt better when I reversed my procedures. Perhaps it would take me some time before the irritating pink light came to feel as natural a sign of my own sleepiness to me as heavy eyelids, or dryness in the throat as natural a sign of needing food as a tugging in the stomach. Nevertheless, there is reason to think that eventually I would feel "normal" once again. (In a celebrated series of modern experiments, subjects were given goggles to wear that contained inverting lenses. For some days – Phase A – they saw the world "upside-down." After a few days, however – Phase B – they began to see things in the usual way. When they took the goggles off, they saw things "upside down" for a few days – Phase C – until the effect wore off – Phase D.)

The Meditator proposes that the connection between a sensation and a disposition to act – to seek out and ingest water or food or to move away from an object – is a learned one. Various other sensations could just as well have been signals of her needing food. As curious as this may seem, some sensation other than the one she knows as "pain" might have been the signal that prompted her to terminate the contact between her body and a sharp object pressing on it. Nevertheless, she can now be certain that she has a personal body. For she knows that there is an external world of extramental objects, and she knows that she has sensations and experiences of moving amongst, touching, grasping, and ingesting these extramental objects. Unless God is a deceiver, she must really be moving, touching, grasping, and ingesting, not just seeming to do so. Without a personal body, she could not do any of these things. If she did not have a body to mediate between her mind and the world, she could neither receive signals nor act appropriately.

"My" body is the particular material object that conveys informative signals from the world beyond its boundaries and that instructs me as to which movements are conducive to its survival. No other body mediates, signals, and instructs me in the same way and so I am entitled to call this one "mine." What, though, is this "nature" that has instituted the signaling system of sensation?

The Meditator now introduces the idea of nature as an orderly system that is established by God. Nature is not, however, something apart from God. Nature "considered in its general aspect" is the same thing as God:

> [I]f nature is considered in its general aspect, then I understand by the term nothing other than God himself, or the ordered system of created things established by God. And by my own nature in particular I understand nothing other than the totality of things bestowed on me by God. (VII:80)

God has so ordered nature that when I feel the sensation I call "pain," there is (usually) something wrong with my body and when I feel the sensation I call "thirst" (usually) my body needs water, and so on. God–Nature, one might say, had to set up *some* system for informing me when there was something wrong with my body or that it needed water, though it was not necessary for Him–Her to set up this particular signaling system.

The Meditator observes that she spontaneously believes not only that she has a personal body but that, as long as her body is alive, she forms a unit with it. One might wonder at this point whether, if the nature of the mind is to occupy itself with intellectual matters, this unification is problematic. What benefit can the mind possibly derive from association with a body? Isn't it a nuisance and a distraction?

Recall that the use of the visual imagination, as it is employed in geometry, earlier suggested to the Meditator the existence of a body closely related to her mind (Ch. 9 Sec. 1). When imagining, the mind seems to turn towards a body and to look at something in the body. It seems that I could not do geometry without my body. For, if I were a wholly incorporeal being, I could not imagine or see the necessary figures – the triangles, circles, and lines needed to construct proofs. This realization might lead us to suspect that, if we can acquire knowledge of physics, astronomy, and medicine, we will need our bodies to do so. Some aspects of these sciences depend on the perception of material objects such as pendulums, billiard balls, planets, stars, and internal organs. Other aspects require only the use of the visual imagination. Although the discovery that the senses are not constituted so as to inform us of the real nature of things but chiefly their harmful and beneficial qualities reinforces the Principle of Intellect Priority, it is hard to see how the mind can engage even in what we might think of as "purely intellectual activities" such as geometry and physics without the body. The body provides content for the mind to think about.

So the mind–body partnership that endures for my whole life is a genuine partnership. My noncorporeal mind is not just "stuck with" or "weighed down by" or "held up on account of" a lumbering physical body that needs food and drink, gets sick, aches, wants to do lots of things my mind disapproves of, and generally behaves like a petulant nuisance. The experience of embodiment is normally not like the experience of having to carry around a fussy, demanding accessory. So far is it from being the case that I am stuck with my body, that I rarely observe what is happening in it as though I were a separate entity from it. On the contrary, I feel immediately what is happening in it; the partnership is so close that I feel that, with my body, I compose one human person.

> Nature also teaches me, by these sensations of pain, hunger, thirst and so on, that I am not merely present in my body as a sailor is present in a ship, but that I am very closely joined and, as it were, intermingled with it, so that I and the body form a unit. If this were not so, I, who am nothing but a thinking thing, would not feel pain when the body was hurt, but would perceive the damage purely by the intellect, just as a sailor perceives by sight if anything in his ship is broken.
>
> (VII:81)

Sensations of hunger, thirst, and pain, as well as experiences of colors, scents, sounds, and so on, the Meditator concludes, are "nothing but confused modes of thinking which arise from the union, and, as it were, intermingling of the mind with the body." The mind cannot "intermingle" with the body as a vapory soul, distributed through the limbs and organs, would. The intermingling is an as-it-were intermingling, an *impression as of* intermingling that is itself an idea. The idea of an animating soul nevertheless arises from the real union of the Meditator's mind with her own body.

Corporeal things are now known to exist extramentally and to be causes of our sensory ideas. The notion of a material object is gradually losing the flimsiness that afflicted it earlier in the *Meditations*. Why, then, does the Meditator continue to describe her perceptions of material objects, as well as the sensations she feels in her body, as "confused?" Sensations can, after all, be sharp, acute, and distinct: think of a searing pain.

The answer to this question is that sensations defy neat categorization as mental or physical. Pain and hunger cannot be properties of extended substance. Pain, however, is not merely the thought expressed by the proposition *This stimulus is noxious*, and hunger is not merely the thought expressed by the proposition *I need to eat*. Pain and hunger cannot be understood clearly as modes either of corporeal substance or of mental substance, when each is considered in isolation. These sensations seem to arise out of a condition that in fact does not obtain, though we experience it as obtaining: namely, the intermingling of mind and body.

The Meditator's knowledge-state is now that represented in Figure 28.

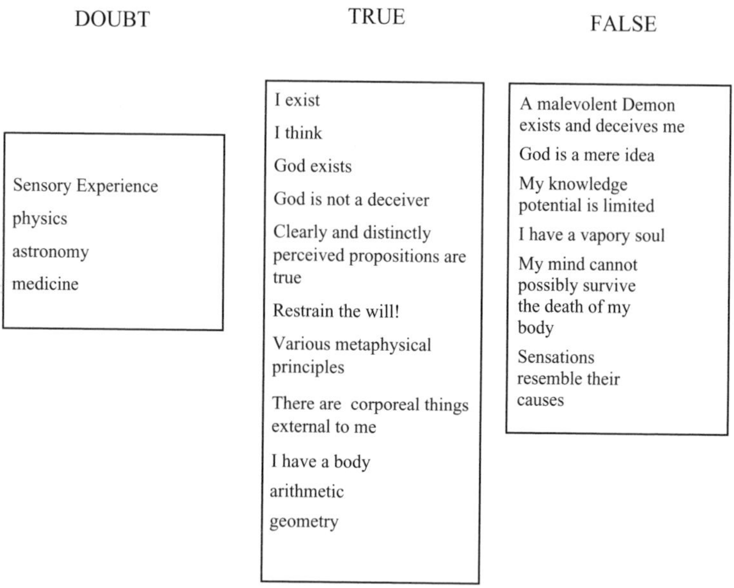

DOUBT　　　　　　　　　　TRUE　　　　　　　　　　FALSE

| Sensory Experience
physics
astronomy
medicine | I exist
I think
God exists
God is not a deceiver
Clearly and distinctly perceived propositions are true
Restrain the will!
Various metaphysical principles
There are corporeal things external to me
I have a body
arithmetic
geometry | A malevolent Demon exists and deceives me
God is a mere idea
My knowledge potential is limited
I have a vapory soul
My mind cannot possibly survive the death of my body
Sensations resemble their causes |

Figure 28　The Meditator's knowledge-set in *Meditation Six* p. 81.

3　THE RESEMBLANCE THEORY OF PERCEPTION QUESTIONED – (AT VII:81–3)

[F]rom the fact that I perceive by my senses a great variety of colours, sounds, smells and tastes, as well as differences in heat, hardness and the like, I am correct in inferring that the bodies which are the source of these various sensory perceptions possess differences corresponding to them, though perhaps not resembling them.

(VII:81)

The view that internal sensations can resemble states of the body is untenable, but the theory that perceptions of the external world are copies of material objects and their configurations is still in question. The Meditator reflects that the following judgments may all be "ill-considered": "that any space in which nothing is occurring to stimulate my senses must be empty; . . . that the heat in a body is something exactly resembling the idea of heat which is in me; . . . that when a body is white or green, the selfsame whiteness or greenness which I perceive through my senses is present in the body." The Meditator grasps that her sensation of hunger – the tugging in her stomach – in no way *resembles* the objective condition in the world of her needing food. Yet her perceptions, she is convinced, are qualitatively differentiated in ways that correspond to differentiations in the external world. They represent it. She has not established that her perceptions do not represent the condition of the world to her by being copies of parts of the world that resemble those parts. Perhaps sensations are ideas that are merely caused by external objects and states of the extramental world without resembling them, whereas perceptions are caused by external objects and states of the external world, correspond to them, and do resemble their causes.

We naturally think in this connection of scents and colors, by contrast with pains and cravings, as qualities residing "in" external objects. To smell a rose better, one approaches the rose; to see the color of a rose better, one looks at it in strong daylight. If a film or a screen is interposed between the observer and the rose, its color or scent may not be detectable. This suggests that, while my craving for it is obviously not *in* the cup of coffee I sip in the morning, my experience of the color of the rose can resemble the color that is *in* the rose, when I am seeing it in a good light, and that my experience of the scent of the rose can resemble the scent it actually has.

Yet these spontaneous beliefs may be false. The Meditator now asks what God has bestowed on her, not by way of access to self-evident truths, or insight into the ordinary course of nature, but rather in virtue of her constitution as a perceived unity of mind and body. What precisely is the Meditator justified in inferring concerning the relation between her sensory perceptions and their causes?

The "resemblance theory" offers one way of conceiving the representation-relation between ideas and the objects that cause them. According to the resemblance theory, when I gaze out the window at my wintry garden, I have a complex visual idea involving damp, bare trees, grass, fallen leaves on the ground, and a blue sky behind it all. My experience is like a picture of the scene I am viewing. For this picture could remain in my mind even if the external world were to vanish, and the scene itself could remain even if I were to be annihilated. If I close my eyes, I suppose the scene to remain just as it is, with every leaf and every twig in place if it is a still day. When I open my eyes again, everything is still there. The scene I am viewing, which I suppose to be the cause of my experience, and my experience of it are therefore two distinct things. The experience seems to be a derivative copy of the scene itself, for the Causal Noninferiority Principle might be taken to suggest that the scene can cause my experience of it to come into being, while my experience cannot cause the trees, leaves, grass, and sky to exist.

Does it make sense, though, to suppose that my experience of the garden is a derivative copy of the garden? Recall that the Meditator decided earlier in *Meditation Six* that, when an idea represents a particular object, that is when the idea is received and recognized as the idea of a particular object, the object must contain "formally" whatever is in the idea "objectively." One way to interpret this claim is as meaning that all recognizable representations are like good pictures. A good picture of Mary is one that actually looks like her. Intuitively, a picture of Mary's elbow that looks like anyone else's elbow is not a good picture of Mary. Much of what is formally in Mary, one might say, is not objectively in the picture, making it a bad picture of her.

The resemblance theory of visual perception explains very well certain features of our perceptual experience as we ordinarily think of it. We suppose that perception involves two distinct things, an experience, and the thing, or configuration, or state of affairs it is an experience of, and that the two should match. If, when the scene before me was a wintry garden, I had the experience of a three-ring circus, it would have to be said of me that I was hallucinating, not perceiving. If, when the object before me was a paper bag, I had the experience of a stone, it would have to be said of me that I was undergoing an illusion. So, resemblance between the scene or the object perceived and the experience seems critical for distinguishing between perceiving and hallucinating and between perceiving veridically and having an illusion. We know that our perceptions can be veridical or delusory – what could this mean except to say that our perceptions are like good pictures or bad pictures of some sector of extramental reality?

Matters are not so simple, though. Reflecting on the resemblance theory, the Meditator realizes that, even if we tend spontaneously to believe in a resemblance between objects and ideas, nature has not, in fact, taught us to infer the truth of the resemblance theory from our experiences:

> My nature... does indeed teach me to avoid what induces a feeling of pain and to seek out what induces feelings of pleasure... But it does not appear to teach us to draw any conclusions from these sensory perceptions about things located outside us without waiting until the intellect has examined the matter. For knowledge of the truth about such things seems to belong to the mind alone, not to the combination of mind and body.
> (VII:82–3)

In fact, the Meditator realizes, we do not believe in the resemblance theory consistently. For example, we have no tendency to believe that a star that looks no bigger than a spark really is no bigger than a spark. We might think of or describe the stars as "tiny, twinkling points of light," but we do not *believe* that they are tiny points. When we apply our intellects to the question of the actual characteristics of the stars, we come actively to disbelieve that they are tiny, twinkling points.

Analogously, we might first think of our sensory idea – our experience – of heat as a copy of something in hot objects. We do not, however, the Meditator decides, really accept the resemblance theory when we apply our intellects to the question what heat is. We come to disbelieve that the hot feeling is in the hot object and we are right to do so: "[A]lthough I feel heat when I go near a fire and feel pain when I go too near, there is no convincing argument for supposing that there is something which resembles the heat any more than for supposing that there is something that resembles the pain." Pain, or anything "resembling" pain, cannot be *in* the object – for example a sharp knife – that causes us to feel it. High C, or anything resembling High C, cannot be *in* the vibrating string that causes us to hear it. And if pain or High C cannot resemble its cause, why should I suppose that my visual or olfactory experiences resemble their causes?

There are other reasons to be wary of the resemblance theory of perception. We cannot set scenes or objects and the experiences we have of them side by side, as we can set Mary next to her picture and look back and forth, comparing one to the other. So we cannot compare the two, and confirm that a scene or object and our idea of it resemble each other. Furthermore, we can get different visual experiences from the same object. If I walk around a rectangular white piece of cardboard, it will take on different shapes from different angles, and if I shine differently colored lights onto it, it will appear in different colors. The different experiences are not copies of each other. So how can they all be copies of the object? If only one experience really resembles the object, which is it?

Taken together, these difficulties create considerable trouble for the resemblance theory and suggest that it should be discarded. One consequence of discarding it, the Meditator decides, is that I should not suppose that what I see (in the sense not just of *seeing$_1$*, but also of *seeing$_2$* [cf. Ch. 3 Sec. 2]) is a reliable guide to what there is:

[E]ven though there is nothing in any given space that stimulates the senses, it does not follow that there is no body there. In these cases and many others I see that I have been in the habit of misusing the order of nature. For the proper purpose of the sensory perceptions given me by nature is simply to inform the mind of what is beneficial or harmful for the composite of which the mind is a part; . . . But I misuse them by treating them as reliable touchstones for immediate judgements about the essential nature of bodies located outside us. . .
(VII:83)

The world as I perceive it, and the entities and qualities I take to be in it on the basis of my perceptions, should not be confused with the world as it is and bodies as they exist in themselves. But doesn't this imply that what we call "perception" is really illusion? What is it to perceive if not to have a sensory idea that resembles the object of which it is an idea in just the way that a good picture resembles its subject? These puzzles are addressed in section 4.

4 THE FUNCTIONAL BODY-MACHINE – THE SEMANTIC THEORY OF SENSATION AND PERCEPTION (AT VII:83–4)

The Meditator now understands that her sensory ideas contribute to her survival as a living organism; indeed their main purpose is to prolong her life. She realizes that, as an embodied creature, she does not merely passively experience the tastes, smells, and colors of objects outside her own body. She is not like someone idly strolling though a department store with no particular intention of buying anything. On the contrary, the experience of the embodied self is that material objects are harmful, hurtful, or neutral with respect to her. She is active in the world and the world poses a set of challenges to her.

> I am also taught by nature that various other bodies exist in the vicinity of my body, and that some of these are to be sought out and others avoided . . . [T]he fact that some of the perceptions are agreeable to me while others are disagreeable makes it quite certain that my body, or rather my whole self, in so far as I am a combination of body and mind, can be affected by the various beneficial or harmful bodies which surround it.
>
> (VII:81)

Suppose my internal bodily state is such that my body is slightly dehydrated and needs water. To keep my body functioning well, I need to find water, and to do so I must be able to find the way to my kitchen tap, get a glass from the shelf, and fill the glass with water. To accomplish this, I need to use my senses. To be sure, if I were blind, I could find my way around by touch and alleviate my thirst. However, if I were blind and numb as well, and yet mobile, it seems that I could not do so. I could not feel the ground under my feet, or discern when my hand had touched a glass or the tap, or even be sure that water was flowing into my mouth and down my throat.

Suppose I was mobile and rational, but lacked the external senses of sight, smell, touch, taste, and hearing, though I could experience the internal sensations of hunger, thirst, cold, pain, and so on. Is it conceivable that I could keep myself alive and comfortable for a certain interval of years and reproduce before my life was over? This seems doubtful. Since I could not react or respond to anything in my environment, I would have to be "programed" like a robot with a series of motions conducive to survival. Since the supposition is that I am mobile and rational, but blind, deaf, numb, and lacking the ability to smell or taste, the programming could not make use of sensory inputs: patterns of light waves or sound waves, changes in pressure, or chemical signals. In a changing and demanding environment, in which food did not fall into my open mouth – in which I had no way of telling whether my mouth was open or not – and in which I was surrounded by other mobile creatures, criss-crossing my path, and even trying to injure or consume me, how could any advance programing adequate for all situations that did not utilize sensory information succeed?

Having senses that can react and respond to objects and creatures in the environment is essential for a mobile creature. My rationality would be of no use if I had no external senses. Perhaps it is somewhat "costly" for nature to supply me with equipment that focuses and reacts to light and sound waves, to pressure, and to the molecules that stimulate smell and taste. Nevertheless, it would be even more costly for nature to try to program my movements in advance in a world in which I must range quite widely and in which the environment is variable, hostile, and somewhat unpredictable. My body can therefore be considered as a receptive machine that reacts flexibly to changes in its environment by co-ordinating sensory information and movement.

Indeed, the Meditator suggests, the human body might be considered as a clock-like machine that can run without any input from the mind, to the extent that acts of free will are ignored:

> I might consider the body of a man as a kind of machine equipped with and made up of bones, nerves, muscles, veins, blood and skin in such a way that, even if there were no mind in it, it would still perform all the same movements as it now does in those cases where movement is not under the control of the will or, consequently, of the mind.
>
> (VII:84)

The notion that the external senses have the function of adjusting our behavior to conditions of the external world helps to break the grip of the resemblance theory. Our perceptual experiences of objects and scenes are not mere copies or images of the external world, as the resemblance theory posits. Rather, they are presentations that "inform the mind what is beneficial or harmful for the composite of which the mind is a part." The color of ripe fruit triggers an impulse to pluck it when we are hungry. A bitter or rancid taste prompts us to spit out an offending substance. The sight and sensation of an insect or small animal crawling on the body produces the response of swatting or calling for help; the touch of a mate or a child calls forth a different response. As the Meditator realized earlier in connection with internal sensations, it does not matter what the quality of a sensory experience is, so long as it provides signals that are consistently useful.

If the Meditator is on the right track, the experience of blue in no way resembles any objective condition of the world, though it corresponds to and signals a condition of the world. Various other color-experiences – for example, the experiences we call "purple" or "yellow" – could have been used by nature to signal whatever condition of the world blue happens to signal to us. Our belief that bluebirds, blueberries, the sea on a sunny day, and other such things have a property of blueness that resembles our color experience of blue merely reflects our habituation to our familiar signaling system.

Perhaps, though, there is a reason why I see things that are in a certain objective condition as *blue*, and perhaps an inverted spectrum or some other color-system would not work as well to enable me to find food, avoid obstacles, and evade dangerous situations. Or perhaps it would be too difficult for nature, or even displeasing to God–Nature, to construct a different system of correspondences.

Perhaps, for reasons having to do with physical measures, such as the wavelengths associated with various colors, the fact that some colors are not easily seen at dusk, or the nature of the optical system that processes incoming light, it is good that we should experience blue and not yellow or purple under the conditions in which we do.

The Meditator decides that, even if various sensations would work in a signaling system, "the best system that could be devised is . . . [the one in which the external stimulus] should produce the one sensation which, of all possible sensations, is most especially and frequently conducive to the preservation of the healthy man." A sensory idea, then, whether it is a sensation felt in the interior of the body, like hunger and thirst, or on the surface of the body, like coolness and pain, or an unlocalized emotion, or the perception of a "quality" of an object or a part of my own body, can best be understood as a meaningful (and perhaps even optimal) signal. The signal is registered by an organism that has to be taught by nature or has learned, to understand it and that is disposed to react, or can choose to react, differently to different messages in standardized ways. This is what is meant by a "semantic" theory of sensory experience. Someone who was convinced that P-F-E-R-D was intrinsically similar to or resembled a living horse would be under the spell of the same illusion as the naïve theorist who supposes that our experiences of corporeal things are similar to or resemble them as they are in themselves.

5 OBJECTIONS TO *MEDITATION SIX* (II)

The seven Objectors have little to say about Descartes's theory of sensory ideas as it is advanced in *Meditation Six*. Perhaps this is because the semantic theory developed by the Meditator in conjunction with her theory of the body-machine is new and unfamiliar; perhaps it is because they do not see much relevance to the problems of authority and religion with which they are overwhelmingly concerned in Descartes's discussion of sensory ideas. Arnauld has already voiced his reservations over Descartes's theory of qualities (Ch. 7 Sec. 2), but it is only some years later that he will become involved in a dispute over the Cartesian theory of perceptual ideas with the second-generation Cartesian Nicole Malebranche.

Contemporary commentators, by contrast, have been intrigued by Descartes's theory that sensory ideas represent the world without resembling it and that objects as they are represented in our minds are very different from objects as they are in themselves. Corporeal substance, considered in isolation, has only Category 1 properties, according to Descartes (Ch. 8 Sec. 1). Does this make all Category 2 properties illusory? This seems to be a reasonable inference. But what about veridicality? What is it to be perceiving, not hallucinating or suffering an illusion, on a theory that posits no resemblance between the scene perceived and the perceptual experience?

The Meditator does not address this point, or not adequately. She indicates that, when we perceive veridically, the object we perceive can be said "formally" to contain the content of the perceptual idea we have. Think of the angel and the stone. Both can produce the visual experience of a stone in me. So can a paper bag. The angel, however, in virtue of his not containing stoneness "formally" but only "eminently" can only produce the hallucination of a stone, and the paper bag can only produce the illusion of a stone. Neither the angel nor the paper bag can cause me veridically to perceive a stone in the absence of a stone. But what is a stone really? Like the paper bag, it is just a set of corpuscles, extended, figured, mobile, that cause an experience in me. How can they contain stoneness "formally?"

Our intuitive perceptual theory, when amalgamated with a Cartesian analysis of ideas, qualities, and their causes, seems to incorporate an "inconsistent triad":

> Thesis 1: There is a difference between veridical and non-veridical perception.
> Thesis 2: When conditions are normal and our perceptual systems are functioning properly, we perceive objects and scenes veridically.
> Thesis 3: We never perceive the world as it really is.

Later philosophers of perception have tried to resolve the inconsistency in several ways. One way is to reject Thesis 3 and to try to explain "veridical" perception without appeal to the notion of a comparison between a visual experience and an object or scene "as it really is." Philosophers have suggested that veridicality is to be understood in terms of dispositions to productive action (I cannot use an illusory stone to prop open a doorway); agreement with other perceivers (who do not share my hallucination); the fulfillment of the perceiver's expectations (moving closer to or touching the paper bag I took for a stone, I get a surprise); and other such notions.

Thesis 3 implies that our perceptual representations of the world are flawed because the world does not look like a swarm of extended, figured, mobile corpuscles, or whatever else we may suppose it really to be. Yet a representation can be a good representation without resembling its object in the same way that a studio portrait of Mary resembles Mary. A Magnetic Resonance Image of Mary's brain, or an X-ray of her wristbones, may be much better representations of Mary for certain purposes. They can give us much-needed information about what we ought to do.

Of course, often what we want in a representation is resemblance of the studio portrait variety. We may need a picture for some purpose in which resemblance is critical – as photo ID, for example, or to remind us what it is like to have Mary around. What we need our experiences for, however, may be such that resemblance between our experiences and what they are experiences of is not important, so long as they can give us much-needed information about what we ought to do. It remains, however, to be seen whether we can resolve the inconsistent triad or are hopelessly confused by our fondness for the philosophically incoherent resemblance theory.

CHAPTER 11

Meditation Six (III)
The Meditator learns how her body is organized, and discovers why her illnesses, like her errors, suggest that God is benevolent, and determines that she can proceed confidently in all the sciences

1 SENSORY ERROR – THE SICK BODY AND ITS SENSATIONS – THE NERVOUS SYSTEM (AT VII:84–9)

A few major questions are still unanswered. First, how do the mind and body actually co-operate to give us experiences? Second, why do our experiences sometimes mislead us? How is sensory error possible if God is veracious and has set up the mind–body relation to enable us to function well as living organisms engaged in various intellectual and nonintellectual activities?

The Meditator tackles these questions in reverse order.

Consider a person who devours tasty food that is poisonous to humans and who subsequently dies. Her sensory system has failed to give her the message that this food should have been avoided and has failed to instruct her not to eat it. She was unable to taste the poison and was misled into consuming it. This shows that her sensory system is not perfect; she is not repelled by all poisons and there are some she cannot taste at all. Now, the Meditator has already acknowledged in *Meditation Four* that she has various imperfections. Such defects in her sensory system do not threaten her view that God has provided for her well. The only inference that can be drawn, she decides, is that the poisoned victim is not omniscient when it comes to correctly identifying harmful substances: "And this is not surprising, since man is a limited thing, and so it is only fitting that his perfection should be limited."

Consider, through, some harder cases that seem to test God's veracity and benevolence more rigorously. At times, Nature, not only fails to warn a victim, but positively encourages him to do something harmful. I might develop a taste for absinthe, which is not a healthy liquid to ingest, at least not in substantial quantities over an extended period. One might call this taste "abnormal" or "perverse," but why has God constructed me in such a way that I am able to develop this taste at all? Why am I liable to harmful addictions to alcohol, tobacco, and opiates? If I develop the disease known as dropsy, I will acquire a ferocious thirst when drinking water is bad for me. It is clear that I am "sick," but this designation, as the Meditator notes, does not solve the problem. How can there be abnormal, perverse, unhealthily addicted, or simply sick creatures if we are creations of a good God, who has made us as we are?

In a sick body, the sensation of thirst will indicate to the creature that it needs water, and it will automatically drink water if water is available, worsening its condition. Now, the Meditator reflects,

A sick man is no less one of God's creatures than a healthy one, and it seems . . . a contradiction to suppose that he has received from God a nature which deceives him. Yet a clock constructed with wheels and weights observes all the laws of its nature just as closely when it is badly made and tells the wrong time as when it completely fulfills the wishes of the clockmaker . . . Admittedly, when I consider the purpose of the clock, I may say that it is departing from its nature when it does not tell the right time; and similarly when I consider the mechanism of the human body, I may think that . . . it too is deviating from its nature if the throat is dry at a time when drinking is not beneficial to its continued health.

(VII:84–5)

It is "in the nature" of a clock to tell time. Nevertheless, if a *particular* clock is broken and does not tell time, it does not follow that something is wrong with Nature. We should not think of Nature as a force that tends to make clocks good, or that could prevent a clock from being bad. A healthy body does not have bizarre appetites that tend to worsen its own condition and a sick body sometimes does, but the latter is just as much a human body as the former. Both are equally natural. There is, the Meditator decides, a nature that is not merely a "label" and that is "found in the things themselves." This is the Nature that consists of certain laws that operate in the same way in a good clock or a bad clock, and in the same way in a sick body or a healthy body.

Amplifying on this thought, the Meditator reflects that one difference between mind and body consists in this: a body is always divisible, whereas a mind is indivisible. There are no "parts" of the mind, even if it has different faculties such as willing, understanding, and perceiving.

> By contrast, there is no corporeal or extended thing that I can think of which in my thought I cannot easily divide into parts; and this very fact makes me understand that it is divisible.
> (vii:86)

The human body, then, is multiple, while the mind is a unity. The human body is composed of a brain in the skull, itself quite complex and differentiated, and various limbs, organs and tissues located at some distance from the brain. The limbs are connected to the brain by cord-like nerves. There is "one small part" of the brain that is, in a sense, "adjacent" to the mind. The configuration of that part of the brain determines the experience of the mind by presenting it with certain signals.

By yanking on one end of a cord, I can produce a certain movement at the other end. If we were attached by a cord, I could communicate with someone in another room by yanking on my end, causing her end, the tiny segment of cord directly adjacent to her hand, to twitch and thus presenting her with a signal. Interestingly, I can produce exactly the same twitch and so send the same signal by yanking on the cord, not at its end, but in the middle.

> In similar fashion, when I feel a pain in my foot, physiology tells me
> that this happens by means of nerves distributed throughout the foot,
> and that these nerves are like cords . . . When the nerves are pulled in
> the foot, they in turn pull on inner parts of the brain to which they are
> attached, and produce a certain motion in them: and nature has laid it
> down that this motion should produce in the mind a sensation of pain,
> as occurring in the foot. But . . . it can happen that . . . [if] one of the
> intermediate parts . . . is pulled, the same motion will occur in the brain
> as occurs when the foot is hurt, and so it will necessarily come about that
> the mind feels the same sensation of pain. And we must suppose that the
> same thing happens with regard to any other sensation.
> (vii:87)

Applied to the case of the dropsical patient, a movement of the nerves
that normally originates in the tissues as the result of a lack of water,
and that communicates itself to the brain, can originate somewhere
else when the tissues do not lack water. The movement can even
originate inside the brain. In any case, the creature will feel thirsty.

It should now be clear why some forms of sensory error are virtually inevitable. The need for a physical connector between the "distal"
parts of the body and that part of the brain that is in direct communication with the mind leaves us vulnerable. Without such *connectors*,
the body-machine could not function. The machine must operate,
as a clock does, according to certain laws of nature that cannot be
suspended or adjusted. So God, or God–Nature, had no choice but
to create a machine that is defective in that its sensory experiences
can induce it to behave in ways harmful to it. Yet the machine that is
produced may be the best that can be produced, the one that induces
harmful behavior less than other possible machines do.

Generalizing, we can infer that illness in the sick body does not tes-
tify to its poor overall design, given what it is meant to do. The structure of any machine, including the bodily machine, is constrained by
certain features of the corporeal world, including the fact that bodies
and their parts tend to fall apart, get tangled, develop obstructions,
and run out of supplies. Another feature of the corporeal world is
that we wander around in it and discover new things. Before humans
happened upon alcohol, tobacco, and the opiates, and learned how

to produce, grow, or process them in large quantities, there were no harmful addictions. Strange appetites and harmful addictions develop when well-adapted bodies are presented with new forms of stimulation. Yet just as intellectual and moral errors of judgment are inevitable, given the truth- and goodness-seeking impulses of the mind, and are no cause for either intellectual or moral pessimism, so injuries and illnesses are inevitable, given the complexity of the bodily machine and all that it can accomplish for our benefit. The development of addictions and aberrant tastes is inevitable as well, given the complexity of the world.

We should not be discouraged by our medical and psychological frailty any more than by our epistemological and moral frailty. There is nothing in our constitutions that does not "bear witness to the power and goodness of God." There is no purpose to our frailties, no need to ask what they are for. Indeed, with further investigation, we can hope to come to an understanding of the underlying mechanisms involved and intervene to make adjustments, wherever our weaknesses cause excessive trouble and grief.

2 THE END OF DOUBT (AT VII:89–90)

The Meditator has decided that physiology and medicine are promising areas of inquiry. For her discussion of the communication of motion from the foot to the brain that results in our feeling pain in the foot recognizes that macroscopical and microscopical examination of human and animal anatomy are sources of knowledge. Doubt and confusion in this branch of science can be overcome.

From a formal point of view, the decision to acknowledge a positive role for the senses in empirical inquiry was premature. Perhaps the Meditator should have given an explicit defense of the roles of autopsy and observation in physiological studies, but she hastens to repair the oversight. For she decides on the basis of several quickly assembled considerations, that "I should not have any further fears about the falsity of what the senses tell me every day; on the contrary the exaggerated doubts of the last few days should be dismissed as laughable." Experimental science is thereby vindicated, provided the senses' testimony with respect to investigations into the structure and function of the human body can be considered just as reliable as their

DOUBT   TRUE

FALSE

Various still-undecided empirical and mathematical propositions

I exist
I think
God exists
God is not a deceiver
God's essence implies existence
Clear and distinct thoughts are true
I have a body
Restrain the will!
There are corporeal things external to me
Sensory experience is confused
Sensory experience teaches us what is harmful and what is beneficial
Various metaphysical principles
Clearly and distinctly perceived and previously proved propositions of arithmetic and geometry are true
Propositions of physics, medicine, and astronomy can be known to be true if clearly and distinctly perceived

A malevolent Demon exists and deceives me
My knowledge potential is limited
I have a vapory soul
My mind cannot possibly survive the death of my body
Sensations and perceptions resemble their causes

Figure 29   The Meditator's knowledge-set at the conclusion of *Meditation Six*

testimony in more ordinary contexts. Reasonable, though not total, confidence in our faculties is accordingly supported by the following considerations:

1) The senses are generally to be trusted since they belong to a standardized signaling system.
2) Where a message is unclear or misleading, another sense can be brought to the aid of the first. (Touch, for example, can dispel optical illusions.)
3) My memory must be fairly reliable, for I know that God has not made me a seriously defective epistemological subject.
4) My intellect, when it does not jump to conclusions concerning what it does not perceive clearly and distinctly, is an admirable and trustworthy instrument.

The Meditator's knowledge-condition can now be represented as it is in Figure 29. The category of DOUBT has been transformed. Its old contents have been sorted into what is now known to be TRUE and what is known to be FALSE and new additions introduced. Many individual propositions of physics, medicine, and astronomy, as well as mathematics and metaphysics, remain doubtful and UNDECIDED. Not every proposition that can be framed as a sentence in the language of one of these disciplines is TRUE; most are FALSE. Nevertheless, these branches of science do allow in principle for certain knowledge. Many important and interesting propositions can be known to be TRUE, and the Meditator's discovery in *Meditation Three* that her knowledge-set is potentially as unlimited as God's suggests that these truths are eminently worth pursuing. These results established, the Meditator dismisses the old reasons for uncertainty regarding her ordinary experience. She can be certain that she is not dreaming, on the grounds that "dreams are never linked by memory with all the other actions of life as waking experiences are."

> [W]hen I distinctly see where things come from and where and when they come to me, and when I can connect my perceptions of them with the whole of the rest of my life without a break, then I am quite certain that when I encounter these things I am not asleep but awake. And I ought not to have even the slightest doubt of their reality if, after calling upon all the senses as well as my memory and my intellect in order to check them, I receive no conflicting reports from any of these sources. For from the fact that God is not a deceiver it follow that in cases like these I am completely free from error. But since the pressure of things to be done does not always allow us to stop and make such a meticulous check, it must be admitted that in this human life we are often liable to make mistakes about particular things, and we must acknowledge the weakness of our nature.
>
> (VII:90)

It is appropriate to ask at this stage how far the Meditator has progressed with respect to her original aim of contributing something stable and lasting to one or more of the sciences.

Of course, many empirical propositions belonging to the observational and experimental sciences are still undecided and doubtful. Yet the Meditator has made substantive progress towards understanding the structure of her world and its basic elements and their interactions. She knows that the study of the corporeal world can be approached through the application of mathematics since, essentially, matter is extension, divided into parts and susceptible of motion. The Meditator's earlier thoughts often turned to the sun and the stars, as well as to animals and stones. She now appreciates that nature is a single system that can be conceived as an aspect of God. She knows that Nature is orderly and structured by laws that are backed up by divine omnipotence and by the constancy of God's will. She has acquired a general grasp of the constitution of the body-machine that is common to men and animals, a comprehension of the respective roles of sensation and intellect within the unity they compose in human beings. She now has insight into the causes of illness, error, and moral failing. Even the emotions – which have traditionally been considered as fundamentally irrational and therefore as not worth trying to explain rationally – hold the promise of being fitted into the overall framework of experiences considered as elements of a signaling system. Further, the Meditator has discovered an effective filter, a sorting-procedure that will reliably separate true propositions from false and doubtful opinions. In short, the progress made by the Meditator towards her initial goal of contributing something stable and lasting to the sciences is not negligible. As a finite substance, the somewhat limited range of her thoughts and ideas and her liability to error prevent her from attaining the knowledge-condition of an ideal scientist. Her representation of the world will never approach God's omniscience. Yet her potential for knowledge is unlimited. Provided she continues to seek out new experiences, while at the same time controlling her tendency to embrace the semblance of truth, she can became a possessor of nonobvious truth.

The Meditator's discovery that sensory ideas are elements of a representational system that is geared towards the preservation of the body, contains some important scientific lessons. She realizes, in the course of considering and rejecting the resemblance theory of perception, that just because nothing appears to us in a certain space, it does not mean that nothing is there. The impression of empty space indicates that it is not particularly useful for us to represent space as full of matter for the purposes of getting about and preserving our lives. However, our perceptual experience may not give us the information we need to do everything that it is beneficial to us to do. Micro-entities, lying beneath the threshold of ordinary perception, may turn out to furnish the essential terms of physics and physiology, hence of medicine.

The apparent inadequency of our perceptual apparatus for acquiring such useful knowledge raises the question of God's benevolence and veracity. If knowledge of micro-entities is important for the prolongation of life and the enhancement of our happiness, why has God–Nature given us a sensory system that fails to represent them? Perhaps reality *can* only be grasped through the intellect, since anything we can actually *see* or visualize is only a perceptual effect, or a representation of a perceptual effect, and not reality. Certainly this is one way to understand the significance of the Principle of Intellect Priority (Ch. 3 Sec. 3). In any case, questions concerning the intentions and motives of God lie beyond the limits of our knowledge. The fine anatomy of corporeal things and of the human body, as obscure and hidden as it is, fortunately does not.

It might seem strange that the culmination of the Meditator's inquiry does not appear to be the revelation of an important moral or theological message concerning her purpose and destiny, but the discovery of some details of pathological and normal functioning in her body, including the central role played by her own brain. Were the Withholding Policy and the supposition of the malevolent Demon really necessary to establish these details? Why didn't Descartes just make some anatomical observations and experiments and write up his hypotheses together with the evidence for them?

The Reader who is puzzled by the endpoint of the *Meditations* should pause and reflect on what has been established along the way and the resistance that each point leading up to the final results has met with from the Objectors. Is it right to say that the Meditator has not acquired a deeper understanding of morality and religion? Could these results have been arrived at in a mere ninety or so pages without the Withholding Policy and the Demon?

By the end of *Meditation Six*, Descartes has, through his presentation of the Meditator's careful train of reasonings, sketched the form of a new science of nature, based on the principle that corporeal substance is extended, divisible, and movable, but otherwise devoid of qualities and powers. Meanwhile, he has taken issue with a body of established doctrine, especially the teaching that we would do better to concentrate on the states of our souls than inquire into the mysteries of nature, and that our weaknesses and sufferings are the fault of our knowledge-seeking ancestors Adam and Eve and are irremediable. He has shown that the notion of a soul animating the body, in virtue of which we live, move, and sense, is a confused idea of the mind. At the same time, he has dissociated himself from the doctrines of the materialists and from the disturbing possibilities, of which he is constantly reminded by his critics, that it is the body that thinks, that God is one of its intramental ideas, and that death is necessarily the end of us.

3 OBJECTIONS TO *MEDITATION SIX (III)*

Objector 3, Hobbes, argues that there could be a person who dreamed that he did not know whether he was dreaming or not, and that this dream could include the memory of a long coherent series of past events. So how does the Meditator know at the end of his meditations that he is not dreaming (VII:195)?

Hobbes points out that Descartes seems to hold the view that *only if* the Meditator comes to believe that God exists and is not a deceiver, can he know that his doubts, with their associated memory of a long series of events, are not dreamed. Hobbes says that this implies that an atheist cannot know that he is awake, even if his experience is coherent. Descartes swallows this slightly peculiar conclusion. An atheist, he says, can infer that he is awake because his experience seems coherent, but he cannot know that the coherence criterion supplies him with certainty that he is awake (VII:196).

Gassendi, Objector 5, takes issue with the Meditator's notion that there is a particular part of the brain where the mind meets the body and accepts its messages. There is no point in the brain where all the nerves are observed to meet, he insists (VII:341). Suppose, through, there is a region of the brain where mind and brain meet or communicate. Maybe, Gassendi suggests, the Meditator is just that small, but still extended part of the brain and not an immaterial substance adjacent to it (VII:340). Moreover, since (as he had explained elsewhere) Descartes's theory of voluntary action depends on the mind's being able to alter the flow of "spirits" in the nerves, how could an immaterial mind existing and acting at a point effect this?

> [Y]ou must explain to us how this "directing" of movement can occur
> without some effort – and therefore motion – on your part. How can
> there be effort directed against anything, or motion set up in it, unless
> there is mutual contact between what moves and what is moved? And
> how can there be contact without a body when, as is transparently clear by
> the natural light, "naught apart from body, can touch or yet be touched."
> (VII:341)

Gassendi further wonders how, if corporeal substance is extended
and divisible and mental substance is not, pain can reside in mental
substance, since pain results from dividing and pushing (VII:345).
How can the corporeal communicate with the incorporeal? How can
there be a union of mind and body (VII:344)?

Gassendi also suggests that immortality is more intelligible on a
materialist theory of the soul than on the theory that the soul is
incorporeal. However, a materialist should not expect to retain the
capacity to think after the death of his body:

> [Y]ou can exist without your solid body – just as the vapour with its
> distinctive smell can exist when it passes out of the apple and is dispersed
> into the atmosphere . . . Indeed, supposing you are some corporeal or
> tenuous substance, you would not be said to vanish wholly at your death
> or to pass into nothingness; you would be said to subsist by means of
> your dispersed parts. We would, however, have to say that, because of
> this dispersal, you would not continue to think, or be a thinking thing,
> a mind or a soul.
> (VII:342–3)

Descartes waves these questions about the interaction between
mind and body and their union aside: you are not producing objections to my arguments, he tells Gassendi. You are merely raising
up doubts which "arise from your desire to call in the imagination to
examine matters which are not within its proper province" (VII:390).
The interaction between mind and body, their communication, he
explains elsewhere, is experienced. We can be certain that it occurs,

but it cannot be represented by our imaginations. It is not, he implies, the sort of process that empirical science could explain, since one of the entities involved does not and cannot present itself to the senses.

Descartes irritably insists in the Appendix to the *Fifth Set of Objections* that he does not does not need to address interaction questions, or to disprove Gassendi's rival materialistic hypotheses, for his own arguments to be valid: "The most ignorant people could, in a quarter of an hour, raise more questions of this kind than the wisest men could deal with in a lifetime, and this is why I have not bothered to answer any of them" (IXA:213). In any event, Gassendi's problems arise from what Descartes terms a false supposition, "namely that, if the soul and the body are two substances whose nature is different, this prevents them from being able to act on each other." According to a commonly accepted view, he proposes, heat and weight are "real accidents" that can act on bodies, and there is more difference between accidents and substances, he says, than between substances (IXA:213). So why shouldn't substances act on one another?

His replies to the Sixth Set of Objectors show Descartes trying to make his views about the union of soul and body more graphic and to find analogies that will render the relationship more intelligible.

He explains that he used to think of heaviness, hardness, the power to heat, attract, and purge as real qualities inhering in solid bodies (VII:440–1). In that way, he was, he says, implicitly thinking of these qualities as though they were substances, just as the clothes hung on a man are substances with respect to themselves, but qualities with respect to the man (i.e., his being well dressed, or dressed in red, is a quality of his).

The mind can be seen as a quality of the body (a woman can be said to have a quick or a dull mind) but it is also a substance. And one way to think of the mind is as related to its body more or less as, on his old view, gravity was related to heavy bodies. Gravity, he thought, was not an extended substance. Further, gravity, on his old view, had the interesting property of being coextensive with the heavy body – a piece broken off from a body would have its own gravity – but still acting as though it exercised all its force in one point. This is how he now claims to understand the soul. It is coextensive with the body, but it exercises all its powers with respect to any part you choose (VII:442).

The analogy is none too clear. It is also somewhat peculiar to use a discarded theory of qualities to explain an actual relation. For Descartes insists that his more recent view is that:

> [N]othing whatever belongs to the concept of body except the fact that it is something which has length, breadth and depth, and is capable of various shapes and motions; moreover, these shapes and motions are merely modes which no power whatever can cause to exist apart from body. But colours, smells, tastes and so on, are . . . merely certain sensations which exist in my thought, and are as different from bodies as pain is different from the shape and motion of the weapon which produces it. And . . . heaviness and hardness and the power to heat or attract, or to purge, and all the other qualities which we experience in bodies, consist solely in the motion of bodies, or its absence, and the configuration and situation of their parts.
>
> (VII:440)

Gravity, he came to see, could not be a tendency of a body to move to the center, since no object without a mind could know where the center was or intend to move towards it (VII:442). So heaviness has to be explained in some other way – as it turns out, by the pressure of circumambient bodies.

Gassendi's view that Descartes's treatment of the unity of mind and body is unsatisfactory is shared by many commentators. Descartes is often criticized for having driven a wedge between mind and body so completely that they cannot be brought together again. How egregious, though, is Descartes's fault in this regard?

Descartes's view is that we are confused when we think of ourselves as minds intermingled with a body, or as bodies with particular intellectual capacities, just as we are confused when we suppose that there is redness in the rose or whiteness in chalk. We experience the unity of mind and body. Ignoring Descartes's misguided attempt to understand the soul on analogy with gravity, or weight, we might add that this experience does not correspond to a phenomenon of the outer physical world. We cannot give a theoretical account of it, for we have no theoretical models available for this purpose.

Our theoretical models of composites are derived chiefly from our experience with material objects of various sorts. Two metals can be amalgamated or fused, wood can be cemented to glass, a perfume can pervade a room, and numerous ingredients can be blended in a batter. Two substances with no properties in common, however, cannot be amalgamated, fused, cemented, or dispersed through one another. The visual imagination and our recollections of experiences with corporeal substance are not useful in understanding the union and interaction of mind and body, or, for that matter, God and the world.

This granted, we might look for models of unity and interaction in another familiar realm: mind-to-mind relationships. The relationship of God to the world is sometimes conceived in this manner: God is said to command, for example, and creatures in the world to hearken and obey or disobey. In other contexts, God and the world are said to be related by mutual affection, with concern on one side and gratitude on the other. The view that affection can create imaginary wholes out of two things is advanced by Descartes in his treatise on the emotions, the *Passions of the Soul*:

> Love is an emotion of the soul . . . which impels the soul to join itself willingly to objects that appear to be agreeable to it . . . in using the word "willingly," I am not speaking of desire, which is a completely separate passion relating to the future. I mean rather the assent by which we consider ourselves henceforth as joined with what we love in such a manner that we imagine a whole, of which we take ourselves to be only one part, and the thing loved to be the other.
> (xi:387–8)

It was conventional in the Renaissance to describe the relationship of the soul to the body as one of love. Did Descartes have affectionate partnership in mind as a model for mind–body unity? There are hints of this view in his suggestion that we regard our bodies with solicitude and benevolence and do not merely appreciate intellectually when they are wounded or in need, but feel the most distressing sensations. Mind and body have a kind of partnership, and, as we saw (Ch. 10 Sec. 2), there are good reasons for the mind to rejoice in the existence of a body to which it is united, since, without the visual imagination, it cannot engage in its favored intellectual activities, including mathematics and science. Perhaps – though the Meditator does not enlighten us on this point – consciousness, reason, and language, the characteristics that animals lack and that we possess in virtue of having incorporeal souls, make some reciprocal contribution to the human body's well-being.

However, models of mind–body unification deriving from mind–mind relationships are unsatisfactory as well. The emotion of love has to be explained, according to Descartes, as "caused by a movement of [bodily] spirits" as this is registered by the soul. While certain sensations caused by the flow of nervous fluids and their effects on our brains doubtless underlie and give rise to our feelings of embodiment, and while these sensations perhaps arise in order to signal to us the usefulness of our bodies to us, we cannot construct a theoretical account of the unity of mind and body on the basis of mutual affection and need arising between body and soul.

Descartes's considered view was that the unity of mind and body was not a phenomenon in the physical world of the sort that natural philosophy could explain. The accusation that he had not explained it was, accordingly, in his view, hollow. He had discovered, he thought, the essential nature of the mind, the essential nature of corporeal substance, and the basic organization of living bodies. He had advanced, in other words, the true theories of mind and body, and the true theory of the animal body. There could, however, be no true theory of human mind–body unity and it would be lost labor to inquire after one.

CHAPTER 12

Descartes in context

I THE ENIGMA OF THE *MEDITATIONS*

Descartes's intellectual activities, including his researches in mathematics, optics, and anatomy, and his publication of three scientific *Essays* and the *Discourse on Method* in 1637 have been described in the Introduction. Why did the *Meditations*, a hundred-page treatise on metaphysics and epistemology appear four years later and what can be concluded from Descartes's manner of presenting it to the world?

In the *Meditations*, doubt and subjectivity are taken to their logical limits to yield, not uncertainty and relativism, but truth and objectivity. The argument begins with the single hypothesis propounded by the Meditator: "A malevolent Demon is thoroughly deceiving me." As in a mathematical *reductio ad absurdum* proof, the hypothesis is shown to be false; it contains a hidden contradiction – if I am deceived, I exist, and if I exist, God exists and is not a deceiver. Considered as a thought experiment, Descartes's procedure discloses important features of reality by artificially forcing the natural way of thinking out of its usual patterns. But why did Descartes decide to take up such abstract questions as the nature and existence of God and the nature of material and mental substance? Why does he employ such scholastic terminology as "formal and eminent causes," "essence" and "existence," as though he were writing to appeal to a traditional university audience when the structure of his argument is so novel? To answer these questions as well as to give an account of the *Meditations*, it will be useful to explore further some features of Descartes's intellectual context.

Expressions of dissatisfaction with the accomplishments of ancient philosophers and naturalists were becoming commonplace in the first quarter of the seventeenth century. A number of Descartes's contemporaries, including Johann Baptiste Van Helmont and Francis Bacon, declared their contempt for the scholastic natural philosophy that was a blend of Aristotelianism and medieval Christian theology, and for Aristotelian ontology and logic. Yet Bacon's program for the renewal and completion of the sciences was synthetic: it was to involve the work of many hands guided by the prescriptions of his method. Bacon advocated the systematic recording and comparison of the results of physical experiments which, he said, would, lead inquirers to the "forms," the underlying arrangements of the hidden parts of bodies that, together with the "spirits" permeating bodies, accounted for their properties and powers. Helmont favored a mixture of experimentation and mystical intuition into the inner guiding principles of natural things.

Descartes's starting point was different from that of these two hopeful renewers of natural philosophy. Unlike Bacon, he was convinced of the necessary unity and integrity of creative intelligence. He saw in architecture and city planning the difficulty of making any significant advance when one had to accept as given, and to work on, the constructions of others. He tried to imagine how the sciences would look if, instead of representing compromises and accommodations, they issued from a single mind which took full responsibility for them and had full control. Although Descartes had no more esteem than Helmont for the Aristotelian syllogism, he was not hostile to abstraction and formalism. Descartes loved mathematics and he saw the possibility of an analogy between proof in mathematics and proof in metaphysics and in the sciences: a proof was a long series of statements, each of which could be derived from the last by clear and indubitable, not mystical, intuition.

It will be recalled that Descartes decided to withhold the two short treatises of natural philosophy written around 1630, later published as *The World*, or the *Treatise of Light*, and the *Treatise of Man*. There are a number of ideas of particular importance in these earlier writings. In the *Treatise of Light*, Descartes distinguishes between the experience of light and the physical cause of the experience of light, and between the world as it appears to our eyes, as composed of different objects of characteristic shapes, sizes, colors, and consistencies, and the physical world as it exists in itself, "a real, perfectly solid body

which uniformly fills the entire length breadth, and depth of . . .
space" (XI:33) that was subsequently divided into parts and ultimately
into particles. Space is entirely filled with subtle matter – if there
were a void anywhere, the light of the distant stars would not reach
our eyes since the transmission of light, though it does not imply
the movement of particles from the stars to our eyes, depends on the
transmission of an impulse through a medium.

The World and the *Treatise of Man* were not creationist accounts
of the formation of the cosmos and its inhabitants, at least not in the
usual sense. Descartes suggested that the stars and planets were not
made by God but simply emerged from an initial chaos of matter in
motion. Though he described the human body as a machine made by
God, he insisted that it too was entirely material. One of Descartes's
first coherent philosophical ideas did not concern God or the human
mind. It was the thought that animals did not have souls and did not
have thoughts and experiences as we do. Neither animal warmth and
motion, nor the manifestations of intention, affection, and cunning
in animals, nor their ability to reproduce, pointed to the existence
of a soul or a principle of vitality. Confronting directly the scholastic philosophy of substances and powers that represented nature as
teeming with vital and architectonic principles, that formed, maintained, and repaired plant and animal bodies, Descartes portrayed
matter as lifeless and inert and argued that there was no intelligence,
intention, or awareness in non-human nature. Animals were like the
moving figures on cleverly contrived clocks – indeed, they were like
clocks. They reacted automatically to sensory signals – for example
patterns of light falling on their retinas. The human body was also an
automatic machine, so that, in a sense, humans as well were no more
alive than clocks. However, Descartes stated, humans were endowed
by divine fiat with minds, in virtue of which they were conscious,
able to use and understand language and to reason abstractly.

The arrest and confinement of Galileo in 1632 is alleged to
be the cause for Descartes's suppression of his two early treatises.
Galileo had ridiculed Aristotelian cosmology and had defended the
Copernican view that the Earth was an ordinary planet circling
the sun along with the rest, in his *Dialogue Concerning the Two
Chief World Systems*. He had also argued that sensory qualities result from the interaction between our minds and the minute particles

composing material objects, advancing a doctrine directly at odds with the Christian–Aristotelian philosophy of substances. Descartes, as a Copernican, had reason to be wary. His two treatises are even more forthright in their materialistic commitments and less favorable to the Christian dogmas of creation and transubstantiation than Galileo's writings.

Unlike the classical atomism that is the basis of the atheistic work of Titus Carus Lucretius, *De Rerum Natura*, Descartes's corpuscularianism does not posit indivisible units of matter, or conceive individual atoms as tumbling about, aggregating, colliding, and separating in a void. Cartesian physics is based on the notion of a *plenum* – matter does not so much fill empty space as constitute the extended universe – and on the imposition of *laws* of nature describing the regular behavior of portions of matter in motion. Though, according to Descartes's later exposition, God had created matter, divided it (or allowed it to abrade) into three grades of corpuscle, and established (or allowed to form) numerous celestial "vortices" or systems of whirling ethereal matter carrying planets around their suns, He had not intervened thereafter. Impulses are transmitted through the plenum as an impulse is transmitted when a rope is snapped. Hence the stars do not waste away by emitting luminous matter, and it is only an impulse in the "nervous fluid" and not the fluid itself that travels from the periphery to the brain and vice-versa in animal sensation and motion. Otherwise, Descartes's system closely resembles that of the ancient materialists who claimed that there were only atoms and the void, that there were many worlds, that the soul was material and mortal, and that there was no supervisory Providence.

Whether or not *The World* ever left his hands, we know that a version of Descartes's *Treatise of Man* was shown to a few close friends. In the late 1630s, Descartes came into contact with Henry Regius, a philosopher and theorist of medicine. Regius propounded an interpretation of Cartesianism as simple materialism and thereby unleashed aggressive disputes and political turmoil at the University of Utrecht, for Protestant theologians controlled the Dutch universities just as Catholic theologians controlled the French. Related disputes, to Descartes's dismay, later broke out in Leyden and other Dutch universities over whether the Cartesian theory of the physical world was dangerous, un-Christian, and unsound.

Descartes's reputation in France was not improved by his publication of his *Essays* and the *Discourse*. In a letter of 1642 to his former teacher, the Jesuit Father Dinet (vii:563–603), a man whom he believed to possess considerable influence in the Church's hierarchy, Descartes expresses his worries over the new "system of philosophy" he plans to publish. The "system of philosophy" in question was that of the soon-to-be-published *Principles of Philosophy*, a greatly expanded version of *The World* and the *Treatise of Man*. The *Principles* would offer a comprehensive treatment of physics, cosmology, terrestrial phenomena, sensory physiology, and mental and physical health, covering some 325 printed pages. He was anxious as to the reception of the *Principles* in a climate of what he refers to as "the envy and hostility of others." In the letter to Dinet, he explains that, while the reception of his essays by those few persons intelligent enough to understand them was very favorable, a minority – more precisely, those who had "mastered the technique of acrimonious debate over scholastic controversies" – was threatened by them and "seethed with hatred towards me": "These people were afraid that once the truth was discovered . . . their own speciality would become wholly despised" (vii:576). What was the basis of the earlier reaction to the *Essays* and how did Descartes propose to avoid unleashing it again with the *Principles*? Descartes's Letter helps us to understand how he intended the *Meditations* to clarify his theological position and defuse hostility.

First, as he points out, the system he proposes to lay out in its entirety is the work of one man. Descartes tried to answer with little reference to past authority the questions what the fundamental physical elements of nature are and what principles of action are needed to explain planetary motions, the weather, the heat and light of the sun, why the sea is salty, how animals come to be born, how we see, smell, taste, and feel, and how to be virtuous. The system that answered these questions was a departure from the "opinions commonly accepted in the Schools," based on Aristotle's and Plato's writings, and the theology and moral philosophy of the Church Fathers, amplified by many generations of commentary. Descartes admits that "It may hardly seem likely that one person has managed to see more than hundreds of thousands of highly intelligent men" (vii:578–9).

Second, Descartes knew that his system resembled that of the atheistic materialists, Epicurus and Lucretius. In the *Principles*, while reassuring his readers that "there is no doubt that the world was created right from the start with all the perfection it now has," with the sun, moon, stars, and living plants and with Adam and Eve "created as fully grown people," he ventures that "if we want to understand the nature of plants or of men, it is much better to consider how they can gradually grow from seeds than to consider how they were created by God at the beginning of the world" (IXB 99-100). Though the ancient atomists had allowed some vague existence to the gods – happy immortal beings existing somewhere else in the cosmos – they intimated at the same time that the gods were dreamed or hallucinated, or that they had only ideational reality: that they were, as we would say today, "social constructions." Certainly, they allowed them no role in creation or supervision and were hostile to what they considered to be religious superstition. They too described the origin of plants, animals, and men in atomic "seeds" and denied the immortality of the soul. Since every individual was fated to die, consolation was to be found in the expectation that the cycle of generations would continue to renew the world and that each animal would play its part as lover and as parent. They gave pleasure, though not wild self-indulgence, a central role in their ethics. Some Epicureans in Paris in the first quarter of the seventeenth century, however, took the advice to seize the day to degenerate levels. Even if such excesses could be contained, Descartes had to allow that "some people maintain that the new philosophy should be prohibited and suppressed at the earliest opportunity, in case it should attract large numbers of inexperienced people who are avid for novelty, and thus gradually spread and gain momentum, disturbing the peace and tranquility of the Schools and universities and even bringing new heresies into the Church" (VII:579).

We now come to the *Meditations*. They were written, Descartes tell us in his Preface, for the Doctors of the Sorbonne, the University of Paris, at the urging of his friends, and intended to fulfill the injunction of Pope Leo X and the Fifth Lateran Council. The Pope had insisted that philosophers should not ignore or set aside the dogmas of the Christian religion, but devote their efforts to proving them. Descartes's readiness to assume this task was hardly disinterested.

We can infer his motivations from the content and structure of the *Meditations*, as well as from his correspondence and the overall pattern of his publications. He wrote, circulated, and published the *Meditations* in the hope that they would secure a good reception for the long-suppressed system of natural philosophy that he wished to bring out. It was to address the ambient alarm and hostility that he had aroused amongst Catholics and Protestants alike and to settle his official position with respect to atheism and materialism that Descartes took the trouble to perfect their elegant architecture. The letter to Father Dinet indicates that the reaction he received from the Objectors was not precisely what he had hoped.

Descartes's task, it must have seemed to him as he embarked on the writing of the *Meditations*, was clearly defined and fell into two parts. He had to convince Parisian readers – and most especially the clerics who controlled the curricula of the Sorbonne – that his system of the physical world was solidly founded and distinctly superior to the supposed knowledge sifted and synthetically pasted together from all the authorities. He had to persuade them that only the pettiest, most anti-intellectual motives could prompt resistance. Second, he had to convince them that his philosophy was not only true but innocuous with respect to theology and morality. This meant showing that his system was consistent with two central doctrines. These were: the existence of an omnipotent and benevolent God and the immortality of the human soul. In the Dedicatory Letter, he states that his chief purpose in writing the *Meditations* is to show that these two theses need not merely be accepted on faith: both are capable of being demonstrated to be true.

A number of other background conditions are relevant to the interpretation of the work.

Skepticism about the reach of the empirical sciences – physics, mathematics, physiology, medicine – perturbed seventeenth-century philosophers. Could there be effective knowledge of nature? How could mere humans – afflicted by the corruption of their faculties after the Fall – presume to understand the workings of the heavens, the composition of the stars and planets, the mysterious agency of the "vital soul" in the body that kept it warm and active, the puzzle of the generation of animals from their parents? The *Essays* of Montaigne bemoaned the fact that human nature was shifting and inconstant and concluded that even knowledge of oneself was impossible, since one changed in tastes and habits from year to year and even from day to day. The reality of sorcery and witchcraft were much debated. Travelers' tales of strange plants and animals and exotic cultures in distant places increased and strained credulity at the same time. Interminable religious conflict between Catholics and Protestants over narrow points of doctrine and procedure caused reflective people to wonder whether rational theology was to be preferred to irrational faith and what exactly was at stake in being right. With the recovery of pagan texts of great philosophical sophistication, some wondered whether there was a truth to religion at all.

Meanwhile, many theologians insisted that inquiry into nature was not a worthy or even a permissible activity, especially not when knowledge of nature was associated with power over nature. St. Augustine had portrayed the close observation of nature as wrongly diverting the mind from the contemplation of the only truly worthy object – God. Preoccupation with "things of the world" – whether other human beings or material goods – had been castigated by the most influential Christian writers. Further, if nature was ordered and supervised by God, the application of technology could be considered an affront, as attempted interference with God's plans. Technology was still associated with magic and the demonic.

The *Meditations* were intended to show that it could be rationally demonstrated by philosophers that God existed and that the soul was immortal. Descartes shows that inquiry into nature is not futile and brings definite results, that scientific research is morally permissible, and that a form of genuinely Christian research is possible.

In the *Meditations*, Descartes shows that inquiry into nature can be pursued. For nature is just extended substance. It contains no mysterious forces or powers that cannot be explicated in terms of the size, shape, and motion of bodies. There are no souls in nature except the human soul, so life is not, in principle, a mystery. Our access to the constitution and workings of the material world requires the use of the intellect. Our intellects cannot be fatally flawed, since we are creatures of a benevolent God, and provided we use our intellects in the proper cautious and critical spirit, we will not go wrong.

Further, Descartes shows that inquiry into nature is permissible. Technology does not interfere with God's plans, since God ordains the laws of nature, which apply to the motions and interactions of bits of corporeal substance, not particular effects. To heal a sick person is not to interfere with God's plans anymore than repairing a broken clock constitutes interference with them. Because there are no souls in material things, the transformation of nature cannot possibly involve trafficking with demons.

Finally, Descartes attempts to show that it is possible to be a scientist without being an atheist. The same train of reasoning that reveals that corporeal things are not mere ideas of a thinking subject also reveals along the way that God is not a mere idea, or a social construction. Further, according to Descartes, one cannot be a confident scientist without being a believer, since one will not have the same level of trust in one's perceptions and demonstrations. As well, the science one arrives at will not have the character of the science of the atomists. One knows oneself to be investigating the order of things laid down by a supremely powerful and benevolent God. The atomists propounded explanatory hypotheses based on the action of unobservable particles. This was creditable, but they did not understand the lawfulness of nature or its dependence on the sustaining power of God. Moreover, the sensuality of their writing – their focus on the color and texture of corporeal objects and their fascination with the generative powers of nature – reveals the superficial character of their investigations. Aestheticism, as Descartes's treatment of the "piece of wax" shows, has no place in scientific inquiry. The mortalism of the atomists, finally, was based in their erroneous assumption that the soul of a human being was composed of subtle matter or fine particles, and no modern scientist, in Descartes's view, has reason to adopt this position.

2 SOME REACTIONS TO CARTESIANISM

The *Meditations*, then, attempted to legitimate the enterprise Descartes had begun earlier without proper foundations – that is, without settling the issues of the possibility, permissibility, and moral–theological acceptability of the acquisition and application of knowledge of nature. This legitimation could not be entirely successful, however. Descartes's new system rejected too many precious doctrines, or at least failed to assert them in strong and unambiguous language. The Objectors – not only Gassendi, but Hobbes, Mersenne, and the Sixth Set of Objectors – constantly refer to materialism and to the doctrine that thinking is a motion in the brain as rival hypotheses. Whether they are sympathetic to Epicureanism or not, they claim to be unconvinced that Descartes has succeeded in proving that the human soul is an immaterial substance. Recognizing that Descartes has effectively denied that there are any souls, considered as principles of life, they wonder how his nominal identification of the human soul with the mind can support hopes and sustain fears of the life to come. They are mostly unconvinced that Descartes's various arguments for the existence of God show that God is more than an idea in our minds.

In short, Descartes's critics were puzzled and suspicious. God, as Descartes conceives Him in the *Meditations*, plays no part in the affairs of the world, neither watching over his creatures, nor supplying their particular needs. Our world was not, in his scheme, like a city governed by a wise ruler who knew his subjects, and whose rewards and penalties upheld good conduct amongst the citizenry. God's governance consisted in his upholding the laws of nature and assuring the continuing existence of substances, material and mental. This sort of God could hardly be supposed to be interested in the deeds of individual humans, and it was difficult to suppose him concerned with their rewards and punishments after death when he took no notice of them in life. Was it not more consistent with what Descartes was rumored to think, and with the tenor of the *Essays*, that humans did not have immaterial souls and that thinking and awareness were simply performed by the bodily machine?

Descartes tried to assuage his critics' concerns. He insisted on the sincerity of his convictions in many of his contributions to the *Objections and Replies*. Despite his efforts, his critics found much to complain of in his theology.

First, the relationship Descartes posited between God and the world could not satisfy theologians. God seemed both to do too much – He sustained the world in existence from instant to instant, through a process of continuous creation – and too little – He laid down the laws of nature and perhaps fabricated the bodily machines of animals, but did nothing further. Prayer, therefore, would seem to be useless. Recovery from an illness could only be brought about

through the ordinary course of nature or through human technolog-
ical intervention. Descartes supplied no reason to identify God with
the Christian God, the Father of Jesus Christ. He did not – as several
critics pointed out – really try to prove the immortality of the soul,
only to show that it was not impossible. Further, since the articles of
the specifically Christian faith were filled with mysteries and obscurities – not only the Resurrection, but Transubstantiation, and the
Trinity – that could never be understood clearly and distinctly, and
with miracles that contravened the laws of nature, it was not difficult
to infer that Descartes was urging readers not to believe them, or at
least not to regard them as true in the same way that his physical
theory was to be regarded as true.

Second, Descartes's account of sensation and experience was con-
fusing. In *Meditation Two* the Meditator finds herself convinced that
she is having conscious experiences of seeming to see, hear, feel, etc.,
whether or not she has a body. It is unclear whether Descartes thought
that the account of experience as resulting from the union of mind
and body he gave in *Meditation Six* invalidated this perception, showing it to be not clear and distinct after all. Did the Meditator discover
that, although her mind can exist apart from her body, she cannot
have visual, auditory, tactual, olfactory, etc., ideas without a body? If
so, is immortality really such a desirable state, given that we will be
deprived of all sensory experience and, what's more, of all memories
of our previous sensory experience? On a darker note, can one punish a creature for its sins if it has no memory of its previous sensory
experience?

Third, the method to be pursued in acquiring knowledge of nature was not spelled out sufficiently clearly or convincingly to satisfy
Descartes's scientifically minded critics. The doctrine that corporeal
substance was better known by the intellect than by the senses did
not seem conducive to the attainment of precise knowledge in the sciences. If the qualities and powers of wax – its stickiness when melted,
its ability to preserve objects embedded within it – are not essential to
it, and if wax is essentially extended substance, then it is essentially no
different from bread. Indeed, it follows that all substances are essentially the same. This view does not seem to provide a good foundation
for an effective knowledge of chemistry. How should the intellect
go about discovering the causes and cures of diseases, the efficacy

of drugs? Since experiments are judged experientially, the doctrine that sensory experience does not represent to us the world as it really is seems to undercut the possibility of experimental knowledge of nature.

Fourth, the problem of the interaction between different substances was waved away by Descartes, who said that he was not required to offer an explanation for how voluntary motion or sensation could take place and what the nature of the mind–body interface was. The problem of mind–body interaction was echoed in the problem of God–world interaction: how could those two substances interact? What was the nature of their interface?

Cartesianism accordingly raised new questions it could not answer to the satisfaction of its critics. It was vulnerable at a number of points and many of the systems of Descartes's successors are developed around these problems, insoluble within the ontological and epistemological constraints of Descartes's own theory. Descartes had to concede to his critics that his arguments for the immateriality of the soul did not really establish its immortality. He failed, moreover, to prevent the most serious attack on his doctrine of the immateriality of the soul – the criticisms of Pierre Gassendi – from appearing with the rest. To Descartes's great annoyance, these criticisms – along with the Gassendist attack on his physics as "imaginary and fictitious" – remained attached to the published versions of the trio of *Meditations*, *Objections*, and *Replies*.

3 RECEPTION AND REPERCUSSIONS OF CARTESIAN DOCTRINE IN SEVENTEENTH- AND EIGHTEENTH-CENTURY PHILOSOPHY

Though after Descartes's death, the *Meditations* were placed on the Catholic Church's Index of Prohibited Books, they did help to smooth the way for the acceptance of his physical theory in the late seventeenth and early eighteenth century, especially in France. In England, Descartes fared less well. He was attacked not only by those more sympathetic to Bacon and Gassendi, like Locke, but also by the Cambridge Platonists, who rejected his mechanism, and by Isaac Newton, whose theory of universal gravitation built on Cartesian physics but discredited Cartesian vortices. It is nevertheless fair to say that most major philosophers of the seventeenth and eighteenth centuries were occupied intensively with Cartesian materials.

The paths of influence and reaction are multiple. We can distinguish a current of idealism in the history of modern philosophy, which leads through Malebranche's and Leibniz's metaphysics to certain themes in Kant and Hegel. But there was also a materialist version of Cartesianism that influenced La Mettrie, who pretended to scorn Descartes, and the French *philosophes*. Some positive and negative reactions to his philosophy are sketched below for the benefit of readers interested in Descartes's influence on his immediate successors.

Baruch Spinoza (1632–1677)

Spinoza fastened his attention on Descartes's claim that there were three kinds of substance, God, corporeal substance, and each individual human mind, realizing that there were apparent contradictions in his treatment. While Descartes characterizes substance as "a thing capable of existing independently," he seems at the same time to deny that matter or our minds can exist without God. God, for Descartes, is the only substance that is self-caused and self-sustaining: "I . . . readily admit that there can exist something which possesses such great and inexhaustible power that it never required the assistance of anything else in order to exist in the first place, and does not now require any assistance for its preservation, so that it is, in a sense, its own cause, and I understand God to be such a being" (VII:109). Further, Descartes conceived substances as related to one another and interacting as follows:

1) God *created* corporeal substance and *creates* each individual human mind

2) Minds *cause motion in* corporeal substance through the exercise of their wills

3) Corporeal substances and God *cause sensations and ideas* in minds

4) God *sustains* the laws of nature followed by corporeal substance through His will

5) God *sustains* the continuing existence of minds through His will.

Spinoza appreciated that Descartes implicitly, though not openly, denied the following interactive thesis:

6) God *confers benefits and punishments* on individual persons after death, and perhaps in life as well.

He was also doubtless aware both of Descartes's identification of God and Nature in *Meditation Six* and of his remarkable statement that "this entire universe can be said to be an entity originating in God's thought, that is, an entity created by a single act of the divine mind" (VII:134).

Spinoza approved of Descartes's presentation of the world as a vast machine whose operations were dictated by the laws of nature, and of human bodies as machines within that larger machine. However, he found the interactive theses (1)–(5) no more credible than interactive thesis (6). If a substance is truly self-sufficient, he reasoned, there cannot be more than one infinite substance and there cannot be both an infinite substance and some number of finite substances in the same totality. For if something is not self-sufficient and capable of existing without the assistance and support of another thing, it cannot be a substance. Descartes's three-substance system is incoherent; for, insofar as matter and individual minds depend for their original and continuing existence on God, they cannot be true substances. If there were two self-sufficient, non-interacting substances in the universe – for example God and matter – each would have to be understood as limiting the other. In that case, though, neither would be truly self-sufficient; its perfection, comprehensiveness, or independence would be affected by the existence of the other. Therefore, God, who alone is self-sufficient and infinite, must embrace the totality of substance.

How, one might wonder, can the existence of a material world, the ordinary course of nature, and our voluntary motions and sensations be explained if there is only one substance and It is divine? For surely these phenomena are not illusory. Spinoza's solution was to assert that the phenomena in question do not require the interaction of substances. They are, in effect, appearances of a single underlying substance. God is not a being over and above the world, and the mind is not a being over and above the body. Each is the other. Echoing the Sixth Set of Objectors, Spinoza pointed out that we do not know what can be done by bodies by way of producing the aspects of mentality. Since God and the human mind cannot be distinct substances, individual creatures have to be recognized as modes of the single divine (and at the same time natural) substance.

Spinoza inferred that free-will was an illusion. Together with his denial of reward and punishment in the afterlife, this left him with the problem of explaining and motivating morality and human aspiration. His chief work, the *Ethics*, is devoted to the solution of that problem and the description of an ethical life in a mechanistic universe in which God and Nature are not distinguished, and in which the terms "good" and "evil" refer to perceptions of things and events from an "interested" human, not from an objective, perspective. Despite his view that it makes no sense to speak of what is objectively good and objectively evil and his insistence that God has no anthropomorphic attributes, Spinoza is often considered a religious philosopher. He echoes the thought expressed by Descartes at the end of *Meditation Three*: intellectual love of God brings the greatest joy of which humans are capable.

John Locke (1632–1704)

Locke, an approving reader of Gassendi, expressed skepticism over the hypothesis of the immaterial soul. Like Gassendi, he insisted that we have no clear idea of "substance" other than as an "I-know-not-what" – a prop for qualities, something assumed to underlie and support them (Ch. 3 Sec. 4). Our personal identity and persistence as subjects, Locke thought, are not to be explained by the indestructibility of our mental substance. Our consciousness of being "selves" depends upon our memories of past events and our present self-awareness. Being a thinking, self-aware entity was consistent, Locke hinted, with materialism. He argued in Book IV of his *Essay Concerning Human Understanding* that it was conceivable that God had implanted in suitably organized material bodies the power to think, without implanting immaterial souls in them. If that was the case, then there was no interaction problem, though it was then difficult to say in what free will consisted. Locke suggested that freedom could be understood situationally, as a lack of external constraint on what one wanted to do, or else psychologically, as associated with the familiar experience of moving oneself by one's own power.

Where scientific knowledge was concerned, Locke agreed with the Cartesians that qualities such as color, taste, and odor resulted from the action of particles endowed with only "bulk, figure, number, situation, and motion upon sensitive observers." He termed the latter "primary qualities" of body and the former "secondary qualities." "Tertiary qualities," such as the power of the sun to blanch linen, should also, he thought, be referred to the primary qualities of bodies, which belong to bodies themselves. Human eyes, however, even with the help of microscopes, could probably never perceive the smallest parts of bodies upon which their qualities depended. Locke thought that only experiments on and observation of macroscopic objects could generate knowledge outside of pure mathematics and that scientific certainty was an unattainable ideal. We could attain practical efficacious knowledge in chemistry and medicine by trial and error and careful recording of the results. It was impossible, however, that we should ever come to understand the qualities and powers of particular substances in terms of the magnitude, figure, and motion of the subvisible particles of which they were composed. While hypotheses concerning their contribution to observed effects could be framed, it was not profitable, in his view, to emulate Descartes in doing so. Locke appreciated the promise of mathematical physics in the form of Newton's theory of gravitation, but he seemed to regard it as an isolated discovery, not as a model scientific result.

Nicole Malebranche (1638–1715)

Devout Father Malebranche was enchanted with Descartes's description of the animal and human body as a machine and fascinated by the details of Descartes's optics and theory of vision, which he built on and extended. Like other philosophers, he was perturbed by the interaction problem, and he perceived that Descartes had not satisfied his theological critics.

Dealing with both problems at once, Malebranche denied that either mind and body or body and body can interact. Rather, events in one entity are "occasional causes" of events in another. God is the only agent with causal powers. Humans can initiate volitions, but they cannot move matter – not even the limbs of their own bodies – with their minds. God co-ordinates sensory experiences with brain-states and states of the external world, and volitions and brain-states with bodily movements. God also produces the illusion of causal interaction amongst material objects by recreating the universe in a slightly different configuration at each instant. The doctrine of continuous creation – revived by Descartes in *Meditation Three* – was originally a feature of medieval Islamic theology and philosophy.

Malebranche dealt extensively with the problem of evil along the lines laid out in *Meditation Six*, in which Descartes explains why human illness is not inconsistent with the perfection of the bodily machine. God is a supremely benevolent being, yet the world shows us misfortune and disaster. Evil can only be understood as a by-product of the laws of nature. God has willed to create the best system He can in terms of the production of a variety of effects from simple, universal laws of nature. The perfection of the system as a whole engenders and deserves our admiration, but particular events are not always perceived as gratifying from the subjective perspective of individual humans.

Gottfried Wilhelm Leibniz (1646–1716)

Like Malebranche, Leibniz thought that Descartes's substance theory raised a problem of interaction without securing as a conclusion the immortality of the soul. He found the Cartesian claim that animals had no conscious experiences and that there was a sharp divide in this respect between animals and humans highly implausible. At the same time, he rejected Spinoza's claim that there was only one substance as having the horrifying implication that human beings were only "modes" of that substance and hence only semi-real.

Leibniz's definitive view of substance is hard to pin down, but one interpretation of his ontology, as presented, for example, in his *Monadology*, is this: there is an infinite number of substances, each of which could exist without any of the others. They are like the indivisible corpuscles of the atomists, except that they are incorporeal and no two are alike. Each substance (which he later termed a "monad") is an incorporeal mind that contains from its creation all the experiences it will ever have. The monads constitute a series graded according to their power and knowledge with God's mind at the top of the hierarchy and less perfect minds below. What we call "bodies" or "material objects" are appearances founded on incorporeal monads, rather than on material atoms. There is no free will in the sense of an influence of the mind on the body. Yet the monads are "spontaneous": their experiences unfold from their own depths, without being triggered by external causes. Minds do not interact with bodies, or with one another, but the experiences of each are co-ordinated with the experiences of each of the others. Animals have perception and appetite, as do plants; and even a seemingly inert object like a rock is teeming with (and perhaps made up of) smaller living creatures, each of which has at least a rudimentary capacity for perception and appetite.

Leibniz thought that a mechanistic physical science of bodies (which were in a sense only appearances) was possible and much needed. He denied, however, that extended substance and its motions furnished an adequate conceptual foundation. He argued that, despite its obscurities, *force* had to be acknowledged as a central term in physics, and that it could only be understood on analogy with the appetites and strivings observed in living creatures. God's goodness, he thought, following Malebranche, could be inferred from the order and beauty of the world, and especially from an appreciation of the laws of nature, and was not put in question by human suffering. Suspicious with regard to Descartes's religious sincerity, he insisted that the Cartesian universe was as ethically neutral as Spinoza's and denied that the Cartesian God could be considered not only powerful but also intelligent and benevolent. Though his solution to the problem of evil, like Malebranche's, is not unlike Descartes's own, his insistence against Descartes that we can have insight into God's intentions and purposes supports his distinctive philosophical optimism. Though he agreed that God establishes once for all an unchangeable order, Leibniz insists against Descartes that God is responsive to goodness, that He has a distinct preference for objectively better states of affairs, and that His creative activity always has a purpose that humans can, in many cases, come to understand.

George Berkeley (1685–1753)

Berkeley, an Anglican Bishop, was repelled by the corpuscularian hypothesis shared by the majority of his immediate predecessors. Unlike Leibniz and Malebranche, he did not try to reconcile the hypothesis with religious faith and Christian ethics. He insisted in his early writings that corpuscularianism could not be purified of its Epicurean implications of atheism and mortalism. Beginning from the standpoint of Cartesian subjectivity, Berkeley argued in the *Three Dialogues between Hylas and Philonous* and the *Principles of Philosophy* that matter – corporeal substance – does not exist. There are only minds, human and divine, and their perceptual ideas. To be is to be perceived: *esse est percipi*. To acquire knowledge is to acquire new beliefs and expectations concerning the relationship of perceptual ideas, namely, beliefs and expectations about which perceptions accompany or follow others, or exclude them. Locke, Berkeley thought, was wrong to suggest that nature cannot really be known because we have no access to the primary qualities of bodies on which all their perceptible qualities and actions depend. Skeptical views like Locke's were dangerous, according to Berkeley, for if skepticism about our knowledge of material objects on the grounds of their obscurity was agreed to be reasonable, what was to prevent anyone arguing that knowledge of God and morality is equally obscure?

Berkeley tried to preserve theism and certitude by dispensing with the Cartesian category of corporeal substance, which he argued to be confused, contradictory, and ultimately useless. He echoed Malebranche's claim that the existence of extramental corporeal things was never proved by Descartes. Descartes takes it to be a reasonable conjecture in light of the assumption of God's benevolence and his pre-existing disposition to believe in those objects, but this falls well short of a demonstration. For Berkeley, one of the points Descartes makes in *Meditation Two* is key: even if corporeal substance, which Berkeley refers to simply as "matter," does not exist, all my experiences can be the same as they are right now and as they always have been. My experiences underdetermine the answer to the question "Do material objects (or corporeal substance) exist?"

Since Berkeley requires God to sustain material objects in existence by thinking of them when they are not being perceived, the question might be raised whether Berkeley's God is a malevolent Demon, since it seems that we do tend to believe in material objects independent of our ideas. Berkeley's implicit answer to this question is that, while some *philosophers* might believe in material objects, the ordinary person can be shown to have no such belief. The position of "common sense," he insisted, is the Berkeleyan one – there are only ideas. God, he claims, does not deceive anyone, and the philosophers only mislead themselves. Because he denies that sensory ideas are caused by or represent anything material, Berkeley avoids the troubles associated with the resemblance theory of perception (Ch. 10 Sec. 4). He offers an account of veridical perception based on the notion of an expectation of a future experience.

Immanuel Kant (1724–1804)

Kant denied that demonstrations that possessed the certainty of mathematics could be formulated involving the metaphysical concepts of God, the soul, and the world. It is a feature of mathematics that, if a convincing and acceptable demonstration of P can be given, no convincing and acceptable demonstration of –P can be given. Metaphysics, Kant pointed out, does not seem to possess this feature. There are fine and impressive arguments for the existence of an immaterial soul – and just-as-good arguments for its impossibility. There are fine and impressive arguments for the existence of God – and just as sharp refutations of these arguments. So nothing consequential, Kant thought, can emerge from the sort of "rationalistic" argument engaged in by Descartes. Pure reason cannot establish that we are doomed to extinction or immortal, or, for that matter, whether the world was created or just emerged from chaos, whether we have free will or are deterministic machines. The empiricists, like Locke and later Hume, were right to suspect that our knowledge is limited by our experiences and by the experiments we can actually perform. What experience or experiment could assure us that there is life after death, or that God designed and supervises the world? Metaphysical questions, said Kant, are permanently undecidable.

We are not in a position, according to Kant, to say how many substances there are – one, two or three – and what the modes of their interaction might be. What he called "critical idealism" – the view that *something* extramental is the "ground" of our experiences, even if matter as traditionally conceived cannot "cause" our experiences – seemed to Kant a good compromise between Berkeleyan idealism and Epicurean materialism. His attempt to explain the system of critical idealism, his reasons for thinking it the only tenable system, and its moral–theological implications occupy many daunting pages of his *Critique of Pure Reason*.

Kant argued that we will live, experience ourselves, and behave differently if we believe that the world arose by chance and that death is the end, instead of believing that God created us and will punish and reward us in a future life. We cannot prove that the world did not arise by chance and that death is not the end, but no one can prove that these hypotheses are true. Moreover, we will have worse lives, he thought, if we adopt these views. If we cannot decide between two hypotheses by either rational or experimental methods, we are entitled to accept the hypothesis, Kant insisted, that best fits with our other convictions. The convictions that we have to accommodate to are that there exists moral right and wrong, that we live under a moral law, whether we always choose to obey it or not, and that there will be some recompense for those who make sacrifices in order to obey it. These convictions do not sit well with the hypotheses of fatalism, mortalism, and atheism, which must therefore be rejected in favor of the hypotheses of free will, a life to come, and theism. Our acceptance of these hypotheses does not, Kant insisted, constitute *theoretical* knowledge like that delivered by mathematics and natural science, but only *practical* knowledge. While this conclusion might seem at odds with Descartes's rationalism, it turns out to be surprisingly close to Descartes's own conception of morality as requiring practical – indeed pragmatic – decisions, where certainty is unobtainable.

4 DESCARTES AND THE FORMATION OF MODERNITY

It is often said that Descartes was the founder of modern philosophy. What is the meaning of "modern" in historical studies and what is the basis of the attribution? What is the Cartesian legacy and what is its place in what is often referred to as our "postmodern era?"

The modern era, beginning near the end of the sixteenth century, is distinguished from the ancient, Medieval, and Renaissance eras with respect to the social and political organization of Western Europe. In broader terms, the modern era is associated by intellectual historians with the extinction of feudalism, the reconsolidation of monarchical and imperial power, and the spread of capitalism. Though it is not easy to distinguish causes from effects, these changes are held to have stimulated democracy, or at least republicanism, and a broadening of participation in politics beyond a narrow circle of aristocrats and high-ranking church officials. Modernity implied new possibilities for social advancement through the attainment of formal qualifications such as academic degrees through merit and effort, and a corresponding rejection of hereditary privilege. The great increase in the number of printed books, the founding of scientific societies and establishment of learned journals were indicative of and encouraged greater freedom of expression and association. The relevance of science to technologies of war, engineering, manufacturing, agriculture, and medicine was recognized. The belief that better legal, economic, and political institutions could be constructed, and human suffering on earth remedied, by the application of rational government policies is an element of secularization: the acceptance of human responsibility for the world. According to critics of modernity, the rise of the commercial classes, the rationalization of power, and the more orderly flow of information implied more extensive state control of private life, institutionalized persecution and oppression, disruption of human relations, the degradation of the environment, the exploitation of workers, and the exclusion of women from the new meritocracies.

Certain – though not all – of these features of modernity in the historian's sense can be read into Descartes's *Meditations*, as well as into his other writings. Though Descartes remained a man of faith, a feudal *rentier* living off the proceeds of his family's estates, and although he retained a breadth of literary and scientific interests more typical of the Renaissance than of later eras, his scientific optimism, especially in his earlier years, is characteristically modern. An effective medicine, including what we would now refer to as psychotherapy in addition to internal medicine and pathology, had to be based, in his view, on physics – on a physiological understanding of the mechanisms underlying vital phenomena. His conviction that the ordinary human intellect can discover important truths unassisted by learned experts is at least proto-democratic, and his esteem for reason and for autonomous, reflective conduct in place of obedience frequently set him at odds with educational and theological authorities.

It is sometimes said that a feature of modernity is a new importance attached to the *subject* of experience and Descartes's *Meditations* are exemplary in this respect. The thinking, perceiving, imagining self, its experiences of color and sound, its awareness of its own body and of its own powers, its ability to form and contemplate images are treated with a seriousness unprecedented in the philosophical literature. Descartes's meditative exercises do not, as they did for the Fathers

of the Church, reveal faults and vices, or, as they did for his immediate predecessor, the essayist Michel Montaigne, contradictions and
inconsistencies, but – despite his frailties – his own underlying health
and soundness, and the coherence of his ideas. It would be fanciful to
see the decidedly cerebral adventures of the introspective first-person
narrators of Chekhov, Proust, Woolf, Joyce, Beckett, and Kafka and
their followers as influenced by Descartes. Yet the notion that a person's experiences and internal struggles in his ordinary environment –
his own room, in Descartes's case – not bloodshed and bold deeds
in far-off lands, are supremely meaningful and worth recounting to
others underlies modern literary tastes.

Descartes did not intend to be the father of modern philosophy.
He would have been startled to learn that he had initiated a tradition
of "Cartesian idealism" or "Cartesian skepticism." He thought of
himself rather as putting an *end* to philosophy, settling once for all
the major questions of ontology, epistemology, and metaphysics so
that the experimental and observational investigation of the self and
the world could proceed on a secure basis. In his *Reply* to the Sixth
Set of Objectors, he restated his confidence in his own achievement
in the *Meditations* as follows:

> [M]y arguments . . . possess complete truth and certainty; in particular,
> they are deduced step by step, not from principles which are obscure and
> unknown, but, in the first place, from total doubt about all things, and, in
> the second place, from principles which appear to be utterly evident and
> certain to the mind, once it has been set free from preconceived opinions.
> (VII:446)

The system of the physical world that Descartes held for true and
certain, that he hoped would have a permanent place in the scientific curriculum of the universities, has faded from the memory
of most scientists and philosophers. Yet contemporary science pre-
serves his notion of the fundamental laws of motion and his commitment to explanation in terms of subvisible interacting particles,
even while the majority of his specific claims and explanations have
been discarded as unfounded conjecture. His contributions to pure

mathematics, especially his discovery that geometry problems can be represented and solved algebraically, are enduring. Where epistemology and metaphysics are concerned, Descartes's ongoing influence is less neatly summarized. His claims for a special privilege for humans over other animals in virtue of their capacity for language, and for the irreducibility of consciousness to a "mechanical" process or the effect of one are echoed by some prominent philosophers of mind, though by few psychologists.

In contemporary philosophy, "Cartesianism" is a term often used pejoratively to signify an unscientific faith in a mysterious distinction between soul and body and a conviction that introspection gives incorrigible epistemological results. The Cartesian, it is alleged, believes himself to be a mind that can have all its ordinary experiences, whether or not it *is* attached to a body, while at the same time believing himself to be attached to a body in some way that he admits he is helpless to explain. Further, the Cartesian believes that he has incorrigible knowledge of his immediate experiences, which serve as the building blocks of his scientific representation of the world. Astute readers will at once understand how these views – Dualism and Foundationalism – came to be designated as "Cartesian," while being aware of the ways in which they are distortions of Descartes's more nuanced, though admittedly somewhat ambiguous, views. Another view commonly expressed by contemporary theorists is that Descartes exalted the mind over the body and is prone to intellectualist excesses. If one is interested in the theme of the denigration of the body in Western philosophy, however, Plato and the Fathers of the Early Church offer more rewarding material. The Principles of Intellect Priority and Mind Priority are enunciated, to be sure, in *Meditation Two*, establishing Descartes's affiliations with Plato and Augustine against the atomists, with their occasionally worrisome sensualism. Descartes's most abiding interest, however, was in the somatic basis of perception, sensation, and emotion; it is this preoccupation that unifies his early and late writings. The account of the mutually beneficial soul-body partnership is the culminating statement of the *Sixth Meditation* and perhaps the most original and significant result stated in the *Meditations*.

Contemporary philosophers continue to discuss what has come to be known as the mind–body problem, incorrigible and *a priori* knowledge, the Ontological Argument, the possibility of immortality, the relationship of pure mathematics to physics, the relationship of the emotions to morality, the freedom of the will, the discrepancy between the sensory appearance of the world and the world as it exists in itself, the nature of sensory qualities and their relationship to behavior, and the difference between subjective and objective perspectives. They are living from – though not exclusively from – the Cartesian legacy. One example of this legacy is the persistence of the problem of consciousness.

The senses as purveyors of information can be considered from an engineering point of view as an efficiency for a mobile animal inhabiting a changing environment and this is precisely how Descartes conceived them. In the absence of sensory signals that register changes in the external environment and its internal milieu, an animal cannot negotiate a complex and unpredictable world or respond to its own states in ways conducive to survival. Evidently, sensory information does not have to be registered consciously in order to fulfill the role of mediating behavioral adjustments, and Descartes can be credited with the insight that a sensory system does not need to be a conscious system in order to work. At the same time, experiences "like ours" – conscious experiences – seem particularly useful as mediators between the environment and behavior.

The preservation of the human body is, however, no more demanding a task than the preservation of the body of an eagle or mouse. Humans, eagles, and mice all face precisely the same environmental challenges – finding food and water, recognizing mates and offspring, avoiding obstacles and predators, keeping warm enough and cool enough. If consciousness contributes to biological survival, these animals must be conscious just as we are. Why should they possess a dimmer or vaguer form of consciousness? Alternatively, if consciousness does not contribute to biological survival, and if eagles and mice do not possess it, why should we?

Descartes's answer was that we share our admirable unconscious sensory engineering, fully adequate to all the demands of life, with eagles and mice, but that we have also been endowed, as a direct gift from God, with consciousness, the power of language, and the ability to construct and discern rational arguments. Other creatures elsewhere in the universe may have received other equally wonderful gifts. The notion of a supernatural endowment bestowed upon an entire species is foreign to our contemporary way of thinking. So is the notion that consciousness, language production, and rationality cannot be studied by empirical science. Yet we are far from understanding what consciousness, language, and rationality might actually be for – or, indeed, whether they are for anything. Perhaps – as Descartes's view suggests – they are only ornaments, acquired at some moment of our evolutionary history, that we use, enjoy, and admire. Descartes's view that we have no insight into final causes and purposes and should restrict ourselves to asking *how* and not *why* is a central feature of the scientific orientation towards the world that might well be invoked in this connection. We may some day understand why, from an evolutionary perspective, we are conscious, rational, animals who use language, but meanwhile we are a long way from understanding even what is involved in our being animals of this sort.

Appendix: the Objectors

OBJECTOR 1

Johan Caterus (1590–1655). A Calvinistically inclined Dutch priest who was chiefly concerned with the theological aspects of the *Meditations*, especially Descartes's proofs for the existence of God.

OBJECTOR 2

Marin Mersenne (1588–1648). A long-time friend and proponent of Descartes and opponent of Aristotle who wrote his own anti-skeptical treatise, the *Véritez des sciences* in 1625. Mersenne did not author the entire Second Set of Objections but collected them from his circle.

OBJECTOR 3

Thomas Hobbes (1588–1679). The English materialist and political philosopher, author of the *Leviathan*, for a time resident in France. Hobbes insisted that there could be no incorporeal substances and that thinking was a mechanical operation. He regarded theology as obfuscation by priests.

OBJECTOR 4

Antoine Arnauld (1612–94). A young Jansenist theologian, strongly influenced by St. Augustine. To all appearances, the most aggressive and focused of Descartes's critics, but later a defender of Descartes and considered to be a Cartesian.

OBJECTOR 5

Pierre Gassendi (1592–1655). The chief seventeenth-century proponent of the systems of Epicurus and Lucretius, which he endeavored to reconcile with Christianity. Gassendi believed that atomic mechanisms underlay natural phenomena but doubted that humans were able to reveal and understand them.

OBJECTOR 6

Friends of Marin Mersenne of unknown identity, some of them described as "philosophers and geometers." They raise Scriptural and other theological objections to Descartes but also find his theory of the incorporeal soul insufficiently grounded.

OBJECTOR 7

Pierre Bourdin (1595–1653). Early on, a Professor of Humanities at La Flèche, later a prominent and well-connected Jesuit mathematician and author of several treatises. The insults and mockery which Bourdin and Descartes hurled at one another were prognostic of the later hostility of the Jesuits to Cartesianism.

Glossary

Authority Principle. The principle that the opinions of a particular designated Authority (for example: elders, technical journals, religious authorities) are decisive in determining what is true and what is false. The application of the principle to epistemological and scientific matters is rejected by the Meditator.

Awareness thesis. Descartes's claim that "We cannot have any thought of which we are not aware at the very moment when it is in us."

Cartesian Circle. The fallacy allegedly committed by the Meditator when he bases his argument for the existence of a veracious God on clear and distinct ideas and bases the veridicality of clear and distinct ideas in turn on God's veracity.

Causal Noninferiority Principle. The principle that a cause must be greater than or equal to the effect it produces.

Clarity and Distinctness Filter. A filter for separating true from untrue beliefs that lets through only propositions that I clearly and distinctly perceive.

Conformity Policy. The principle that whatever (and only what) most other people believe ought to be deemed true and that whatever (and only what) most other people reject or fail to believe ought to be deemed false. (Cf. Authority Principle.) The application of the principle to epistemological and scientific matters is rejected by the Meditator.

Corpuscularianism. The theory that all material objects are composed of small, mobile corpuscles existing below the threshold of ordinary perception that cause sensations of heat, color, taste, etc. without having these properties.

Dualism. The theory that there are two substances, e.g., mental substance and corporeal substance. Technically, Descartes is not a dualist since he acknowledges a third, infinite substance (God) in addition to finite mental and corporeal substances.

Epicureanism. The ancient philosopher Epicurus' doctrine that there exists a multiplicity of *cosmoi* containing animals and people assembled by chance from the motion of atoms and that everything perishes.

Epistemology. The theory of knowledge. Epistemologists are concerned with the justification of beliefs and with what can be known with various degrees of certainty or probability.

Hierarchy of Ideas. The ordering of ideas according to the clarity, excellence, and importance of what they represent.

Hyperbolic doubt. Philosophical skepticism that far surpasses what a reasonable person would normally be led to doubt. It is induced in the Meditator by the supposition that there exists a malevolent Demon.

Idealism. The theory that only minds and their ideas (human and/or divine) are real and that matter is an illusion. (Not to be confused with *Psychologism.*)

Incorrigibility. A proposition is known incorrigibly if the person who is convinced of its truth cannot be wrong. If I cannot be wrong in my belief that I am perceiving a tree, then my claim "I perceive a tree" is incorrigible.

Intellect Priority. The principle that reason is a source of knowledge superior to the senses.

Material falsity. An idea is "materially false" if it is a confused image of something that cannot be distinctly conceived except as an absence or privation of something real. Examples: cold, dark, void.

Materialism. The theory that only matter is real and that minds and their ideas are products of organized matter or manifestations of material states and processes. (Cf. *Idealism.*)

Metaphysics. The branch of study devoted to causality, time, existence, substance, divinity, the soul, and other such abstract subjects.

Mind Priority. The principle that the human mind is easier to come to know than are material objects.

Modality. Most centrally, the feature of propositions that make reference to logical possibility, impossibility, and necessity.

Mortalism. The doctrine that the human mind does not survive the death of the body with which it is associated.

Ontological Argument. The attempt to deduce God's extramental existence from the definition of His essence as an absolutely perfect being.

Ontology. The study of being. A given philosopher's "ontology" is the set of objects and relations he or she believes exists.

Psychologism. The view that some designated entity or type of entity has only intramental existence. (Not to be confused with *Idealism.*)

Radical mistrust. The policy of never believing information from any source that has ever been untrustworthy in the past. This policy is rejected by the Meditator.

Realism. The view that some designated entity or type of entity has extramental existence.

Resemblance theory. The theory, rejected by the Meditator, that one's experiences (especially one's visual experiences) are like pictures or copies of extramental objects.

Skepticism. The refusal to assent to commonly accepted or plausible opinions.

Substance. Something capable of existing independently of anything else. Usually conceived as the underlying "stuff" in which various qualities and modes, such as color, shape, size, motion, perception, and other attributes "inhere."

Syllogism. A pattern of valid argument consisting of two premises and a conclusion. *If* the premises are true (which they need not be) the conclusion of a syllogism *must be* true. The following are examples of good syllogistic reasoning: (1) *All men are mortal; Socrates is a man; Socrates is mortal.* (2) *No cats are black; All pigs are cats; No pigs are black.* Descartes insisted that *I think* is not one of the premises in a syllogism whose conclusion is *I exist.*

Withholding Policy. The policy adopted by the Meditator of refusing to believe and actively doubting any proposition that it is possible to doubt.

Further reading

1 MODERN SURVEYS OF DESCARTES'S LIFE AND WORK

Boros, Gábor, *René Descartes' Werdegang: Der allgütige Gott und die Wertfreie Natur.* Würzburg, Königshausen & Neumann, 2001.

Cottingham, John, *Descartes*, Oxford, Blackwell, 1986.

Gaukroger, Stephen, *Descartes: An Intellectual Biography*, Oxford, Clarendon, 1995.

Rodis-Lewis, Geneviève, *Descartes, biographie*, Paris, Calman-Levy, 1995. English translation by Jane Marie Todd, *Descartes: His Life and Thought*, Ithaca, Cornell University Press, 1998.

Sorell, Tom, *Descartes*, Oxford, Oxford University Press, 1987.

2 STUDIES OF THE *MEDITATIONS*

Broughton, Janet, *Descartes' Method of Doubt*, Princeton, Princeton University Press, 2002.

Curley, Edwin, *Descartes Against the Skeptics*, Oxford, Blackwell, 1978.

Gueroult, Martial, *Descartes selon l'ordre des raisons*, Paris, Aubier, 1953. English translation by Roger Ariew, *Descartes's Philosophy Interpreted According to the Order of Reasons*, 2 vols., Minneapolis, University of Minnesota Press, 1984.

Kenny, Anthony, *Descartes: A Study of his Philosophy*, New York, Random House, 1968.

Miles, Murray, *Insight and Inference*, Toronto, University of Toronto Press, 1999.

Sarka, Husain, *Descartes' Cogito: Saved from the Great Shipwreck*, Cambridge, Cambridge University Press, 2003.

Williams, Bernard, *Descartes: The Project of Pure Enquiry*, Sussex, Harvester, 1978.

Wilson, Margaret, *Descartes*, London, Routledge and Kegan Paul, 1978.

3 SPECIAL STUDIES OF DESCARTES

Almog, Joseph, *What am I?: Descartes and the Mind–Body Problem*, New York, Oxford University Press, 2002.

Ariew, Roger and Green, Marjorie, *Descartes and his Contemporaries: Meditations, Objections and Replies*, Chicago, University of Chicago Press, 1995.

Baker, Gordon and Morris, Katherine J., *Descartes's Dualism*, London, Routledge, 1996.

Caton, Hiram, *The Origins of Subjectivity*, New Haven, Yale University Press, 1973.

Clarke, Desmond, *Descartes's Philosophy of Science*, Manchester, Manchester University Press, 1982.

Des Chene, Dennis, *Spirits and Clocks: Machine and Organism in Descartes*, Ithaca, Cornell University Press, 2001.

Frankfurt, Harry, *Demons, Dreamers, and Madmen*, Indianapolis, Bobbs-Merrill, 1970.

Garber, Daniel, *Descartes Embodied: Reading Descartes through Cartesian Science*, Cambridge, Cambridge University Press, 2001.

Gilson, Étienne, *Discours de la méthode, texte et commentaire*, Paris, J. Vrin, 1962.

Grosholz, Emily, *Cartesian Method and the Problem of Reduction*, Oxford, Clarendon, 1991.

Nadler, Steven, "Descartes's Demon and the Madness of Don Quixote," *Journal of the History of Ideas* 58 (1997), pp. 41–55.

Röd, Wolfgang, *Die innere Genesis des cartesianischen Systems*, Munich, E. Reinhardt, 1964.

Rozemond, Marlene, *Descartes's Dualism*, Cambridge, MA, Harvard University Press, 1998.

Schouls, Peter, *Descartes and the Enlightenment*, Edinburgh, Edinburgh University Press, 1989.

Verbeek, Theo, *Descartes and the Dutch: Early Reactions to Cartesian Philosophy (1637–1650)*, Carbondale, IL, University of Illinois, 1992.

4 COLLECTIONS OF ESSAYS

Cottingham, John, ed., *The Cambridge Companion to Descartes*, Cambridge, Cambridge University Press, 1992.

Gaukroger, Stephen, Schuster, John and Sutton, John, eds., *Descartes's Natural Philosophy*, London, Routledge, 2000.

Moyal, G. J. D., ed., *René Descartes, Critical Assessments*, 4 vols., London, Routledge, 1991.

Rorty, Amélie, ed., *Essays on Descartes's Meditations*, Berkeley, University of California Press, 1986.

5 ARTICLES

Baker, Gordon P. and Morris, Katherine J., "Descartes Unlocked," *British Journal for the History of Philosophy* 1 (1993), pp. 5–27.

Bennett, Jonathan, "Descartes's Theory of Modality," *Philosophical Review* 103 (1994), pp. 639–67.

Boros, Gábor, "Ethics in the Age of Automata," *History of Philosophy Quarterly* 18 (2001), pp. 139–54.

Harrison, Peter, "Descartes on Animals," *Philosophical Quarterly* 42 (1992), pp. 219–27.

Hatfield, Gary. "Force (God) in Descartes' Physics," *Studies in the History and Philosophy of Science* 10 (1979), pp. 113–40.

Hintikka, Jaako, "Cogito Ergo Sum: Inference or Performance?" *Philosophical Review* 71 (1962), pp. 3–32.

Jacquette, Dale, "Descartes' *Lumen Naturale* and the Cartesian Circle," *Philosophy and Theology* 9 (1996), pp. 273–320.

Kaufman, Dan, "Descartes on the Objective Reality of Materially False Ideas," *Pacific Philosophical Quarterly* 81 (2002), pp. 385–408.

Kennington, Richard, "The Finitude of Descartes's Evil Genius," *Journal of the History of Ideas* 32 (1971), pp. 441–6.

Kim, Jaegwon, "How Can My Mind Move My Limbs? Mental Causation from Descartes to Contemporary Physicalism," *Philosophical Exchange* 30 (1999–2000), pp. 5–16.

Loeb, Louis, "Is There Radical Dissimulation in Descartes' *Meditations?*" in *Essays on Descartes' Meditations*, ed. Amélie Oksenberg Rorty, Berkeley: University of California Press, 1986.

Menn, Stephen, "Descartes and Some Predecessors on the Divine Conservation of Motion," *Synthèse* 83 (1990), pp. 215–38.

Newman, Lex, "Descartes on Unknown Faculties and our Knowledge of an External World," *Philosophical Review* 103 (1994), pp. 489–531.

Popkin, Richard, "Skepticism at the Time of Descartes," *Dialogos* 69 (1997), pp. 243–253.

Scott, David, "Occasionalism and Occasional Causation in Descartes's Philosophy," *Journal of the History of Philosophy* 38 (2000), pp. 5–16.

Shapiro, Lisa, "Princess Elizabeth and Descartes: The Union of Soul and Body and the Practice of Philosophy," *British Journal for the History of Philosophy* 7 (1999), pp. 503–20.

Simmons, Alison, "Sensible Ends: Latent Teleology in Descartes' Account of Sensation," *Journal of the History of Philosophy* 39 (2002), pp. 49–75.

Voss, Stephen, "Scientific and Practical Certainty in Descartes," *American Catholic Philosophical Quarterly* 67 (1993), pp. 569–85.

6 THE SEVENTEENTH-CENTURY BACKGROUND TO THE *MEDITATIONS*

Buchdahl, Gerd, *Metaphysics and the Philosophy of Science,* Oxford, Blackwell, 1969.

Burtt, E. A., *The Metaphysical Foundations of Modern Science*, London, Routledge and Kegan Paul, 1932 (repr. 1972).

Rogers, John, *The Matter of Revolution: Science, Poetry and Politics in the Age of Reason*, Ithaca, Cornell University Press, 1996.

Shapin, Steven, *The Scientific Revolution*, Chicago, University of Chicago Press, 1996.

Willey, Basil, *The Seventeenth-Century Background: Studies of the Thought of the Age in Relation to Poetry and Religion*, London, Routledge and Kegan Paul, 1986.

Index

266